W9-BEZ-203

The Professional Chef's® Guide to Kitchen Management

The Professional Chef's® Guide to Kitchen Management

John Fuller
Oxford, England

John B. Knight
Cornell University
Ithaca, New York

Charles A. Salter
Academy of Health Sciences
Fort Sam Houston, Texas

CBI

A CBI Book
Published by Van Nostrand Reinhold Company
New York

A CBI Book.
(CBI is an imprint of Van Nostrand Reinhold Company Inc.)
Copyright © 1985 by John Fuller
Library of Congress Catalog Card Number 84-22100
ISBN 0-442-22624-1

All rights reserved. No part of this work covered by the copyright
hereon may be reproduced or used in any form or by any means—graphic,
electronic, or mechanical, including photocopying, recording, taping,
or information storage and retrieval systems—without written permission of the publisher.

Printed in the United States of America
Designed by Barbara M. Marks

Published by Van Nostrand Reinhold Company Inc.
135 West 50th Street
New York, New York 10020

Van Nostrand Reinhold Company Limited
Molly Millars Lane
Wokingham, Berkshire RG11 2PY, England

Van Nostrand Reinhold
480 La Trobe Street
Melbourne, Victoria 3000, Australia

Macmillan of Canada
Division of Canada Publishing Corporation
164 Commander Boulevard
Agincourt, Ontario M1S 3C7, Canada

This book was inspired by
Professional Kitchen Management by John Fuller,
published in 1981 in Great Britain
by B. T. Batsford Limited.

16 15 14 13 12 11 10 9 8 7 6 5 4 3 2 1

Library of Congress Cataloging in Publication Data

Fuller, John, 1916-
The professional chef's guide to kitchen management.
Includes index.
1. Food service management. 2. Kitchens. I. Knight,
John Barton, 1950–   . II. Salter, Charles A.,
1947–   . III. Title.
TX911.3.M27F85   1985   647'.95'068   84-22100
ISBN 0-442-22624-1

To our wives

Pamela Honor Fuller
Whitney Carol Knight
Carlota Luisa Salter

Contents

Part II. The Kitchen and Management

Preface

The Professional Chef's Guide to Kitchen Management is a practical text for both chef and manager. Beginning with an overview of foodservice history, the authors proceed through chapters covering all operational factors in the management of professional kitchens. Section I, "The Professional Chef," defines the vocation and responsibilities involved. Tools and utensils are reviewed along with sanitation/safety considerations and nutrition. Section II, "The Kitchen and Management," presents all aspects of kitchen organization, from staffing, layout, equipment, and maintenance to menu production, food purchasing, and controls.

The writing style ensures that students as well as industry practitioners will learn the techniques of kitchen operation. Management recipes for learning are provided throughout to present important facts in a clear, concise manner. Illustrations, charts, and photographs all contribute to making the text more understandable and practical. The ultimate purpose of this definitive work on kitchen management is to assist in the development of high-quality kitchen standards throughout the foodservice industry.

Part I.

The Professional Chef

1. History Reviewed

Ancient Times

People have always eaten and enjoyed eating. It is not too farfetched to imagine that even in prehistoric times people differed in their cooking skills. If one person could boil bison or roast rhinoceros better than the others in the region, Neanderthals from nearby caves would probably come around and offer a beaver pelt for the privilege of eating good food.

Such is speculation. But certainly from the dawn of recorded history ancient civilizations regulated establishments for dispensing food and drink. One of the earliest references dates to 2500 B.C. and is recorded on Babylonian tablets of baked clay. The cuneiform characters on these tablets list food items and catering services. Around 1700 B.C., the code of Hammurabi promulgated strict regulations for the food and drink business. A tavern keeper who watered his beer to increase profits could actually be executed. The menu in ancient Greece commonly included goat and lamb, fish, cheese, barley bread, beans and peas, and —for dessert—honey buns or sesame cakes. In ancient Egypt, although the low-cost menu offered only bread and dried fish, the gourmet menu for the rich included roast goose, beef, and fruit.

The Roman Empire had a highly organized system of foodservice establishments. Places to eat were located in every town and along all major highways. The *popina* was like our modern restaurant and served a full course hot meal. The *thermopolium* was like today's snack bar, with a counter service of appetizers and drinks.

The Middle Ages

After the fall of the Roman Empire, various orders of the Roman Catholic Church established facilities to house and feed travelers. For example, at one of the hospices scattered across Europe, a weary traveler could get a meal and a bed free of charge—although donations were welcome.

In 1066, William of Normandy (a French-speaking state, and now part of France) invaded Great Britain. The Norman Conquest had a lasting influence on the customs, language, and cookery of the English-speaking world. The words veal, beef, and pork, for example, are derived from the French *veau*, *boeuf*, and *porc*. French cookbooks provided relatively delicate and involved recipes and described cooking processes that were more refined and varied than the traditional one of sticking the meat on a spit and roasting it.

By 1183, London had public cookhouses offering fish, beef, venison, and poultry. By the end of the Middle Ages, inns serving food had sprung up all over the country, particularly in the larger towns and along thoroughfares.

The Renaissance

In 1536 Henry VIII split with the Roman Catholic Church and suppressed the Catholic religious orders, including their hospices. This stimulated the further growth of privately owned establishments to replace them. The menus in these early English inns at first consisted mainly of meat, bread, and ale. Following the discovery and exploration of the New World in the fifteenth and sixteenth centuries, however, foods such as potatoes, beans, corn, tomatoes, blueberries, strawberries, cocoa, and coffee made their way into the European diet. The bills of fare at most inns soon offered these new foods from America.

The Modern Period

Early Modern Period

In 1650 the first coffeehouse in Britain was established at Oxford. The concept spread rapidly. Within 50 years, there were 200 coffeehouses in London alone. About this same time, the first foodservice establishments were opened in the American colonies. In 1634, the Coles Ordinary was established in Boston. Later the Puritans decreed that every community should have an "ordinary"—a public house at which an ordinary meal could be had for the standard price of sixpence. See figure 1-1. A typical ordinary meal consisted of salmon, fowl, or meat, served with vegetables, washed down with a pint of Madeira wine, and topped off with a pudding.

In 1765 in Paris, Boulanger opened the first true restaurant, thus introducing the concept we know today. A few Americans like Thomas Jefferson loved French wines and recipes (he had served as American minister to France), but for the most part, early American foodservice was more deeply influenced by the British model.

Recent Modern Period

The first great chef to be recognized was Antonin Carême (1783–1833). The sixteenth child in a poor French family, Carême started at the bottom in his field—as a kitchen boy in a catering service—at the age of ten. Six years later, he became an apprentice *pâtissier* and taught himself how to read and write. By 1803, he was *chef pâtissier* to Talley-

1-1. Table setting of an early American tavern (Ordinary at the Hall Tavern, Charlemont, Massachusetts, 1700). Courtesy of the Heritage Foundation; photograph by Samuel Chamberlain; from Lundberg, *The Hotel and Restaurant Business,* 4th edition.

rand, France's foreign minister. In this position, he came in contact with the most famous European leaders of the age. He turned down Czar Alexander's invitation to become Russia's leading chef and instead went to England as *maître chef* at Carlton House in London, where he set standards for other chefs throughout Great Britain. Yet, after two years in Britain, he returned to France, where he lived until his death at 50. His classic books on the art of the chef influenced cooks for generations.

Other great chefs followed Carême during the Victorian era. Jules Gouffé gained fame as *chef de cuisine* of the Paris Jockey Club. His cookbooks, written in French but translated into English, influenced cooks in many countries. Louis Eustace Ude gained fame as the chief of catering at Crockford's Club and the St. James' Club. His book, *The French Cook,* was well-received. Alexis Soyer was also French but gained his greatest fame in Britain. He was the chef at the Reform Club and later served in the Crimean War, improving Britain's military foodservice. Charles Elmé Francatelli, a student of Carême, rose to become chief cook to Queen Victoria. His book, *The Modern Cook,* also became a classic.

In 1829, the first true restaurant in the United States was opened —Delmonico's in New York City. Also in 1829, the Tremont House in Boston became the first hotel to use a printed menu card. This menu offered primarily French cuisine. In 1876, Fred Harvey began the first major restaurant chain which, over the next 20 years, spread throughout the United States. Charles Ranhofer, a chef at the by then well-established Delmonico's, wrote a famous cookbook called *The Epicurean* in 1894.

As the grand hotel movement swept the United States and Europe (figure 1-2), the last of the great chefs flourished in France. Auguste Escoffier (1846–1935) was considered the premier cook in the world. Cesar Ritz, the founder of a famous chain of hotels, admired Escoffier and brought him to London, where he created such new dishes as *Filet de Sole Waleska* and *Pêche Melba.* Escoffier's ideas and techniques emphasizing "exquisite simplicity" influenced cooks throughout the western world. This "chef to kings and king of chefs" wrote a book called *Guide to Modern Cookery* which is still in use, half a century after his death.

Current American Situation

The age of the world-renowned hotel chef seems to be yielding to that of the chief proprietor, exemplified in France by such internationally known craftsmen as Paul Bocuse, Michel Guérard, and others who were associated with *la nouvelle cuisine.* Although America still has its great hotel restaurants and famous independent restaurants, from Brennan's in New Orleans to Delmonico's in New York, these establishments are famous for their own names, not the names of their chefs. Writers of cookbooks also lack the following they once had. There is too much competition and too much specialization into various ethnic

1-2. The kitchen of the Old Palmer House Hotel, Chicago, about 1890. The kitchen is departmentalized and not too different from some kitchens seen in old resorts today. From Lundberg, *The Hotel and Restaurant Business,* 4th edition.

styles of cooking (such as Italian, Chinese, and Greek) for any one writer to command universal attention.

Even if fame seems a distant possibility, there are more jobs in the food preparation field than ever before. Many of these pay very well, especially positions at the larger, better-known establishments. Throughout the country, hotel and motel restaurants, airport, train station, and bus depot restaurants, specialty restaurants, cafeterias, coffeeshops, fast-food restaurants, lunch counters, and snack bars are open. In addition, many companies have staff cafeterias, schools and universities have student cafeterias, hospitals have foodservice for their patients, and military units must provide food for their troops. Of all the employees in the half-million varied institutions that serve food, about 15% are cooks and chefs.

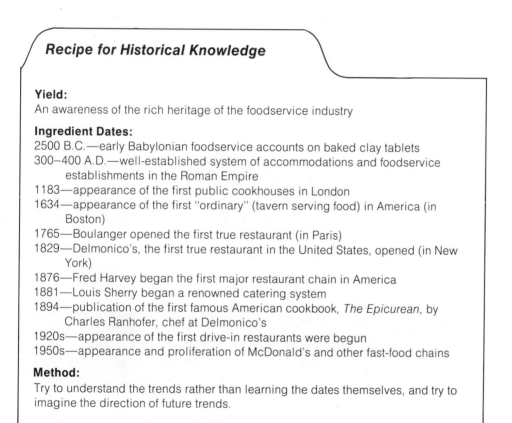

Recipe for Historical Knowledge

Yield:
An awareness of the rich heritage of the foodservice industry

Ingredient Dates:
2500 B.C.—early Babylonian foodservice accounts on baked clay tablets
300–400 A.D.—well-established system of accommodations and foodservice establishments in the Roman Empire
1183—appearance of the first public cookhouses in London
1634—appearance of the first "ordinary" (tavern serving food) in America (in Boston)
1765—Boulanger opened the first true restaurant (in Paris)
1829—Delmonico's, the first true restaurant in the United States, opened (in New York)
1876—Fred Harvey began the first major restaurant chain in America
1881—Louis Sherry began a renowned catering system
1894—publication of the first famous American cookbook, *The Epicurean*, by Charles Ranhofer, chef at Delmonico's
1920s—appearance of the first drive-in restaurants were begun
1950s—appearance and proliferation of McDonald's and other fast-food chains

Method:
Try to understand the trends rather than learning the dates themselves, and try to imagine the direction of future trends.

2. Vocation Defined

Advancement of the Culinary Arts

While there may be no world-famous chefs like Escoffier today, the position of the regular chef is becoming more prominent and prestigious because of the following six factors:

1. Increased educational opportunities. Vocational and technical schools train foodservice people. Many universities now offer degrees in foodservice. McDonald's and other franchise chains have their own training centers.
2. Increased activity of professional organizations. The National Restaurant Association (NRA), the National Institute for the Foodservice Industry (NIFI), and the American Culinary Federation (ACF), among others, benefit foodservice people by setting standards, encouraging legislation, and informing the public.
3. A trend in the industry toward certification. The organizations just mentioned provide certificates to properly qualified people to distinguish them from others. The ACF, for example, certifies chefs.
4. Improved technology. New equipment and techniques enable chefs to produce high quality menu items routinely.
5. A growing demand for trained professionals. As the industry expands, more chefs and other foodservice staff are needed. Foodservice establishments increasingly compete with each other for high-quality people, offering more money, fringe benefits, or autonomy.
6. An increase in eating out. As Americans eat out more frequently, they become more selective about where they go. They seek out and patronize establishments whose food is superior.

The Professional Chef

As the foodservice industry grows and the position of chef gains prestige, who stands to benefit? Not the unmotivated, haphazard person who wanders in off the street to become a short-order cook; but the trained professional chef *will*. The following are traits that distinguish the true professional from the salaried amateur:

Chef Read Manager

Personal Attributes

The chef is not only an artist and a craftsman, but an executive who is expected to organize and direct the activities of other people, watch costs, plan and compile menus, order supplies, and handle paperwork. These duties demand certain obvious personal qualities:

1. *Tact and understanding*. The professional chef must be able to foster a spirit of cooperation so that all staff members can work together smoothly and efficiently.
2. *Integrity and honesty*. The chef's character and ethical standards should be above question—just as any professional person's should be.
3. *Temperance*. The chef should avoid excessive drinking, smoking, or eating, thus setting an example for the entire staff. This is of particular significance in hotelkeeping and catering, where special precautions against overindulgence on the part of lower level staff are often necessary.
4. *Level-headedness*. Acting like a vain "hot shot" is no longer acceptable. The professional should deal with problems and crises in a calm, logical way.
5. *Immaculate appearance*. Hygiene is of top importance in the kitchen. The chef should set the standard for others with clean clothes, clean hands, and a neatly groomed appearance.
6. *Knowledge of the field*. The professional chef should be at ease and at home in cultured surroundings, in order to cultivate the ability to make menus and dishes varied and appealing to comparably cultured "men and women of the world."

Creativity and Responsibility

Many famous chefs have the skills and imagination to create dishes that are recognized as works of art—however temporary such works might be. Even those who are not artists, however, must be highly skilled at their craft if they are to fulfill their role successfully. Artists can create original works; craftspeople can follow a pattern and recreate

---

Recipe for a Professional

Yield:
A competent person qualified to play a profitable role in an expanding industry

Personal Ingredients:
Tact and understanding
Integrity and honesty
Temperance
Levelheadedness
Immaculate appearance
Knowledge of the field

Method:
Cultivate the above ingredients in all situations at all times.

dishes of equal quality time and again.

The creative aspect of cookery depends upon personal taste, manipulative skill, urge to create, interest in food, mastery of cooking technique, practice, and patience.

A genuine interest in food and cookery is the key with which the aspiring chef unlocks the door to creativity. The same interest is also a powerful factor in ensuring the development of taste and judgment. Certainly, without genuine interest in the craft of cookery, a person who possesses technical ability and craft at the stove will never reach the pinnacle of the profession.

The chef should constantly strive to serve the public and should find satisfaction in doing so. Not only must food look, smell, and taste good, but it must be wholesome and safe, nutritious and clean. The best type of chef, therefore, is one who has a sense of duty, strong pride in the cooking craft, and a desire to serve the public well.

Demands of the Job

Though working conditions in the kitchen have greatly improved in recent years, and though total hours of work compare favorably with those in many other industries, many chefs will be required to work hours other than the common nine to five. Consequently, chefs must feel sufficiently interested in their vocation to remain happy with a career in which their working (and free) hours differ from those of many of their friends. They may need to pay more than usual attention to the organization of their leisure time.

Overall Qualities

It is not easy to express with mathematical precision the human qualities required of a successful chef. But to sum up, the essential qualities and characteristics of a good chef include the following:

Sufficient education and intelligence

Capacity for and willingness to undertake hard work (both physical and mental)

Honesty

High personal standards in physical hygiene and moral responsibility

A sense of vocation, including a commitment to integrity and high standards of quality

The Chef's Attire

Although a *chef de cuisine* works behind the scenes, the chef's attire is perfectly familiar to the average person. It includes the white, starched cap, the white, double-breasted jacket, the white neckerchief, the blue and white checked cotton trousers, the white apron, and the kitchen cloth. See figure 2-1. Its distinctiveness and recognizability confer prestige and status. It should be carefully maintained and worn with pride.

2-1. The chef's attire. From Culinary Institute of America, *The Professional Chef's Knife.*

History

This professional attire is the outcome of gradual evolution and became completely standardized only in this century.

In medieval kitchens, cooks wore a variety of costumes. The only common denominator was the apron. By Victorian times, portraits reveal chefs and ordinary *cuisiniers* in white clothing. *Chefs de partie* generally are shown wearing white caps. Carême is credited with having introduced to Britain the toque or high, starched hat, which superseded the "night cap" type. Alfred Suzanne, in his book *La Cuisine Anglaise* (1894), gives 1840 as the year when the toque began to achieve popularity. But even after that, as great a chef as Alexis Soyer wore a tasseled black beret instead of the toque.

12

In Great Britain, a similar black skullcap is still worn by the master cook (the equivalent of the *maître chef de cuisine*) at the famous English-style restaurant Simpson's in the Strand. However, the darker, closer-fitting cap, even though it conveys effectively the prestige of top rank in the kitchen, is less cool and comfortable for working at the stove than the airy toque.

Styles

In addition to outward garments, underclothing and socks should be selected with care. In some warmer sections of the kitchen, physical activity causes considerable perspiration. A generous number of undergarments of an absorbent material such as cotton are therefore essential. Undergarments and socks should be changed daily. It is equally important to wear sound shoes that are in a good state of repair; bad footwear leads to tripping and accidents, as well as to discomfort and poor hygiene.

The Chef's Cap. The cap should be laundered regularly whether it is obviously dirty or not. Telltale marks such as perspiration stains around the band must particularly be avoided. Disposable caps of paper or some other inexpensive material are worth considering for reasons of hygiene and economy.

The Neck Cloth. There are many modes of tying and wearing the neck cloth. The original purpose of this appendage was to absorb facial perspiration, but the trend now is toward wearing it as a close-fitting, neatly knotted tie. No doubt this has occurred because kitchen heat is less intense than it was in the old days of open fires.

The Jacket. The accepted chef's jacket is a double-breasted or crossover style, and the type with cloth buttons is generally favored for an elegant appearance. The sleeves of this garment are never rolled up; instead, the chef simply turns back the cuffs, which are adapted with a slit especially for this purpose. The sleeves are kept long in order to protect the chef's arms from splashing hot liquids and fats and from contact with hot oven doors, saucepans, and so forth.

The Trousers. The chef's trousers are made of washable blue and white checked cotton material. Because the lower part of the leg, for example, can easily become splashed and soiled, it is important that the trousers be washed frequently.

The Apron. The white apron takes the worst of the workaday soiling and will almost certainly need at least daily changing (reversing the apron once is permissible). Folding at the waist to camouflage staining can also extend the wear time. But folding cannot be done indefinitely or the apron will become too short.

The "Rubber." The "rubber," a linen kitchen cloth, is tucked into the apron string, usually at the rear left. It has an almost infinite number of uses, but most of them are associated with the protection of the hands when moving objects around stoves and in the ovens (the kitchen cloth should not substitute for the thick oven cloth, however). The kitchen cloth should not be abused as a floor swab or duster, since it is an item of apparel. It should be kept clean and odor free during the day.

Personal Hygiene

Unusually high standards of personal hygiene are required of a chef. Dress and hygiene should combine to produce a professional appearance: well-groomed, with due attention to a neat hairstyle; neatly trimmed and clean nails; freshly laundered clothing; and (for men) a close shave, as well as general neatness.

Recipe for Proper Attire

Yield:
A well-dressed chef who takes pride in personal appearance

Costume Ingredients:
4 chef's caps
4 chef's white double-breasted jackets
6 chef's white neckerchiefs
6 white aprons
6 plain (white or unbleached) linen kitchen cloths ("rubbers")
3 pairs kitchen trousers/skirts

Method:
The number of each item allows for delays at the laundry and for the flexibility to change as frequently as necessary.

A scrupulous attention to dress and the competent handling of tools distinguish the truly professional chef. It is a myth that dirty or disheveled dress is evidence of a hard worker. Rather, such an appearance signifies a careless and disorderly cook. Pride in appearance, on the other hand, reinforces pride of craft and consequent efficiency.

Training and Employment

For several reasons, chefs should stay abreast of recent developments in training and employment, even after completing their own training. First, they may often be asked for advice by prospective students and their parents. Second, they will be involved with recruiting newly trained people and should be able to evaluate the quality of their potential employees' training. Finally, every chef serving in a supervisory capacity will be responsible for the continued training of subordinates. This may involve formal teaching in an on-the-job training program or simply making arrangements for staff members to attend other programs.

The primary objective of all good training programs is to produce skilled experts who are able to meet the high standards of kitchen craftsmanship common in the industry today. Certificate or degree programs are designed to prepare people for a lifetime career. Initial training is also available for those who want an introduction to the field but do not plan to specialize in it. At both levels, properly trained staff are more efficient, more productive, and happier. They also have a lower turnover rate than untrained recruits. Everyone benefits from good training—the cook, the cook's supervisors and employers, and the customers.

There are two fundamentally different sources of high-quality formal training: industry training centers and educational institutions.

Industry Training

Nearly every category of foodservice operation has associated with it some type of formal training program, in addition to the normal on-the-job training found in almost every establishment.

Restaurant Chains. Most restaurant chains offer centrally planned and organized training opportunities for employees and managers of the various establishments in the chain. The Mr. Steak chain, for example, has a program of films, charts, and study guides for independent, self-paced study that is administered from the company's headquarters in Denver. On-the-job training follows successful completion of this core material. In addition, by taking more advanced training courses in the company's management development program, participants can earn study credits toward degrees at participating colleges.

Hotel Foodservice. Many hotel chains also have a central program for staff training and development. The Marriott system, for example, uses workshops, videocassette programs, interactive Computer Assisted Instruction, and even teleconferencing, which bounces audio and video communications via satellite from a central office to multiple locations, as needed.

Institutional/Contract Foodservice. Companies that provide foodservice on a contract basis to such institutions as schools, hospitals, and airlines must also provide adequate training for their employees. For example, the training headquarters for Saga Corporation in Kalamazoo, Michigan, offers traditional classroom work, seminars, and role-playing.

Fast-Food Chains. McDonald's, whose golden arches can be seen all over the world, maintains a "Hamburger University" in Elk Grove Village, Illinois, as well as a branch campus in Tokyo, Japan. About 2,000 students each year graduate from the schools as "Bachelors of Hamburgerology." In addition to basic restaurant operations, the program includes courses in management and personnel psychology. Many of these courses are approved for college credit by the American Council on Education.

Independent Foodservice Operations. Practically all foodservice establishments, even "mom and pop" operations, have some form of training for employees. Usually this is of the informal on-the-job training type.

Educational Institutions

A growing number of diploma- and degree-granting educational institutions have instituted foodservice programs of study.

High Schools. Many high schools have vocational preparatory programs specializing in foodservice. Such programs often include traditional courses, such as business math and business administration, and practical experience via work-study programs, summer workshops, laboratory kitchens, and so forth.

Community Colleges. Some institutions have two-year Associate of Arts degree programs for the high school graduate. Miami-Dade Community College in Florida, for instance, has a 66-credit-hour program leading to an Associate in Science degree in Hotel/Restaurant/Institutional Management. This program includes basic courses on such topics as elementary food preparation, volume food management, and food and beverage control. It also includes some general college courses and an internship to provide practical experience.

Culinary Arts Institutes. The Culinary Institute of America offers an Associate in Occupational Studies degree at its campus in Hyde Park, New York. To graduate, each student must earn a total of 72 credit hours in such courses as introductory baking, introductory hot foods, menu and facilities planning, international cuisine, and à la carte food preparation. The program includes a 21-week internship, in which each student works for pay in a real foodservice establishment and is evaluated by both his employer and an Institute coordinator.

Four-Year Colleges and Universities. Many colleges and universities have a department offering bachelor's degrees in foodservice administration. At this level, most programs emphasize management training rather than basic cooking skills, and they include a lot more general college courses in humanities, social sciences, and physical sciences. Cornell University in Ithaca, New York, and the University of Massachusetts at Amherst have such programs. Courses include food production management, foodservice management, personnel management in hotels and restaurants, and hotel, restaurant, and travel law. Many universities with this type of department also offer graduate degrees such as the Master of Science or the Ph.D.

Trade Associations

One of the useful functions of chefs' associations and other trade organizations is to assist members in finding suitable employment. They can also help chefs who are recruiting to find suitable staff. They also may conduct training seminars, publish literature relevant to the industry, sponsor competitions and awards to help set and maintain high standards, and engage in lobbying for pertinent legislation. There are many such organizations in the United States.

American Culinary Federation (ACF). This organization was founded in 1930. It has about 6,000 professional chef members, who are organized into state and local chapters. It sponsors continuing education programs and sends American teams to the international Culinary Olympics. It publishes *The Culinarian* and *Culinary Review*, both monthly periodicals. Address: 3520 N. Rutherford Street, Chicago, Illinois 60634. Phone: (312) 545-8887.

International Chefs' Association (ICA). This organization was founded in 1905 and has about 250 members worldwide. To qualify for membership, an applicant must be a professional chef in a restaurant or hotel. Address: 435 Fifth Avenue, New York, New York 10016. Phone: (212) 686-7479.

National Restaurant Association (NRA). Founded in 1919, this group now has about 13,000 members. It represents most types of foodservice, including caterers, institutional and contract providers, and traditional restaurants. It sponsors foodservice research, continuing education, and public information. It publishes *Washington Report* weekly and other bulletins on an irregular basis. Address: One IBM Plaza, Suite 2600, Chicago, Illinois 60611. Phone: (312) 787-2525.

Council on Hotel, Restaurant, and Institutional Education (CHRIE). This organization was begun in 1946. It now has approximately 600 members, most of whom are affiliated with schools and colleges that offer training programs in food production and hospitality service administration. It publishes the bimonthly *Hospitality Educator* and the semiannual *Journal of Hospitality Education.* Address: Human Development Building, Room 12, University Park, Pennsylvania 16802. Phone: (814) 863-0586.

State and Local Associations. The American Culinary Federation and many other organizations have affiliated state or local chapters. Such subgroups are able to offer more opportunities for members to meet and get to know one another than are the national groups, which may have only one convention a year. In addition, such subgroups probably have more direct information about the employment opportunities in their particular areas.

3. Responsibilities Outlined

Chefs have been called "people in the middle." They are regarded as employees by higher management but are looked upon as members of management by employees below them. In reality they are both. They translate higher management's directives into an efficient food production service. They bridge the gap between policies and action, between goal setting and goal attainment.

In fulfilling the position of supervisor, the chef could until recently rule the kitchen in a rigid, dictatorial manner. The chef was empowered to hire and fire, to promote, and to award pay raises, with little accountability to higher authority. But with the appearance of large hotel groups has come a new managerial philosophy based on a growing recognition that chefs must possess flexible attitudes and develop social awareness if their subordinates are to work at maximum efficiency. Modern chefs must understand how their workplace's informal organization works and how people are motivated. They must be able to adjust their personal styles to changing circumstances, and they must learn to apply fundamental management techniques to kitchen production.

Management Functions

Chefs have several responsibilities with regard to management.

Planning

Planning means determining the best course of action, under a given set of circumstances, for achieving preestablished objectives. Specific targets set by top management are derived from overall company objectives. The chef should be personally committed to these overall goals and then should set intermediate performance goals and basic standards for the rest of the staff. These must ultimately reflect the kitchen's contribution to the company's main objectives. The chef's problem, then, is to ensure that subordinates' work is always directed towards the achievement of the goals and standards set for them.

Many aspects of kitchen work must be planned—food purchasing, for example. Unfortunately, menu-item demand cannot always be forecast with precision, so the chef should work with front office sales managers to estimate the demand pattern for food over the coming week or 24 hours. See figure 3-1. The chef must also plan work rosters and employee schedules that reflect the actual demand for foodservice. In the course of planning, the different abilities of the staff members must be considered so that the right mix of skills exists for each shift or subgroup. An operations manual might also be developed to cover normal, predictable conditions and to inform staff members about where to go for guidance when needed.

Planning is not a one-time operation. Plans must be flexible enough to adapt successfully when unforeseen circumstances arise. Changing conditions may also dictate frequent and regular revision of general plans.

Organizing and Coordinating

Organizing means allocating work to the various staff groups and individuals and providing them with the right materials (equipment and supplies) to do their jobs. In order to carry out this task success-

3-1. Scatter sheet used for economic analysis. From Lundberg, *The Hotel and Restaurant Business*, 4th edition.

SCATTER SHEET

SALES PRICE	MENU ITEM	TIMES SOLD	TOTAL	SALES VALUE
	25% Cost			
$ 1.25	Hamburger	ʘʘʘ ʘʘʘ ʘʘʘ ʘʘʘ - ʘʘʘ ʘ	26	$ 32.50
1.00	Cheese Sandwich	ʘʘʘ - ʘ	6	6.00
1.50	Egg Salad Sandwich	ʘʘʘ - ʘʘʘ	10	15.00
1.00	Jello Salad	ʘʘʘ	5	5.00
	30% Cost			
1.25	Pie, Cherry & Apple	ʘʘʘ - ʘʘʘ - ʘʘʘ	13	16.25
1.00	Ice Cream	ʘʘʘ - ʘʘʘ - ʘʘʘ	15	15.00
1.75	Cheeseburger	ʘʘʘ - ʘʘʘ - ʘʘʘ - ʘʘʘ - ʘʘʘ - ʘʘʘ	30	52.50
2.00	Ham Sandwich	ʘʘʘ - ʘʘʘ - ʘʘʘ	15	30.00
1.50	Waldorf Salad	ʘʘʘ - ʘʘʘ - ʘʘ	12	18.00
7.00	Baked Ham Dinner	ʘʘʘ - ʘʘʘ - ʘʘʘ - ʘʘʘ - ʘʘʘ	25	350.00
5.75	Fried Chicken Dinner	ʘʘʘ - ʘʘʘ - ʘʘʘ - ʘʘʘ	20	115.00
	35% Cost			
2.75	Pork Sandwich, Hot	ʘʘʘ - ʘʘʘ	10	27.50
2.75	Beef Sandwich, Hot	ʘʘʘ - ʘʘʘ - ʘʘʘ - ʘʘʘ	20	55.00
4.50	Shrimp Salad	ʘʘʘ - ʘʘʘ - ʘʘʘ - ʘʘʘ - ʘʘʘ - ʘʘʘ	30	135.00
6.00	Turkey Dinner	ʘʘʘ - ʘʘʘ - ʘʘʘ - ʘʘʘ - ʘʘʘ	25	150.00
6.50	Pork Chop Dinner	ʘʘʘ	5	32.50
1.30	Ice Cream, Sundae	ʘʘʘ - ʘʘʘ - ʘʘʘ - ʘʘʘ - ʘʘʘ	25	37.50
	40% Cost			
6.00	Lobster Cocktail	ʘʘʘ - ʘʘʘ - ʘʘʘ - ʘʘʘ	20	120.00
3.75	Club Sandwich	ʘʘʘ - ʘʘʘ - ʘʘʘ - ʘʘʘ - ʘʘʘ - ʘʘʘ - ʘʘʘ	35	131.25
6.50	Pork Tender, Dinner	ʘʘʘ - ʘʘʘ - ʘʘ	12	78.00
8.50	Filet Mignon, Dinner	ʘʘʘ - ʘʘʘ - ʘʘʘ - ʘʘʘ - ʘʘʘ	25	212.50
2.00	French Pastry	ʘʘʘ - ʘʘʘ - ʘʘʘ	15	30.00
	45% Cost			
6.00	Oyster Cocktail	ʘʘʘ - ʘʘʘ - ʘʘʘ - ʘʘʘ	20	120.00
4.50	Fruit Salad, Plate	ʘʘʘ - ʘʘʘ - ʘʘʘ - ʘʘʘ - ʘʘʘ	23	103.50
7.00	Rib Steak, Dinner	ʘʘʘ - ʘʘʘ	10	70.00
7.25	Rainbow Trout, Dinner	ʘʘʘ - ʘʘʘ - ʘʘʘ - ʘʘʘ - ʘʘʘ - ʘʘʘ - ʘ	31	224.75
9.75	Prime Rib, Dinner	ʘʘʘ - ʘʘ	7	68.25
.50	Coffee	ʘʘʘ - ʘʘʘ - ʘʘʘ - ʘʘʘ - ʘʘʘ - ʘʘʘ - ʘʘʘ - ʘʘʘ - ʘʘʘ - ʘ	46	23.00
.50	Milk	ʘʘʘ - ʘʘʘ - ʘʘʘ - ʘʘʘ - ʘʘʘ - ʘʘʘ - ʘʘʘ	35	17.50
	50% Cost			
2.00	Asparagus Tip Salad	ʘʘʘ - ʘʘʘ - ʘʘʘ - ʘʘʘ - ʘʘʘ - ʘʘʘ	30	60.00
5.00	Prime Rib Sandwich	ʘʘʘ - ʘʘʘ - ʘʘʘ - ʘʘʘ	19	95.00
13.50	T-Bone Steak, 16 oz.	ʘʘʘ - ʘʘʘ - ʘʘʘ - ʘʘʘ - ʘʘʘ - ʘʘʘ - ʘʘʘ	35	472.50
12.50	New York Cut Steak, 12 oz	ʘʘʘ - ʘʘʘ - ʘʘʘ - ʘʘ	17	212.50
2.25	Strawberry Shortcake	ʘʘʘ - ʘʘʘ - ʘʘʘ - ʘʘʘ - ʘʘʘ - ʘʘʘ - ʘʘʘ	35	78.75
	55% Cost			
3.50	Chef's Salad Bowl	ʘʘʘ - ʘʘʘ - ʘʘʘ - ʘʘʘ - ʘʘʘ	25	87.50
6.25	Calf's Liver Dinner	ʘʘʘ - ʘʘʘ - ʘʘʘ - ʘʘʘ - ʘʘʘ - ʘ	26	162.50
12.50	Lobster Tails	ʘʘʘ - ʘʘ	7	87.50
				$3550.75

fully, the chef must not become overextended and exhausted by insisting on retaining all authority. The secret of managerial efficiency lies in the art of delegation. This is not a process of evading work by dumping as much as possible onto others; on the contrary, it involves giving each person the authority required to handle an assigned job directly. The chef still retains ultimate responsibility for the overall standard of the kitchen's food production.

Some chefs may fear to delegate. They may think that, if they do not personally attend to every detail, either the food produced will suffer or they themselves will appear superfluous. But in reality, both chef and staff work better when each concentrates on what each does best.

Coordination ensures harmony within the chef's staff group and cooperation with other departments of the hotel or catering establishment. In particular, the chef should seek close cooperation with the service department and its head, the maître d'hôtel. All too often, friction between these two department heads results in bad restaurant service, which only serves to hurt everyone. Coordination becomes especially difficult in split-shift systems and in systems in which multiskilled employees work in more than one department. The latter concept has been tried with employees who find the varied pattern more fulfilling and elsewhere as a cost-cutting measure. But it places great demands on a chef's organizational skills and ability to communicate and coordinate with other supervisors. Should such practices become more common in the future, the chef's supervisory tasks will become still more demanding. Such new levels of responsibility and authority may even change the nature of the chef's position from that of supervisor to that of manager.

Motivating – very important

Motivating means inspiring subordinates to accomplish their portion of the overall plan. The best method of motivation is reward. Reward is not limited to money (salary, raises, and bonuses); it includes words of praise, public recognition, or even a personal letter of gratitude to the individual concerned. Different rewards work for different people, depending on each person's unique mix of emotional and financial needs. Therefore the chef must constantly strive to understand the individual needs of subordinates in order to know what form of reward will motivate them best.

Higher managers must appreciate that chefs are vital links in the chain of responsibility. The chef, being the individual closest to the production workers, must measure performance and take remedial action when necessary. The unqualified support of those higher up is essential to enable the chef to function properly at the supervisory level.

Controlling

Controlling means evaluating progress and taking corrective action when needed. Without a control system, any plan drawn up by the chef will be unsuccessful. To fulfill any management plan, the person charged with the supervisory role must become aware of underachievement and other problems soon enough to do something about them. In establishing his control system, the chef must be careful neither to overcontrol nor undercontrol subordinates. The system established must be understandable to those who operate within it, must conform to the organizational structure within the kitchen, and must allow for quick reporting of underachievement of standards together with an indication of how and when corrective action should be taken.

Recipe for Good Chef Management

Yield:
A chef who knows how to manage the kitchen

Management Function Ingredients:
Planning
Organizing and coordinating
Motivating
Controlling

Method:
Apply with reason and common sense.

Responsibility and Discipline

In order to achieve individual and group targets, the chef must achieve and then maintain an acceptable level of discipline in the kitchen. This involves encouraging individuals to control their personal conduct in a way that develops individual cooperation and appropriate behavior; after all, employees should not waste time, quarrel, or perform tasks the wrong way. It usually takes years of experience and insight to develop positive disciplinary skills that do not rely on threats of punishment, but the effort is worth it. It may seem easier to rely mainly on punishment, but such an approach produces kitchen staff members who are chiefly concerned with avoiding punishment rather than ones who are totally committed to achieving high standards through cooperative teamwork. Punishment, therefore, should be limited to the rare instances when positive efforts fail.

Basically, the positive philosophy is supportive rather than vindictive. It seeks to explain standards and to obtain kitchen workers' inner commitment to them. To accomplish this, the chef uses personal example, explanation, and individual encouragement to foster a secure environment in which individual creativity and group cooperation can flourish. Cooperation among all workers throughout the organization must be promoted. A fair grievance procedure should be established to handle legitimate grievances.

Positive or supportive discipline will be difficult to achieve unless the chef is aware that, alongside the formal organizational structure of any kitchen, an informal social structure also exists. The chef must realize that people form such social groups not to resist authority, but to give themselves a sense of belonging. Rather than trying to disrupt these informal, cohesive groups, the chef should direct their energy towards achieving the standards set for the kitchen. Subordinates who are known and respected as individuals and as workers will come to accept their chef's leadership.

Progress in developing positive discipline may be slow, and many pitfalls will appear. But after all, management concerns human beings, and chefs must deal with individuals who have different personalities, different qualifications, different abilities, and different personal problems as well as different work problems. It is the function of management to weld these diverse personalities into a soundly motivated and efficiently working group.

Recipe for Kitchen Discipline

Yield:
A dedicated staff that works cooperatively as a team

Chef's Managerial Ingredients:
Establish high standards
Explain policies and procedures
Set a good example
Be supportive and encouraging
Avoid punishment when possible
Reward good performance
Handle grievances fairly

Method:
Apply to each staff member on an individual basis, recognizing that differences exist among people.

Management of People

Recent developments in the field of management may suggest that there is a continuous supply of new difficulties to overcome. But most experts in management training stress that the problems have neither changed nor increased; they are just being approached in newer and more sophisticated ways. Take, for example, the old kitchen dictum, "A place for everything and everything in its place." That is an old-fashioned and simpler way of expressing a concept which is today the basis for the more complicated approach called *method study.* Chefs have always sought to identify and then simplify the component parts of each task, and to reduce unnecessary movement of personnel and material. See figure 3-2. Rather than having each chef reinvent the wheel, however, specialists, consultants, and advisors are available today who can make substantial contributions to streamlining kitchen work. Chefs and caterers would be unwise to reject the aid of such specialists. Despite individual differences, human behavior, motives, and reactions

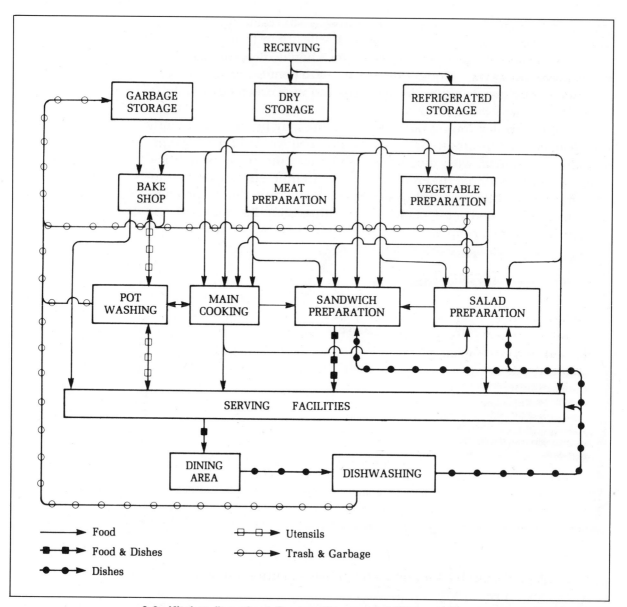

3-2. Kitchen flow chart. Source: Commercial Kitchens, The American Gas Association, from Lundberg, *The Hotel and Restaurant Business,* 4th edition.

are basically consistent, so what works in one industry or establishment will probably work in another.

To achieve maximum productivity in the kitchen, the chef must practice efficiency in management of both equipment and people. The latter is considerably more difficult. In larger establishments, personnel issues are handled by a separate department. But chefs or caterers in such establishments must not regard the presence of a staff manager or personnel officer as eliminating their responsibility and concern for the human beings on the staff. These people are not robots impersonally putting out work units; they are individuals with whom the chef must work. In any case, it is not possible to concentrate all personnel matters into a single specialized department. Unlike finance or purchasing, the personnel function must be diffused through all operational and staff departments.

Nevertheless, certain functions stay mainly within the personnel department, including: identifying areas where policy needs to be clarified; developing constructive solutions to current problems in a manner that is consistent with previous company decisions; helping to achieve a balance between employee and company goals; ensuring that heads of departments conform to established company procedures in administering the company's appraisal system; and providing routine services in such areas as maintaining employee records and administering employee pension and insurance systems. In addition, there are many functions that cannot be isolated in the personnel department. These include manpower planning, recruitment and selection of new employees, training, appraisal, discipline, and grievance procedures. The chef must be involved with all of these.

Manpower Planning

The quality of the foodservice offered depends on the skills of those who prepare it and on the effort they put into its production. Quality affects, in turn, the establishment's commercial viability. If the establishment fails to please customers, they will cease to patronize it. The chef should help in identifying the manpower requirements for adequate foodservice. In particular, the chef should consider the kitchen's manpower needs in terms of numbers, skills, and experience. These will be assessed in light of the direction in which the company intends to expand or contract in the future. For example, new technology such as microwave or cook/freeze systems may dictate hiring new employees with different skills or retraining current employees. If perceived manpower needs cannot be met, then company objectives must be modified in accordance with reality.

Recruitment and Selection

Having the right person for each job helps maintain morale. When recruiting for a new position, however, the chef may have difficulty attracting someone who is self-evidently the "right" person for the job. Sometimes the person desired by the chef is not interested because of the pay and/or status of the job. Sometimes the one most eager for the job does not meet the chef's standards. The personnel department can help in the process by conducting preliminary screening of applicants.

In operations where job analysis is practiced, the chef will have on file records for each position that state:

The job title
The type of person required
The source from which the person may be obtained (whether by promotion or by outside recruitment)
The training, experience, and other qualifications the person should have
The duties the person will have to perform (level of responsibility, physical and social tasks, and the like)

Such job analysis records are particularly useful when a detached main office does the hiring and the chef is not available for on-the-spot advice.

In addition to the job analysis information above, the prospective salary, hours of work, and promotional opportunities associated with the post must be considered before a want ad can be written. Normally, when the replies to want ads are received, the recruitment specialist screens for further consideration only those who seem to fit the job description and personnel specifications. Now the selection phase proper begins. Even though a personnel officer may make the final choice, the opinion and judgment of the chef (who will be the future supervisor of the new recruit) will have considerable weight in the final decision. Thus the chef is well-advised to develop interviewing skills that will help identify potential, in terms of both work efficiency and social compatibility with the existing informal groups that new recruits will join. Ultimately, the personnel manager will appraise how effectively the chef conducts the selection function, based on an analysis of labor turnover and the results of final interviews.

Staff Efficiency

After analyzing an open staff position, the chef should prepare brief notes, in the form of either an instruction sheet or a leaflet, that outline the nature, times, and details of the duties to be performed. See figure 3-3. Even when the broad duties required of a position seem traditionally clear, the operational style of the hotel or catering establishment may be unique, and this should be explained. For less experienced workers, this type of leaflet is particularly valuable. Such an instruction sheet also helps when it comes time for the chef to rate subordinates for the establishment's appraisal system. If their performance is matched against what they were told to do, the chef's judgment will tend to be more objective and fair, and the chef will be less likely to confuse personality with performance.

After issuing the instruction sheet, the chef should not wait until the first formal evaluation before giving new subordinates some feedback. To improve efficiency, the chef must provide sympathetic criticism and advice regularly and frequently, thereby informing the employees about how well or poorly they are doing the work defined in their job descriptions. Unfortunately, such communication too often either is not provided or is given in a blunt or uncaring manner. These approaches, however, only signal that the chef is not interested in the staff members as people and is avoiding the responsibility to help them recognize and develop their skills in order to prepare for promotion. Further, by failing to develop and train members of the existing staff, the chef will end up having to seek new skills and experience from outside the organization, and promotion from outside rather than within will seriously undermine the morale of the established kitchen staff. Therefore, the chef should continually seek to improve the efficiency of the existing staff, in order to increase both current productivity and long-term development.

Use of Mixer: Medium-size Bench Model

Steps	Key Points
1. Place bowl in bowl support.	1. Bowl has three hook holes on outside of rim, which are used to hold bowl in position: one in center back, one on each side.
	2. Place bowl into position with center back hook hole in correct contact with hook found in center back of support rim and with two side hook holes over two small posts found on either side of supporting rim.
	3. These three points must be correctly adjusted or paddle (or beater) will not move freely in the bowl.
2. Attach paddle, beater, or dough hook.	1. Have lift handle in lowered position.
	2. Place paddle (beater or dough hook) inside the bowl. Bring top of paddle up onto rod, push up and turn to the right to lock into position.
3. Pull lift handle up.	To bring bowl into position.
4. Set speed.	Correct speed for mixing ingredients is important—otherwise splashing or over-mixing may result. *See instructions on recipe card.*
5. Start motor.	Turn switch to "on" position.
6. Stop mixer when through mixing.	Turn switch to "off" position.
7. Lower the lift handle.	This lowers the bowl.
8. Release paddle (beater or dough hook).	Push up, turn to the left, then pull down.
9. Lift bowl from rack support.	
10. *Safety rule.*	Never put your hand or spatula inside the bowl when paddle is in motion.

SOURCE: U.S. Department of Commerce, *Establishing and Operating a Restaurant.*

3-3. Separating a job into simple, individual tasks. From Eshback, *Foodservice Management,* 3rd edition.

Morale

High labor turnover, particularly in the initial weeks after hiring, is characteristic of kitchen staff. Some of this may be due to personal inadequacies of the workers, but it is also due to inadequacies in the work environment. The chef has little say over many of these factors, such as salaries and fringe benefits, although recommendations can be made to higher management even in these areas. However, the chef can have a substantial impact on morale in the areas of his or her primary responsibility. For example, the chef can and should develop an orientation program to provide newcomers with a warm and friendly welcome.

The chef can also ensure a fair distribution of tasks and work hours by developing a schedule that does not dump all unfavorable times on new people. The schedule should provide adequate time and days off for all and should provide some holidays for each person. The schedule should be prepared and distributed far enough in advance that subordinates can make plans for their leisure time.

The chef should treat all subordinates with respect and try to afford them a sense of dignity by giving proper status and recognition to even the lowliest worker. One way to achieve this is to give a hierarchical title to each position. For example, instead of "veg man," the title "kitchen assistant" might be used, and instead of "dishwasher," the title "kitchen hygiene assistant" or "sanitary assistant." In addition to assigning titles, the chef should make sure each worker has a clean, pride-instilling working uniform and that every staff member's working conditions are decent. Machines should be enlisted to eliminate, or at least reduce, the drudgery of unskilled and semiskilled tasks. The chef should avoid all traces of racism, sexism, and ethnocentrism by treating each worker as a unique individual. Even when periods of high unemployment produce many qualified applicants for each opening, the chef should not succumb to an uncaring attitude toward subordinates.

One other area relating to morale—the facilities for kitchen staff—is not under the chef's direct control, but if the chef does not make the case for better facilities for the staff, no one will. Such facilities are often poor because the owners do not profit directly from them. So the chef's best argument to convince higher management to improve conditions and facilities for staff members is that such an investment will create a work environment in which members are motivated to achieve higher levels of performance. This benefit often exceeds the cost of improving the facilities.

Restrooms constitute one crucial area in which investment may be required to ensure that standards of hygiene are properly observed by members of the staff. Restrooms for staff are often inferior in comparison to those provided for guests, which may directly reduce the kitchen staff's willingness to maintain the required standards of hygiene, as well as to achieve desired levels of production generally, because such facilities suggest that management has an uncaring attitude.

Ideally, adequate staff facilities would include a clean restroom, a place for staff members to shower and change clothes, a dining room where they can eat in a leisurely manner and an area for rest and recreation when they are on breaks. Larger establishments should provide a bright and attractive staff lounge, with recreational amenities such as games, TV, and books.

These are not the only factors that affect morale. If key staff members begin to leave, the chef must make every attempt to discover why, through exit or termination interviews. If the reasons given for leaving show a meaningful pattern, then the reasons for discontent should be dealt with as soon as possible, even if this calls for capital investment or other significant changes.

Recipe for Staff Morale

Yield:
A satisfied staff motivated to achieve and maintain high standards of productivity

Ingredients:
Equitable pay
An attractive benefits package
A good orientation program for new staff
Fair distribution of tasks and work hours
Adequate staff facilities
Status and recognition
Supervision with respect for individual dignity

Method:
The chef should follow these guidelines in areas of direct responsibility and in other areas should make recommendations consistent with them to higher management as needed.

Training

The principal aims of a sound training program for new and established staff members are:

To make the most effective use of people and materials
To ensure efficient use of the plant and equipment
To prevent accidents and consequent loss of time
To encourage high morale through job satisfaction
To improve promotion planning

The chef who avoids the responsibility for training subordinates may jeopardize the smooth functioning of the entire kitchen.

Subordinates usually favor on-the-job training to other arrangements. Whatever approach is selected, the training program should be organized and should not be too time-consuming. It should incorporate standards for measuring trainee progress and it should provide for periodic feedback to trainees. Training should be instituted any time a subordinate reveals a "training gap"—that is, any time the worker is willing but unable to perform a given task to an acceptable standard. In such cases, there should be no suggestion that the subordinate is being punished for failure to perform, but rather that his or her abilities and skills are being further enriched. In addition to filling gaps in current knowledge, systematic training should be instituted to help prepare individuals for promotion and to fulfill long-range manpower plans. When drawing up detailed training plans, the chef should be able to identify skills that are best taught off the job, should be familiar with local training resources, and should be able to differentiate among different training methods so that the most appropriate method under the given circumstances can be chosen.

4. Tools and Utensils

The great chefs of the past could not have dreamed of many modern innovations such as microwave ovens. Yet the tools the chef uses himself and which he owns and carries with him wherever he may work have changed little over the past hundred years.

Personal Tools

The chef's personal tools are relatively few in number and consist mainly of knives, which are required in various sizes to trim and cut vegetables for garnish, to bone meat, to fillet fish, to slice, and to carve. For these and other tasks, individual chefs have their own preferences as to the particular types of knives to have on hand. All good professionals, however, have one thing in common: dexterity with the knife. Careful selection of personal knives and skill in their use not only conserve the chef's time and energy but also aid artistry. Dexterity ensures neatness and allows more time for finishing touches.

Just as some good golfers prefer a limited range of clubs while other equally good players rely on a multitude of irons and drivers, so chefs differ in their range of tools. All good chefs, however, are careful in making their selection. Many knives with fancy shapes and pretty handles are ill-adapted to special tasks, and some are unable to withstand the rigors of kitchen work. One rule the chef is well-advised to adopt early with personal tools is that of neither borrowing nor lending his implements.

In the following paragraphs are presented the more important knives and other tools the chef is likely to find useful in making a personal selection. See figure 4-1.

Couteau d'Office

The *couteau d'office* is a small knife normally of the traditional French shape—having a broad heel and tapering to a point. The blade is seldom longer than 10 centimeters (4 inches), and the size usually preferred is 7.5 or 8.5 centimeters (3 or 3.5 inches). The pointed end is used for tasks such as removing the hard pith where the stem joins the tomato and removing blemishes in root vegetables.

In addition to cleaning and peeling, the *couteau d'office* is used for the skilled task of "turning" vegetables. After the chef has peeled and cut the vegetables into rectangular segments, the *couteau d'office* is

4-1. Kitchen knives. Courtesy: Russell Harrington Cutlery, Inc., Southbridge, MA.

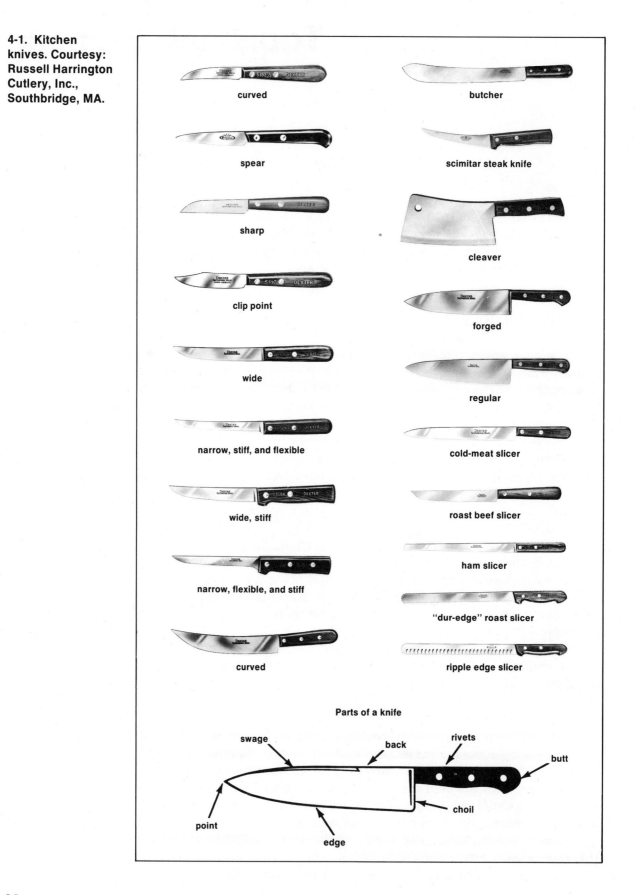

curved

butcher

spear

scimitar steak knife

sharp

cleaver

clip point

forged

wide

regular

narrow, stiff, and flexible

cold-meat slicer

wide, stiff

roast beef slicer

narrow, flexible, and stiff

ham slicer

"dur-edge" roast slicer

curved

ripple edge slicer

Parts of a knife

swage

back

rivets

butt

point

choil

edge

also used to trim off the square edges to produce an oval or rounded shape for vegetable garnishes. Only the point of the knife is used in turning, however. The axis of movement should be from the wrist down so that the hand and the tool make the same motion on round, downward cuts.

Filleting Knife

The filleting knife is a thin, pointed knife resembling an elongated *couteau d'office.* The blade length most favored is 15 to 18 centimeters (6 or 7 inches) long. This knife is used chiefly for removing fish from the bone and for trimming meat.

French Cook Knife

French cook knives vary in size from 20 to 36 centimeters (8 to 14 inches). It is here that the real value of the traditional French shape—the broad heel that tapers to a point—is most appreciated. With only a little practice, the apprentice can soon be taught to slice neatly, using the alternating toe-and-heel movement of the knife and controlling the garnish to be cut with the left (noncutting) hand. The heel does the cutting, while the point serves as a pivot. The fingers of the left hand that hold the foodstuff are slightly tucked under, enabling the left hand to guide the knife's action safely. See figure 4-2.

The beginner must learn to hold the knife correctly by grasping the handle lightly but firmly, with the fingers around and under one side and with the thumb along the other. The knife is designed for the *handle* to be used; the forefinger should not press along the top of the blade itself. See figure 4-3. The cook's knife, in particular, should always be used in concert with a wooden cutting board, not against metal or any other hard surface.

Another way of slicing with a small knife is to hold it vertically and move it quickly up and down, while the hand holding the vegetable ensures that the desired thickness is achieved. This up and down technique requires considerable practice and depends on a sharp knife and a slightly yielding surface on the cutting board. To mince, the knife should be held parallel to the cutting board, with the fingers of the left hand steadying the top of the point end. The knife is then rocked so that the cutting pressure passes from one hand to the other, each stroke gradually progressing across the board away from and then toward the body.

Spatula

The spatula blade ranges in size from 12.5 to 30 centimeters (5 inches to 12 inches), in increments of about 2.5 centimeters. A popular size for general use is a 23- or 25-centimeter (9- or 10-inch) blade. The blade of this knife is rounded at the end and has no sharp edge. It is used for scraping bowls and trays, for turning and removing articles during cooking, and for smoothing and finishing surfaces such as the icing on cakes.

1   **2**

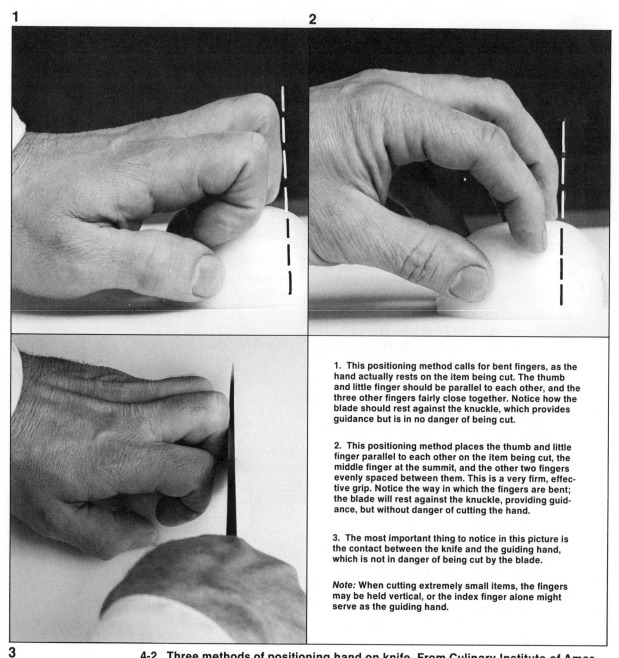

1. This positioning method calls for bent fingers, as the hand actually rests on the item being cut. The thumb and little finger should be parallel to each other, and the three other fingers fairly close together. Notice how the blade should rest against the knuckle, which provides guidance but is in no danger of being cut.

2. This positioning method places the thumb and little finger parallel to each other on the item being cut, the middle finger at the summit, and the other two fingers evenly spaced between them. This is a very firm, effective grip. Notice the way in which the fingers are bent; the blade will rest against the knuckle, providing guidance, but without danger of cutting the hand.

3. The most important thing to notice in this picture is the contact between the knife and the guiding hand, which is not in danger of being cut by the blade.

Note: When cutting extremely small items, the fingers may be held vertical, or the index finger alone might serve as the guiding hand.

3

4-2. **Three methods of positioning hand on knife. From Culinary Institute of America,** *The Professional Chef's Knife.*

Boning Knife

The usual blade size for a boning knife is 15 centimeters (6 inches). This blade differs in shape from a French cook's knife; it has a narrow heel and the blade curves backwards at the tip to a slightly uplifted point. The knife is grasped like a dagger, for the point is the part that does the work of searching out the bone and then cutting very close to it. In boning, unless great care is taken, accidents can happen because frequently cuts must be directed toward the body. It is important that these cuts be directed only obliquely toward the body so that, if there is a slip, the knife will pass harmlessly by.

Carving Knives (Slicers)

The most common carving knives are long, flexible ones that are quite straight for most of their length but curve back at the point. They range in size from 25 to 35 centimeters (10 to 14 inches) and are used for slicing meat.

Serrated Knives

A little knife with a serrated edge can cut grooves desirable in the preparation of fancy garnishes. There are also small knives that produce a single, distinctive grooving cut and that are particularly well-adapted for decorating lemons.

Other Small Tools

A selection of other small tools useful to the chef is shown in figure 4-4.

Cook's Fork. The cook should use a fork with great caution. Normally a spatula is a safer tool for manipulating items during the cooking process because it poses less danger of penetrating meat tissues and causing a consequent loss of juices. A fork should not, under any circumstances, be used to test whether the meat is done. Its main use is for holding meat during carving.

Peeler. Despite the fact that the peeling of vegetables in bulk—for example, potatoes—is usually done by unskilled kitchen hands, a peeler remains a necessary part of the chef's kit. Used at the correct angle, the type with a double-edged blade between which the peeled strip passes is best.

All-Purpose Disher. This implement can be used to provide rounded scoops of everything from ice cream to mashed potatoes.

No chef needs to keep a personal store of all the small tools used in the kitchen, even if they are needed frequently. Each chef, however, has individual preferences for certain items. In addition to those already mentioned, the list could include such items as apple corers, can openers, and kitchen scissors. Whatever pieces of equipment the chef decides to include in a permanent kit should be carefully maintained. A few chefs use a leather sheath on a belt to hold their tools while working. Other chefs use their pockets. Bunching tools into a kitchen cloth or rubber, though common, is not a good idea because it indicates a lack of concern for sanitation and safety.

Knife Care and Safety

Of all personal tools, knives require the most careful handling.

Knife Steels

Knives should be kept sharp so that they do their job effectively and safely. Blunt knives frequently cause accidents because bluntness en-

4-3. Proper knife grip. From Culinary Institute of America, *The Professional Chef's Knife.*

1. Let the knife rest in your open hand, with your four fingers together at right angles to the knife. The exact place where you grip the knife is a function of how the knife fits comfortably and is kept in control in your hand. The thumb should be relaxed and parallel to the knife.

2. Fold your fingers and, at the same time, tighten the grasp of your palm. The thumb should still be relaxed.

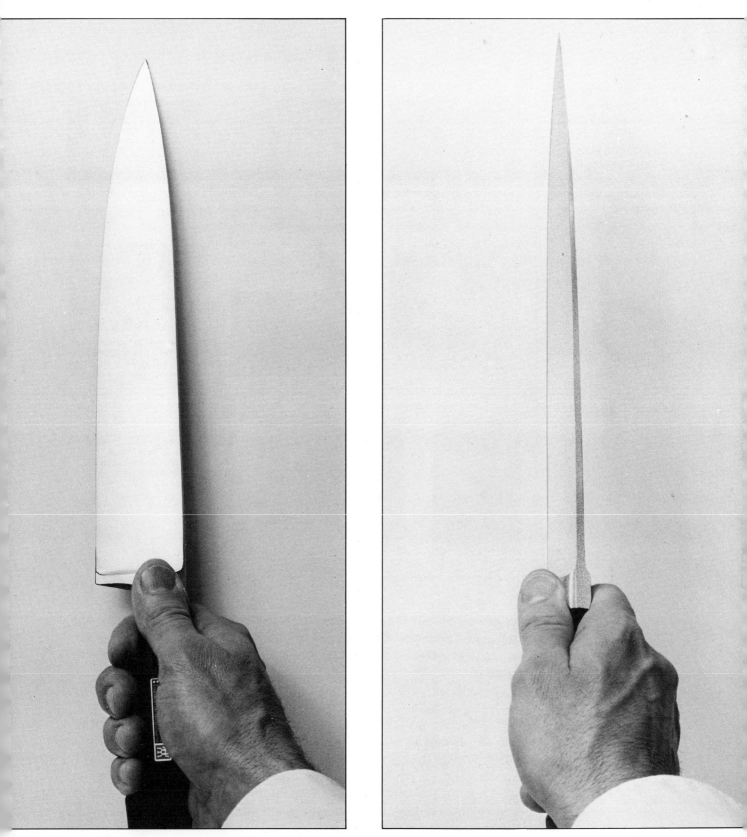

3. Turn the knife so that it is at a right angle to the cutting board, and you are ready to begin. Hold the knife securely, not permitting it to rub your hand as you work, to prevent blisters or sore spots.

4. Now rest your thumb on the knife handle, near the index finger. The strength of the grip should still come from the fingers and palm.

4-4. Kitchen utensils. Courtesy: Russell Harrington Cutlery, Inc.; from Knight and Kotschevar, *Quantity Food Production, Planning and Management.*

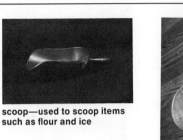

scoop—used to scoop items such as flour and ice

wire skimmer—excellent for skimming hot fat

colander—used to drain all types of foods

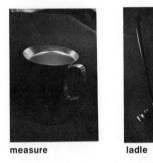

Chinese strainers—used for straining soups, gravies, purées, and other foods

all-purpose disher

wire whisks: piano wire whisk (used for liquid and fluid solids); French wire whisk: (used for mashed potatoes and soft solids)

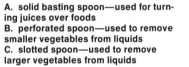

measure   ladle

A. solid basting spoon—used for turning juices over foods
B. perforated spoon—used to remove smaller vegetables from liquids
C. slotted spoon—used to remove larger vegetables from liquids

courages unusually strong pressure. Knives should be sent to an expert as necessary (normally just once or twice a year) for resetting and regrinding. However, they should not be used up prematurely by excessive grinding.

In addition to giving knives periodic professional attention, the chef should own a steel to sharpen knives with. The steel should be held with the thumb on top of the handle on the same side as the fingers, which firmly but lightly grasp the knife. The reason for the thumb's position is that the steel only needs to be held steady; should the knife slip, the thumb is much less likely to be nicked if it is in this position than if it is on the underside of the steel. Proper use of the steel is best learned by observing and imitating a good butcher or chef.

Sharpening and Setting

Oilstones and whetstones can also be used to give a keen edge. Some chefs carry a Carborundum for sharpening their knives, but this is not recommended as it results in excessive wear of the knife and soon produces an uneven edge.

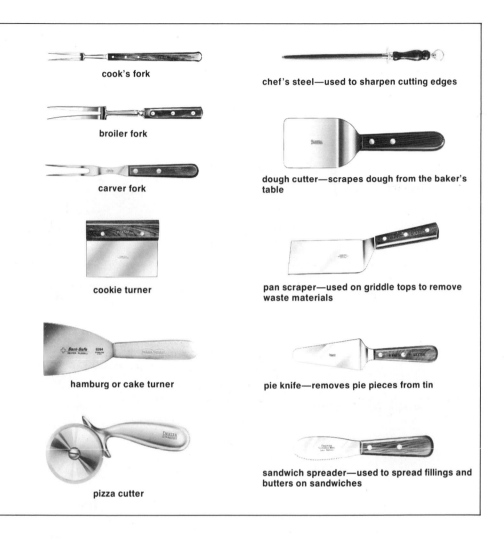

cook's fork

chef's steel—used to sharpen cutting edges

broiler fork

dough cutter—scrapes dough from the baker's table

carver fork

cookie turner

pan scraper—used on griddle tops to remove waste materials

hamburg or cake turner

pie knife—removes pie pieces from tin

pizza cutter

sandwich spreader—used to spread fillings and butters on sandwiches

Nonpersonal Kitchen Tools

In addition to the small knives and tools that form the chef's own kit is a range of instruments that are usually part of the kitchen's permanent equipment. See figure 4-5.

Parsley Chopper

The parsley chopper consists of four curved blades topped by a wooden handle equipped with two handle knobs that permit a rocking action for rapid chopping. The tempered steel blades are about 30 centimeters (12 inches) long; during use these should be scraped from time to time to keep them clear of clinging material from the food being chopped. The blades require grinding at regular intervals.

Choppers and Cleavers

There is little difference between the chopper and the cleaver (see Figure 4-1), the latter being slightly longer but much deeper than the

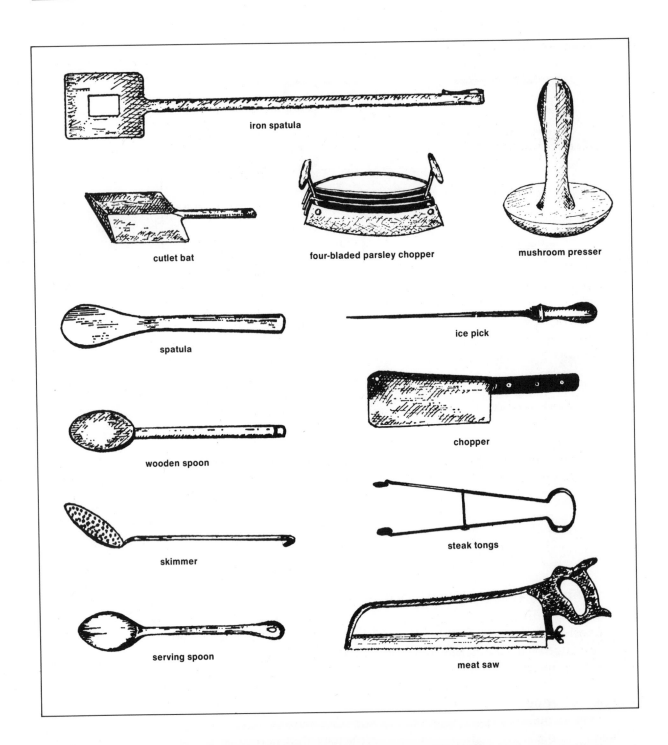

iron spatula

cutlet bat

four-bladed parsley chopper

mushroom presser

spatula

ice pick

wooden spoon

chopper

skimmer

steak tongs

serving spoon

meat saw

4-5. Kitchen tools. From Fuller, *Professional Kitchen Management*.

chopper. Both implements are used in butchery. The chopper is used on meat with relatively soft bones (lamb, for example) or to penetrate hard or gristly parts of meats. The back of the chopper is also used to crack bones. It is about 25 to 38 centimeters (10 to 15 inches) in length.

Meat Saw

The meat saw is simply an ordinary bow-shaped saw, equipped usually with a 35.5 centimeter (14-inch) blade, though sometimes it is adjustable to different lengths. The saw is reserved for severing bones and should not be used to cut through meat itself. For careful butchery work, it is preferable to the chopper because it avoids bone splintering.

Cutlet Bat

The cutlet bat is used to flatten raw meat cuts and fish. During use, the bat should be kept moist. The meat is tapped sharply with the bat, which is allowed to slide sideways off the food after each stroke. This is repeated with the bat sliding, after tapping, in all directions, so that the piece is flattened by a few strokes of this kind and not broken down by continual blows.

Wire Whisks

Whisks (shown in figure 4-4) are made of strong, flexible, tinned wires that curve out from a handle (normally of wood) where they are bound together with thin copper wire. The large type—about 40.5 to 45.5 centimeters (16 to 18 inches) long—is used almost entirely for whipping egg whites and cream. Its design makes it an ideal tool for incorporating air, especially when manually operated. The small type—about 15 centimeters (6 inches) in length—is used for all kinds of preparations requiring beating to ensure smoothness. These smaller whisks or "beaters" are normally used on power-driven mixers.

Wooden Spoon

Wooden spoons range in length from 20 to 45.5 centimeters (8 to 18 inches) and are usually made from hard beechwood. The bowl of the spoon is only slightly concave and tapers to an extremely thin outer edge. Unlike the wooden spatula, wooden spoons are not made for strength and consequently should not be used for heavy mixing. Their primary purpose is to lift ingredients such as meat or fruit out of a pot of liquid when an iron spoon might discolor the liquid or introduce a metallic flavor.

Wooden Spatula

The wooden spatula is a flat piece of wood, usually hard beechwood, available in many lengths from 20 to 122 centimeters (8 to 48 inches). Its shape can be most simply described as that of a flattened spoon. It is used as a preliminary to the wire whisk for any kind of mixing involving ingredients whose consistency is initially too thick for the whisk to operate properly. A typical use would be for making a sauce from a roux base. In this case, the whisk only comes into play at the last moment, for final stirring.

Metal Spatula

The metal spatula is made from tinned steel or iron and consists of a flat rectangular piece of metal with a long shaft bent back at the extremity for hanging. There is sometimes a hole in the center for soup or sauce to pass through when stirring up ingredients that have sunk to the bottom. Because the metal spatula scrapes the pan, it is important that both spatula and pan be properly tinned to avoid discoloration of the food. Sizes vary from approximately 30 to 90 centimeters (12 to 36 inches).

Perforated Skimmer

The skimmer consists of a round, slightly concave, perforated disk, set on a long handle at only a slight angle. The disks range in diameter from 12.5 to 17.5 centimeters (5 to 7 inches). The tool efficiently skims grease off the surface of stock. It can also be used to turn vegetables in boiling water or to remove pieces for testing. The perforated skimmer is better for vegetables than the wire skimmer (described below) because the latter tends to cut delicate foods.

Wire Skimmer

The wire skimmer is similar in shape to the perforated skimmer, but its concave disk is formed by heavy wire. See figure 4-4. The disks range in diameter from 17.5 to 23 centimeters (7 to 9 inches), with handles ranging from 30 to 34 centimeters (12 to 13.5 inches). It should not be used on foods being cooked in boiling water, but rather for deep fat frying, where it can be used to turn and remove food.

Ladle

The ladle consists of a hemispherical bowl riveted at right angles to its handle, which curves slightly back. The ladle is the most effective implement for skimming and serving sauces and gravies. It is better than a spoon for quickly and evenly spreading or coating an item with sauce. It should not be used for serving stews or soups that contain pieces of food; the ladle might break.

Ladles range in bowl-size from 5 to 20 centimeters (2 to 8 inches) in diameter. The most useful size for single portions of gravy or sauce is the 65-centimeter (2.5 inch) bowl, which holds approximately 85 grams (3 ounces) of liquid when two-thirds full. The 15-centimeter (6-inch) bowl, which holds about 195 grams (7 ounces), is sufficient for one portion of soup.

Serving Spoon

The serving spoon is simply a very large metal spoon, 30 to 45.5 centimeters (12 to 18 inches) long. It is used for serving stews and vegetables, rather than for stirring.

Steak Tongs

These metal tongs are normally about 45.5 centimeters (18 inches) long. They are held together by a crosspiece that pushes through a side bar when the tongs are pinched together. For placing, turning, and removing meat in the course of grilling, these are better than forks, which pierce the flesh and cause loss of meat juices.

Ice Pick

The ice pick is used more frequently by kitchen helpers than by chefs. This wooden-handled metal implement bears a superficial resemblance to a knife steel, but its purpose is to break blocks of ice into pieces. The ice pick should be reserved exclusively for this purpose and should not be misused pry open boxes, pierce cans, or the like.

Mushroom Presser

The mushroom presser is named for its shape. It consists of a slightly domed, circular piece of wood with a handle attached to the flat underside. Normally it is about 12.5 centimeters (5 inches) in diameter and is simply used to press food through a sieve. Its rounded shape makes it superior to a flat presser, which allows food to clog up the sieve.

Other Kitchen Implements

Slightly more elaborate implements with very basic uses are shown in figure 4-6.

Mandolin

The superstructure of the mandolin consists of a rectangular wooden frame fitted with a handle. Bolted within the frame are two steel plates. The top plate is fixed; the lower plate, which has a knife edge, forms an adjustable space between itself and the fixed plate. The size of this aperture can be controlled by a wing nut. A potato or other vegetable to be sliced is held in the hollow of the user's hand and pushed downwards against the knife blade repeatedly. If the user's fingers are not kept out of the way, however, they can get cut rather easily. When the mandolin is being used properly, the user's hand should shift the vegetable in a slightly circular movement between passes so that the vegetables will be cut evenly and not at an angle. Mandolins are available in different sizes, but the common size is approximately 30 centimeters (12 inches) long and 10 to 12.5 centimeters (4 to 5 inches) wide.

Mar-For Slicer

The Mar-For slicer is close kin to the mandolin, but instead of having a handle, it is supported by a metal stand that keeps it steady at an angle convenient for use. Instead of two pieces of metal on a wooden frame, the operating portion of the Mar-For consists of three flat pieces and a fourth crosspiece. The center plate is fixed, holding the frame together, and the two end plates are adjustable blades.

The crosspiece, which is simply a bar running through the side frame, has on one side a row of small, wheel-shaped blades about 3 millimeters (0.25 inches) apart and set vertically. Pushing vegetables against these blades produces julienne-style slices. Turning the hand at right angles alternately during slicing produces lace-style slices. Thus the Mar-For offers more variety than the mandolin.

4-6. Mandolin and Mar-For slicer. From Fuller, *Professional Kitchen Management.*

Metals in the Kitchen

Various metals perform differently under kitchen conditions. In cooking, efficient conduction of heat is of supreme importance. Of the metals potentially used for cooking, silver is the best conductor of heat, although today it is too costly to use, except occasionally in chafing dishes. If silver is given a relative figure of 100% conductivity, then copper is 73%, aluminum is 31%, tin is 15%, and iron or steel is 11%.

Other important factors to consider in choosing a metal cooking utensil are resistance to corrosion and absence of toxic qualities. Metals that oxidize (rust) readily in the moist, hot atmosphere of the kitchen or that pit or otherwise corrode due to chemical reaction with food acids either are not used or are plated with corrosion-resistant metals or treated in some other way to extend their useful life. However, some metals that have desirable qualities of corrosion-resistance and durability still can only be used with extreme caution, if at all, in cooking utensils. Lead and cadmium are two such metals whose toxic properties may cause poisoning, sometimes fatal, if consumed in food that has been contaminated by contact with improperly made cooking utensils.

Copper

Copper has a melting point of 1083°C (1,985°F), which compares very favorably to the 232°C (449°F) melting point of tin. It weighs about the same as wrought iron but is three times as heavy as aluminum.

In spite of its weight, copper is used on the heating surface of many pans. Unfortunately, it has some drawbacks. For example, copper exposed to acetic acid (a natural acid contained in vinegar, tomatoes, and other foods) forms a thin, blue-green film of verdigris, which is poisonous. To prevent contact between the copper and the food, copper cooking vessels are lined with tin, a metal that resists corrosion by air, water, and organic acids well and does not harm food. Copper also tends to turn fats, oils, and dairy products rancid, especially in the presence of heat. Coating with tin also prevents this problem, but even scratches in the lining can expose enough copper to produce rancidity.

Tin and Lead

The only significant problem with tin linings is that the tin produced in some countries contains too much lead, minute quantities of which can easily diffuse into food during cooking. Lead is a cumulative poison; if consumed over a period of time, it can cause serious damage to health. Originally, pewter, a combination of tin, copper, and antimony, also contained lead. As it grew dark with age, it became poisonous. Modern pewter, however is bright ahd shiny, containing tin but no lead.

Aluminum

Aluminum, a relatively soft metal, is light, low-priced, and rust-free. Compared with cast-iron and steel, aluminum has high conductivity and has been used with considerable success in vessels for boiling, frying, and baking. However, the metal can easily be pitted by certain foods, especially those containing acids or sulfur compounds.

Long use causes a dark, thin film to form on aluminum surfaces. This discoloration is nontoxic and does not affect food flavors, although it may alter the color of white sauces or other white foods such as potatoes. The film can be removed by boiling a slightly acidic product such as apple parings in the vessel. Fluorinated hydrocarbon resin coatings such as Teflon can be applied to aluminum cooking utensils to make them nonsticking as well as resistant to corrosion and discoloration.

Iron

Because of their relatively low conductivity and their tendency to rust, iron and steel have only specific and limited uses in the professional kitchen. Iron is still widely favored for frying with fat because vessels used for this purpose are not cleaned by prolonged exposure to water, meaning that rusting is not a problem.

Otherwise, when iron is used in the manufacture of cooking equipment, it needs a protective coating to improve its resistance to corrosion. Porcelain enamel, for example, has been used to coat many casserole dishes. Galvanizing, the application of a thin coat of zinc to an iron surface, is also used to protect iron. This retards rusting, but since zinc easily dissolves under acidic conditions, galvanized iron vessels should not be used to prepare acidic foods. Polymers, such as Teflon and Fluon, can also be used as protective coatings on iron pots. These are modern plastics—tough, easy to clean, inert chemical substances made from oil. Such polymers have been widely used to make nonsticking pots and pans. Unfortunately, the coatings are extremely susceptible to scratching, which ruins their nonsticking properties. As a result, special utensils must be used with them, and cleaning must be done carefully to prevent scratching the surfaces. Moreover, such pans should not be overheated, or the polymer may break down and release fluorine, a poisonous gas.

Stainless Steel

Stainless steel is easy to clean and highly resistant to corrosion, but it is very expensive. Because steel conducts heat relatively poorly, stainless steel pans are usually copperbottomed to spread the heat.

Composition and Design
of Equipment

Cooking vessels come in all shapes and sizes, each designed to fulfill a particular function. For example, a shallow pan allows fluid to evaporate very quickly. A tall, narrow pot keeps its contents hot longer because the smaller exposed surface area does not permit much escape of heat. A pan with one long handle does not go into an oven as easily

4-7. Pans. From Knight and Kotsch- evar, *Quantity Food Production, Planning and Man- agement;* Fuller, *Professional Kitchen Manage- ment.*

loaf pan—used for baking, bread, meat loaf, and the like

sauce pans—used for many cook- ing tasks, available in many shapes and sizes

roasting pan

layer cake pan

pie tin

sauté pan

frying pan

straight-sided baking pan—used for baking ham, apples, rolls, and other foods

baking sheet—used for baking or displaying buns, cookies, and simi- lar products

muffin pan

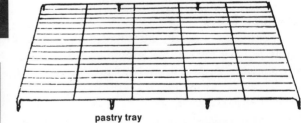

pastry tray

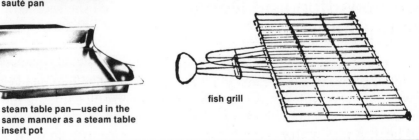

steam table pan—used in the same manner as a steam table insert pot

fish grill

as a pan with two small handles on the sides. Each shape and type of material has a purpose. Wooden spatulas are made of wood because metal scraping against metal would cause discoloration. Covers are tinned because tin does not harm food.

Many of the items shown in figures 4-7 through 4-10 are available in a wide variety of metals, shapes, and sizes. The professional chef will insist on utensils of a size, shape, and material to suit the job at hand.

Deep-Fat Fryers

Deep-fat fryers are usually constructed from cast iron, stainless steel, or aluminum. They vary in depth from 12.5 to 25.5 centimeters (5 to 10 inches). Included with the fryer is a wire drainer that just fits the pan. Drainer handles are, of course, made high to project well above the hot fat. The wire drainer is used to immerse food in and then remove it from the hot fat that does the cooking.

Frying Pan

The frying pan can also be made of cast iron, stainless steel, or aluminum. It may be 15 to 35 centimeters (6 to 14 inches) in diameter and 3 to 9 centimeters (1.25 to 3.5 inches) deep. A good frying pan has a flat bottom to ensure even cooking and rounded angles where the sides meet the bottom for ease of cleaning. Iron frying pans should never be cleaned with liquids; instead, they should be thoroughly wiped with a dry cloth or clean absorbent paper after each use. Thorough cleaning can be effected by spreading coarse salt over the bottom and then heating the pan. This absorbs dirty fat.

Omelette Pan

The omelette pan closely resembles an ordinary frying pan, except that it has curved sides to help shape the omelette. The authentic omelette pan also has a distinctive handle that rises from the side in a slight curve and then straightens almost to the horizontal so that it is almost parallel with the base. This angle facilitates folding and turning out the omelette.

Sautéing Pan

The sautéing pan is similar to a frying pan but shallower, with vertical sides (see figure 4-7). It has a long handle and a flat sheet-metal type cover. The pan is designed especially for sautéing meat, particularly when an accompanying sauce is to be made from the sediment within the pan. In addition to functioning as a lid, the flat cover can be oiled on the underside, turned upside down, and used to hold the uncooked food until the pan is hot enough for cooking. Then all of the food can be slid off the cover into the hot fat of the pan simultaneously. This ensures that all the pieces will be cooked the same length of time and consequently to the same degree. If pieces were put in one at a time, they would all turn out differently.

Fish Pan (*Meunière* Pan)

The fish pan is basically an oval frying pan with a grip handle at each narrow end. Its shape is designed to accommodate fish such as trout and sole fillets, which can lie side by side across the width of the pan.

Baking Sheet

This flat sheet is used for baking cookies, buns, or shaped loaves. It has rims around three sides. The fourth side is open so that baked goods can easily be slid from the sheet.

Colander

Colanders have been produced in a variety of materials, including plastic, aluminum, and stainless steel. See figure 4-4. The colander is simply a hemispheric bowl pierced with small holes less than 6 millimeters (0.25 inches) in diameter. It is used for draining fluids from vegetables and pasta.

Vegetable Drainer

The vegetable drainer is shaped like a saucepan except that it, like a colander, has 6-millimeter holes. It is designed to rest within a saucepan and hold vegetables for reheating over boiling water.

Chinese Strainer

The name "Chinese strainer" is based on the supposed similarity of the sieve's conical shape to that of a Chinese coolie hat. See figure 4-4. Made from wire gauze with fine or large pores, it is used for straining sauces and gravies. The flow of liquid can be facilitated by tapping the top lightly with a ladle or by applying light pressure with a ladle or wire whisk to push solid matter through the mesh.

Double-Wire Grill or Fish Grill

The double-wire grill is another wire implement consisting simply of two grids hinged together and capable of being folded and then clipped together at the handle. For cooking fish on an open grill, the wires, which are set about ⅔ inch (16 mm) apart, are first wiped (the grill should never be washed), and the oiled fish placed onto one grid and then held in position by folding over the other grid and fastening the handles together with a wire ring. The whole contraption is placed over the hot coals, and when the fish is cooked on one side, the wire grill is turned to cook the other side. When the grill is opened, the fish is easily removed with a spatula. The size of the grids is usually about 30 centimeters (12 inches) square.

Wire Rack (Pastry Rack)

This wire stand consists of a simple rectangular grid on short feet. It is used for cooling goods removed from the oven and also for any cooking operation in which a coating must be drained away from the article being coated, such as iced petits fours.

Roasting Pan

The roasting pan is rectangular, with short, straight, vertical sides. It is typically 50.8 by 27.9 by 8.9 centimeters (20 by 11 by 3.5 inches). Strong steel handles are fitted on the ends, projecting upward and outward. This type of pan is used for roasting ham, turkey, and other large dishes. The close-fitting lid helps retain the juices, by reducing evaporation. Otherwise, the intense heat of roasting would scorch the meat and ruin the sediment to be used for gravy.

Saucepans

Saucepans can be used for boiling vegetables or for tossing foods in butter or sauce, as well as for preparing sauces and gravies by reducing liquids through rapid evaporation.

Stock Pot

Stock pots are as broad as they are high, ranging in depth and diameter from 30 to 60 centimeters (12 to 24 inches). The vessels can

double boiler—with water in the bottom pot and food in the top, the double boiler produces an even, low temperature for preparing sauces and keeping foods warm.

stock pot—used for stocks, soups, and sauces; may have a spigot for easy draining.

bain-marie pot and steam table insert—both are used to hold hot food ready to be served. They rest above a shallow vat of hot water that continuously transfers heat to the food product.

4-8. Pots. From Knight and Kotschevar, *Quantity Food Production, Planning and Management.*

be easily recognized by their cylindrical shape, two side handgrips, and (often) a spigot on the lower part. The spigot requires careful attention during cleaning. The stock pot is, of course, used for making meat or poultry stock, sauces, and soups.

Dutch Oven

The Dutch oven is a large iron pot, wider than it is high. The width affords easy access and space to remove grease and residue, and the relatively large surface area distributes heat over the contents so that a gentle simmer results. This vessel also has a tight-fitting, rounded cover, which helps retain juices when cooking meats.

Bain-Marie

The term *bain-marie* is often used to refer both to the large bath of heated water in which pots are kept hot and also to the specially adapted pots themselves. *Bain-marie* pans resemble extremely narrow, deep saucepans. The larger sizes have two side handles, and the smaller sizes have one long, high handle. Both have a sunken lid, fitting in the inside of the pot and equipped with a knob on top for easy removal. These pans are rarely used for cooking, but rather for hot storage of foods over a vat of boiling water.

Double Boiler

The double boiler is a combination of two pots in one. The bottom pot holds boiling water, which heats the food in the top one. This system is used for foods such as custard that require low, even temperatures.

Dessert Molds

Molds are variously shaped containers made of stainless steel, plastic, or aluminum. They are filled with fluids like hot gelatin or soft foods like warm pudding and then chilled so that their contents solidify. Then the mold is removed, leaving the dessert in its attractive shape.

There are many kinds of molds. See figure 4-9. The *timbale mold* is popular for mousse and aspic. The *gelatin mold* is designed for all sorts of decorative gelatins, including multicolored ones and ones with fruit. *Ice cream molds* come in several shapes and sizes. *Pie pans* can also be considered molds since the pie crust is fitted to their shape and then baked.

Other Implements

In addition to metal and plastic pots, pans, and molds, other implements are also used in the professional chef's kitchen. For example, rolling pins are essential for preparing pie crust and other doughs. The rolling pin is commonly made of wood, although metal varieties are available. Loose-handled pins are not as good as rigid ones for gauging the evenness and thickness of dough. Cutting boards are also made of wood and are preferable to metal or laminated plastic surfaces for use with knives. Wooden cutting boards should not be washed with water

timbale

dome-top bomb mold

bomb mold

gelatin mold

pie tin

4-9. Dessert Molds. From Fuller, *Professional Kitchen Management*.

because this causes softening of the wood and a subsequent tendency to splinter and warp. Rather, they should be dry-scraped with a scraper or cleaned with a wire brush by scrubbing in the direction of the grain.

In addition to strainers, there are sieves made from cloth gauze (cotton or nylon) fitted into a round, wooden frame. See figure 4-10. These are used principally for sifting out foreign material from a substance like flour, which passes through cleanly. Passing is assisted simply by tapping or agitating the sieve.

The large kitchen cheesecloth is also useful. It is made from heavy cotton muslin by cutting lengths of approximately 90 centimeters (36 inches) from 67.5 centimeter rolls (27 inches) in width. The technique is to place the cloth over the receptacle, push it in to fit loosely inside, and then pour in the sauce to be passed through it. Two people are required at this point, to lift the cloth at each end and hold it fairly taut. The ends of the cloth are then gathered together. Each person twists and pulls (never relaxing the tautness of the cloth) until all the sauce has been forced through the cloth. Pieces of regular muslin are similarly used in the straining of clear gravies and consommés, but they should never be used with pressure as a cheesecloth is.

4-10. Sieve. From Fuller, *Professional Kitchen Management*.

5. Sanitation and Safety

Introduction to Sanitation

The word *"hygiene"* is derived from Hygea, the Greek Goddess of Health. A dictionary definition of hygiene is: "principles of health, sanitary science." Observance of these principles of health should be part of everyone's life. In certain industries such as foodservice, however, hygiene is of extraordinary importance. All foodservice workers must understand the importance of hygienic practices and the appalling dangers that attend their neglect. Poor food handling is often the cause of outbreaks of food poisoning.

In Great Britain, for example, the number of identified outbreaks of food poisoning rose steeply from under 100 in 1940 to almost 4,000 in 1950. In this same decade, the practice of eating away from the home rose correspondingly. This correlation implicates the foodservice industry as the primary cause. Even one outbreak can harm hundreds, even thousands of people. For instance, in Sweden in 1953, one outbreak poisoned over 8,000 people and killed 90.

Despite continuing research, hygiene training, and legal health standards, food poisoning outbreaks remain at an unacceptably high level. In addition to the hundreds of recorded outbreaks each year, it can be assumed that many more occur that are mild enough not to receive official attention.

Not only is poor sanitation dangerous to customers, but it is bad for business. Customers certainly will not frequent an establishment that looks unsanitary, even if they have never actually become ill from eating there. And the local board of health can close down any establishment after warning the management of health code violations and seeing no improvement.

The professional chef, therefore, will seek to understand how hygienic practices can prevent contamination and disease and will lay down simple, concise, practical rules for subordinates to follow. Even if they do not fully understand the biology or chemistry of disease transmission, they can learn what to do to avoid problems. The chef can instruct them with training films, pamphlets, stickers ("Always wash your hands after using the restroom."), posters, and slogans. Furthermore, the truly responsible chef will not be content merely to meet the minimum standards set by health ordinances and codes but will seek a higher standard of excellence that not only prevents disease, but positively adds to the overall quality of the products of the kitchen.

Causes of Food Poisoning

There are two major types of food poisoning—food-borne intoxication and food-borne infection. Food-borne intoxication is caused by poisons in the food that are produced by bacteria. The person ingests the poisons by eating the food. Food-borne infection, on the other hand, is caused by eating food infested with bacteria that then produce toxins or poisons in the stomach. Both types of food poisoning are usually caused by ignorance or negligence on the part of the person preparing the food. The food preparer either does not realize how bacteria can be transmitted to food or does understand but does not take steps to prevent it. The sources of these bacteria include contamination at the slaughterhouse or food-packaging company, diseases and infections of the food handler, and rodent or insect pests. The professional chef should seek to minimize the introduction of these bacteria into the food being prepared and should use the strictest standards of hygiene to prevent their spread.

Bacteria

Bacteria are microorganisms so small that they can be seen only with the aid of a powerful microscope. See figure 5-1. They occur everywhere in the surrounding environment and in living creatures. Some are harmful to man, others are harmless, and some are even beneficial.

Bacteria grow at the same temperatures at which human beings can survive. See figure 5-2. Some bacteria can grow at temperatures as low as those found in refrigerators (2°–4°C or 36°–39°F), but food poisoning bacteria do not grow until temperatures of at least 6°C (43°F) and above are reached. The higher the temperature (up to a point), the faster the bacteria will grow. They multiply rapidly at the temperature of a warm kitchen (21°–25°C or 70°–77°F) and grow at their fastest rate at human body temperature (37°C or 98.6°F)—a temperature often

5-1. The three cell shapes that occur among bacteria: (a) coccus; (b) rod; (c) spiral. From Richardson and Nicodemus, *Sanitation for Foodservice Workers*, 3rd edition.

a.

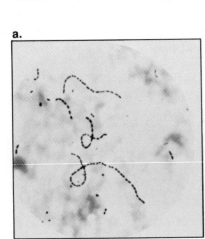

b.

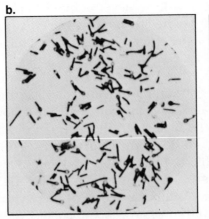

c.

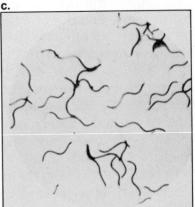

found in food being improperly warmed or kept hot before and during service. Bacteria cannot survive very high temperatures, although some of their spores can resist boiling temperatures for several hours. It is most important to realize that, at the other end of the scale, freezing temperatures do not kill bacteria but merely hold them in suspended animation. Freezing therefore does not make foods bacteria-free. Once the food thaws, the bacteria continue to multiply at an incredible rate.

Species	Growth Range	
	Minimum	Maximum
Staphylococcus aureus	7°C (44°F)	46°C (114°F)
Clostridium perfringens	13°C (55°F)	50°C (122°F)
Clostridium botulinum	3°C (38°F)	48°C (118°F)
Salmonella species	6°C (42°F)	46°C (114°F)

5-2. **Growth range of common food-poisoning bacteria. From Richardson and Nicodemus, Sanitation for Foodservice Workers, 3rd edition.**

Food-Borne Intoxication

The organisms responsible for food-borne intoxications are described in the following paragraphs.

Staphylococci. Staphylococcal bacteria are found in the human nose and throat and on the skin. At least 30% of the public, and up to 80% of food handlers, are carriers of these bacteria at any given time. Even though only 30% of these bacteria are of the type that can cause food poisoning, it is no wonder that staphylococci accounted for more food-borne illnesses than any other bacteria in a recent study year. There is a particular danger of food being contaminated by staphylococci during handling, particularly if personal hygiene is poor. If food becomes contaminated and is left to stand overnight in a warm kitchen, a poison is produced by the growing bacteria. Custards, pastries, pies, cooked meats, gravies, and dressings, as well as improperly processed canned foods, are most likely to foster these bacteria. The incubation period is from 2 to 6 hours. The symptoms—severe abdominal pain and vomiting—usually occur about 4 hours after eating contaminated food. The illness lasts from 6 to 24 hours.

Clostridium Botulinum. This serious, but fortunately rare, type of food-poisoning bacteria is associated with improperly processed canned foods, particularly home-processed ones, and occasionally with vacuum-packed foods, including canned meat products, fish, and soups. The bacteria originate in the soil, in oceans, and in lakes. They will only grow in the absence of oxygen and thus are not associated with freshly prepared foods intended for immediate consumption. The bacteria produce a very powerful toxin in the food, which attacks the nervous system and causes dizziness, muscular weakness, and difficulty in breathing. Outbreaks of botulism are usually accompanied by a very high mortality rate.

Food-Borne Infection

The organisms responsible for food-borne bacterial infection are described below.

Salmonellae. These bacteria owe their name to an investigator named Salmon and not to the fish. During the slaughter of meat animals and poultry, the bacteria can be spread from the animals' intestines to the surface of the meat. If temperature conditions allow it, the organism will multiply and, when present in large numbers, will cause illness. Symptoms include diarrhea and vomiting, often accompanied by fever. But the bacteria are easily killed by heat, and adequate cooking at temperatures over 60°C (140°F) will eliminate the hazard, as long as the cooked product is not reinfected by bacteria from raw meats in the kitchen.

Clostridium Perfringens. This organism is particularly troublesome because it produces heat-resistant spores. The spores are also resistant to dry conditions and to high salt concentrations. The spores may survive for several hours at boiling temperatures, although 15 minutes at the higher temperatures found in pressure cooking, roasting, frying, or grilling will kill the spores. It is quite likely, therefore, that the spores of *Clostridium perfringens* will still be viable in foods that are only boiled or simmered or that are cooked in other ways for insufficient time. If the food is not all eaten immediately after preparation, the spores will then germinate to produce actively growing bacteria as soon as the food cools sufficiently. It is vitally important, therefore, that any food that is to be kept overnight be chilled as quickly as possible and refrigerated within 1½ hours after cooking. This will ensure that the bacteria produced from the surviving spores have no chance to grow. If cooked food is to be kept hot for some time before service, it must be kept above 63°C (145°F) to prevent the spores from germinating and the bacteria from growing. Obviously, it is best to produce food that is eaten as soon after cooking as possible on the day of preparation. As *clostridium perfringens* is found in the feces of animals, a common place of contamination is the slaughterhouse. The incubation period is from 8 to 22 hours, and the symptoms occur from 10 to 12 hours after the contaminated food is eaten. They consist of severe stomach pain with accompanying diarrhea. Because of the time taken for the symptoms to develop, their onslaught is often in the early hours of the morning after the bacteria are swallowed.

Bacillus Cereus. This bacteria is similar to *Clostridium perfringens* in that it, too, produces heat-resistant spores. It is, however, a much slower-growing bacteria, and it has to be present in very large numbers before it can cause poisoning. It is most often found in cooked vegetable products such as rice, potatoes, and corn starch. Wherever possible, only the quantities of vegetables required for immediate service should be prepared at any one time. If there is any surplus, it must be stored in a refrigerator. The symptoms of the illness caused by this organism are so similar to those of salmonellosis that the two have often been confused in the past.

Shigellae. These bacteria produce classic symptoms of dysentery

—diarrhea, sometimes with mucus or even blood in the feces, and possibly some fever and vomiting. Dysentery bacteria take approximately 18 hours to incubate. The spread of these organisms is not necessarily through foodstuffs. It can also be due to poor personal hygiene and contamination from person to person, such as from one young child to another in a public restroom.

Vibrio Parahaemolyticus. This bacteria is particularly associated with uncooked shellfish and is a common cause of food poisoning in Japan. In recent decades, the bacteria have become established in American coastal waters. Most outbreaks occur when cooked seafoods are put in containers that held contaminated uncooked food earlier and were not cleaned properly. Symptoms include nausea, abdominal pains, and diarrhea.

Unsanitary food, drinks, and eating utensils can spread many diseases in addition to food poisoning. For example, an infected food handler can spread typhoid, paratyphoid, hepatitis, diphtheria, and other bacterial and viral infections. Food can also be infested with such parasites as amoebas, trichina worms (pork worms), and tapeworms, all of which can be killed by proper cooking.

Statutory Requirements

Because of the grave dangers presented by negligent food handling, preparation, cooking, and service, law-makers at all levels of government have enacted various pieces of legislation, regulations, and ordinances to protect the public. The chef does not have to be intimately aware of all the legalities affecting the foodservice business, but it is important to be aware of the major trends and to know the specifics of unusually important rules.

Regulatory Agencies

There are many regulatory agencies at all levels of government. At the federal level, for example, the Food and Drug Administration (FDA) publishes "The Model Food Service Sanitation Ordinance" in the *Food Service Sanitation Manual.* This is a sample legal code whose provisions can be adopted by states and municipalities. The FDA also regulates foodservice on airplanes, boats, and other interstate carriers. The U.S. Department of Agriculture (USDA) inspects and grades meat, poultry, dairy, and vegetable products to ensure their quality and safety. The U.S. Center for Disease Control (CDC) in Atlanta, Georgia, investigates food poisoning outbreaks. All such problems should be reported directly to the CDC. In addition to the federal agencies, each state has its own board of health, and each county or municipality has its own health department. Since no particular sanitation ordinance is required by federal law, each state and city has its own laws, and these vary from place to place. The chef, therefore, should check with local authorities if there is any question about which rules apply.

Foodservice Inspections

The local and state health authorities issue permits that allow establishments to offer food and drink for sale. These authorities employ public health officers and sanitation specialists who make unannounced inspections of foodservice establishments to see if they are honoring the local ordinances. The inspectors use an inspection report form (figure 5-3) and give demerits for each violation they spot. If unsanitary conditions are found, the manager is usually given time to correct them. If the manager then fails to do so, or if the violations are very serious, then the health authority can suspend or even revoke the owner's permit to operate.

5-3. Foodservice establishment inspection report. From U.S. Department of Health, Education, and Welfare, *Food Service Sanitation Manual.*

DEPARTMENT OF HEALTH, EDUCATION AND WELFARE
PUBLIC HEALTH SERVICE — FOOD AND DRUG ADMINISTRATION

Food Service Establishment Inspection Report

PURPOSE
Regular 29 1
Follow-up 2
Complaint 3
Investigation 4
Other 5

Based on an inspection this day, the items circled below identify the violations in operations or facilities which must be corrected by the next routine inspection or such shorter period of time as may be specified in writing by the regulatory authority. Failure to comply with any time limits for corrections specified in this notice may result in cessation of your Food Service operations.

OWNER NAME

ESTABLISHMENT NAME

ADDRESS

ZIP CODE

EST. I.D. (1-10) | COUNTY | DIST. | EST. NO. | CENSUS TRACT 11-13 | SANIT. CODE 14-16 | YR MO DAY 17-22 | TRAVEL TIME 23-25 | INSPEC. TIME 26-28

FOOD

		WT. COL.
*01	Source, sound condition, no spoilage	5 30
02	Original container, properly labeled	1 31

FOOD PROTECTION

*03	Potentially hazardous food meets temperature requirements during storage, preparation, display, service, transportation	5 32
*04	Facilities to maintain product temperature	4 33
05	Thermometers provided and conspicuous	1 34
06	Potentially hazardous food properly thawed	2 35
*07	Unwrapped and potentially hazardous food not re served	4 36
08	Food protection during storage, preparation, display, service, transportation	2 37
09	Handling of food (ice) minimized	2 38
*10	In use, food (ice) dispensing utensils properly stored	1 39

PERSONNEL

*11	Personnel with infections restricted	5 40
*12	Hands washed and clean, good hygienic practices	5 41
13	Clean clothes, hair restraints	1 42

FOOD EQUIPMENT & UTENSILS

14	Food (ice) contact surfaces designed, constructed, maintained, installed, located	2 43
15	Non-food contact surfaces designed, constructed, maintained, installed, located	1 44
16	Dishwashing facilities designed, constructed, maintained, installed, located, operated	2 45
17	Accurate thermometers, chemical test kits provided, gauge cock (1/4'' IPS valve)	1 46
18	Pre-flushed, scraped, soaked	1 47
19	Wash, rinse water clean, proper temperature	2 48
*20	Sanitization rinse clean, temperature, concentration, exposure time; equipment, utensils sanitized	4 49
21	Wiping cloths clean, use restricted	1 50
22	Food-Contact surfaces of equipment and utensils clean, free of abrasives, detergents	2 51
23	Non-food contact surfaces of equipment and utensils clean	1 52
24	Storage, handling of clean equipment/utensils	1 53
25	Single service articles, storage, dispensing	1 54
26	No re-use of single service articles	2 55

WATER

| *27 | Water source, safe hot & cold under pressure | 5 56 |

SEWAGE

| *28 | Sewage and waste water disposal | 4 57 |

PLUMBING

| 29 | Installed, maintained | 1 58 |
| *30 | Cross connection, back siphonage, backflow | 5 59 |

TOILET & HANDWASHING FACILITIES

| *31 | Number, convenient, accessible, designed, installed | 4 60 |
| 32 | Toilet rooms enclosed, self closing doors; fixtures, good repair, clean; hand cleanser, sanitary towels/hand drying devices provided, proper waste receptacles | 2 61 |

GARBAGE & REFUSE DISPOSAL

| 33 | Containers or receptacles, covered; adequate number insect/rodent proof, frequency, clean | 2 62 |
| 34 | Outside storage area enclosures properly constructed, clean; controlled incineration | 1 63 |

INSECT, RODENT, ANIMAL CONTROL

| *35 | Presence of insects/rodents—outer openings protected, no birds, turtles, other animals | 4 64 |

FLOORS, WALLS & CEILINGS

| 36 | Floors, constructed, drained, clean, good repair, covering installation, dustless cleaning methods | 1 65 |
| 37 | Walls, ceiling, attached equipment constructed, good repair, clean surfaces, dustless cleaning methods | 1 66 |

LIGHTING

| 38 | Lighting provided as required, fixtures shielded | 1 67 |

VENTILATION

| 39 | Rooms and equipment—vented as required | 1 68 |

DRESSING ROOMS

| 40 | Rooms, area, lockers provided, located, used | 1 69 |

OTHER OPERATIONS

*41	Toxic items properly stored, labeled, used	5 70
42	Premises maintained free of litter, unnecessary articles, cleaning maintenance equipment properly stored. Authorized personnel	1 71
43	Complete separation from living/sleeping quarters. Laundry	1 72
44	Clean, soiled linen properly stored	1 73

Received by: name _____
title _____
Inspected by: name _____

FOLLOW-UP
Yes 74-1
No 2

RATING SCORE 75-77
100 less weight of Items violated →

ACTION
Change 78-C
Delete . . . . D

*Critical Items Requiring Immediate Attention.   Remarks on back (80 1)

FORM FDA 2420 (2/79)   PREVIOUS EDITION MAY BE USED   USE REVERSE FOR REMARKS

The Model Food Service Sanitation Ordinance

The Model Food Service Sanitation Ordinance is long and detailed, and, as already mentioned, each state and municipality is free to modify it in any way. Therefore, only a general summary of the main topics covered is warranted here.

Chapter 1 (General Provisions) — Terms such as *employee* and *tableware* are defined.

Chapter 2 (Food Care) — Food supplies must be from approved sources, must be stored under sanitary conditions and at proper temperatures, and must be prepared in a sanitary manner. They must be transported, displayed, and served in ways that minimize exposure to contamination and the opportunity for bacteria to multiply.

Chapter 3 (Personnel) — Employees with respiratory or skin infections must not be allowed near food. Employees at work must keep their bodies and clothing clean. They should use hair restraints and avoid smoking and unhygienic practices such as picking the nose and sneezing while around food.

Chapter 4 (Equipment and Utensils) — Foodservice equipment and implements should be constructed of safe materials, designed in ways that facilitate cleaning, and installed in sanitary locations that minimize the possibility of soil build-up and insect or rodent infestation.

Chapter 5 (Cleaning, Sanitization, and Storage of Equipment and Utensils) — Tableware should be sanitized after each use. Kitchenware and food-contact surfaces should be cleaned whenever contaminated and at least once a day otherwise. Wiping cloths and sponges should be clean. Heat and/or safe bactericidal chemicals should be used to sanitize tableware and other utensils. Thermometers should be used to ensure that wash water is at an acceptable temperature. Equipment and utensils should be stored in clean, dry locations.

Chapter 6 (Sanitary Facilities and Controls) — The water supply must be safe and uncontaminated. Plumbing, toilets, and sewage disposal should be properly installed and situated a reasonable distance from food areas. Restrooms must have suitable lavatories with soap, water, and sanitary means of drying the hands. Garbage and refuse should be stored in insect-proof and rodent-proof containers, away from food areas. Screen doors, exhaust air ducts, and other openings to the outside should be protected against penetration by insects and rodents. Exterminators should be called in when necessary.

Chapter 7 (Construction and Maintenance of Physical Facilities) — Floors, walls, and ceilings should be constructed so as to allow ready cleaning. They should also be kept in a good state of repair. All physical facilities should be properly cleaned, lighted, and ventilated. Suitable dressing rooms and lockers for employees should be provided. Only essential poisonous or toxic materials (for example, insecticides and sanitizers) should be stored on the premises; these should be properly labelled and safely stored. All the premises should be free of litter, debris, and animals. Soiled clothes and linens must be stored separately from clean ones and laundered promptly.

In addition to these chapters that apply to all foodservice establishments, Chapter 8 deals with mobile food units or pushcarts, Chapter 9 deals with temporary foodservice operations, and Chapter 10 deals with the granting and suspending of permits.

Legal Liability

Foodservice managers face other threats in addition to losing their permits to operate. They can also be sued by customers who get sick or injured as a result of eating their food. Although state laws differ, it is commonly held that food served in a restaurant, cafeteria, or other establishment is a product offered for sale, and that such products carry implied (not written or orally expressed) warranties that they are fit for their intended purpose (to be eaten). If the food makes a customer sick, the customer can sue for damages—an amount of money not only sufficient to compensate for actual medical bills, but also for "emotional damage" or "mental suffering." The amount of money in such cases can be substantial, although customers bringing suits do not always win and do not always get what they ask for even if they do win.

Recipe for an Outbreak of Food-Borne Illness

Yield:
A large number of sick customers who will never return to the restaurant and may try to sue; a Board of Health inspection that may result in suspension of the establishment's operating permit

Ingredients:
Careless inspection of received food
Unsanitary storage and food preparation areas
Food handlers who are infected and/or dirty
Letting cooked food come into contact with uncooked food
Storing at improper temperatures (not cold or hot enough)
Allowing insects and rodents to have access to food or food-handling areas
Failing to clean tableware and food preparation equipment.

Method:
Hire employees who know little about the principles of hygiene and care even less. Do not train them. Just stand back and wait for results.

Food in Preparation, Cooking, Service, and Storage

Foods of all kinds can become dirtied or contaminated at any stage before actual consumption by the guest. Hygienic precautions with respect to food should, therefore, be maintained rigorously throughout the period it is in the kitchen or kitchen storage. Two points particularly to be borne in mind are the need to avoid contamination of food in the first place and the need to kill or prevent the growth of any bacteria already present.

Food Examination

The following simple rules should be observed by the chef and all staff members in dealing with foods entering the kitchen storage or food preparation areas. Food in its natural, unprocessed state should be clean, should look clean, and should have a fresh smell. In particular, meat and poultry—although they are inspected at the slaughterhouse and at meat markets—should be checked before being allowed into the kitchen or kitchen meat storage. Expert inspection should be sought if there is any discoloration or bad smell (bone taint, for example, is sometimes not betrayed until meat is dissected). A special inspection should be made, both at the time of delivery and at the time the meat is stored, for any signs of contamination or deterioration. Similar vigilance is necessary in the case of fish, whose deterioration can be rapid if packing or cold storage is inadequate.

It is very important that garden soil adhering to vegetables and fruits not be allowed to come into contact with other foods. Produce should be washed and prepared in the vegetable storage and preparation room. For hygienic reasons as well as culinary and aesthetic ones, bruised, damaged, or rotting vegetables and fruit should be rejected. Although dry goods such as bread are more resistant to the multiplication of bacteria than moist foods, they become potentially highly dangerous once their preparation into dishes begins. Therefore, dirty and damaged bread should be rejected, as should musty-smelling or weevil-infested flour. Foods such as cereals or sugars that bear the slightest trace of attack by rodents are likewise unacceptable. Wrappings and packings should be intact; suspicions should be raised otherwise. Tin cans with rust, corrosion, or swells should also be rejected.

Food Temperatures

Since bacterial growth is linked closely with temperature, food should be cooked at sufficiently high temperatures to kill bacteria and stored at sufficiently hot or cold ones to prohibit growth. Keeping food in the moderate warmth of the kitchen or on a tepid *bain-marie* is potentially dangerous. In the case of reheated meat and fish dishes, for example, bacteria can multiply at an enormous and dangerous rate if the dish becomes contaminated by any cause whatsoever and then is left in the warm kitchen or noncold storage overnight. Gelatins such as aspic are such a favorable medium for cultivating bacteria that a similar material, agar, is used in the laboratory for this very purpose. Special precautions need to be taken, therefore, with this type of dish. Any food that has been exposed on buffet tables where it can easily be contaminated by dust, air, human breath, sneezes, and coughs should definitely be used on the day of preparation and not stored at all.

Cleanliness of Kitchen and Staff

Premises, Tools, and Equipment

Design of the premises and of kitchen equipment should be strongly influenced by the need for a clinical level of cleanliness. Surfaces of walls and floors should be washable and should be kept clean, as should food shelves and preparation tables. Surfaces on which food is prepared should be of impervious material such as stainless steel, laminated plastic, or marble. Sinks and tanks in which food is rinsed, soaked, or stored should similarly be of noncorrosive metal or of porcelain in an undamaged state.

Disposal of Waste

A crucial feature of the kitchen is the facilities for disposing of food waste. Left in the open, such garbage can contaminate other foods, both directly and by attracting flies and other vermin. Electric waste disposal units allow hygienic disposal of all food waste immediately, preventing its standing around in the kitchen or just outside while awaiting removal. For other garbage, it is important to keep food-waste bins clean (with tightly fitting lids). Bins should stand on a hard surface outside the kitchen so that both they and the area on which they stand can be kept clean, disinfected, and deodorized. Food-waste bins should be washed internally as well as externally at regular intervals, including a periodic scalding out. If large volumes of bulky waste (cardboard boxes, for example) have to be disposed of, an electrically operated waste compactor can be used to crush and bind the waste into neat bales.

Dish Washing

Providing proper facilities for washing dishes, utensils, and equipment is vital. Various devices are available that can clean cooking vessels, plates, and cutlery. The method adopted should include a sanitizing procedure to render plates and cutlery sterile. Chemical cleansers can be used, but immersion of equipment in rinsing water heated to 83°C (180°F) or above is generally considered to be the most effective and most practicable method.

Hand Washing

Foodservice establishments must comply with statutory requirements regarding hand-washing facilities, especially in restrooms. Essential items should include a wash basin with adequate hot water, soap (bacteriocidal gel soap is preferable to conventional bar soap), and a nail brush. (The nail brush should be carefully rinsed after each use to avoid recontamination.) Soap dispensers and water faucets with foot, wrist, or elbow-operated controls help prevent cross-contamination from one person's hands to another's. Since Shigella and Salmonella bacteria are able to live a long time on the skin, especially under the fingernails, each person should lather and rub thoroughly. Hand-drying arrangements should preclude the possibility of recontamination. Ordinary roller towels that can become wet and soiled are particularly unsuitable. The patented type of rollers that allow access to clean portions by pulling down, electric warm-air driers, individual towels, or disposable paper towels all give satisfactory results.

Precautions against Contamination by Vermin

Rodents

Since rats and their kin spread disease and ruin food supplies, it is important that the kitchen staff be able to detect the presence of these pests on the slightest evidence. Invasion by rats and mice is usually discoverable by the following signs.

Damage. This is the most obvious first sign of rodent infestation. Gnawing damage may be caused not only by the rodents' search for food, but also for nesting material. Apart from eating food, rodents gnaw anything that is not too hard to be indented. This activity prevents their front teeth, which continue to grow throughout life, from becoming excessively long. It is well to look for gnawing marks, therefore, not only in foods such as cheese, butter, and chocolate, but on wood, soap, and even lead pipes.

Holes and Scrapes. The beginnings of rat holes are revealed by little piles of earth or debris known as scrapes.

Smears. This is the term used to denote marks made by greasy and dusty fur repeatedly touching a wall or other surface where rats or mice frequently run. Smears may also be left by the tracks of their feet.

Runways. These are simply the tracks beaten down by rodents using the same route repeatedly. Footprints and tail marks can readily be seen in dust, spilled cereal and so forth. As further verification, a powdery substance such as flour can be laid over a suspect area and later checked for signs of rodents.

Droppings. House mouse droppings dry quickly, and consequently their freshness may be difficult to determine. But common rat droppings are moist when fresh and can give a guide to the magnitude of the rodent infestation. Unfortunately, the common rat tends to leave its droppings away from the usual runway.

Disappearance of Bait. In order to test whether rodents are present, bait (which should *not* be poisoned at this point) may be put down and later inspected. Bread mash, sausage casings, flour, and sugar can be used for this purpose.

If rats are in the vicinity, the following precautions should be taken to prevent rodent infestation:

1. Anything that might provide cover, such as rubbish, cartons, or other objects leaning against a wall, should be removed promptly.
2. Holes made through walls for cables, pipes, and drains, should be filled with a rat-proof material such as concrete mixed with glass.

3. Windows that are left open at night for ventilation should be covered with wire screens.
4. Wooden doors and frames opening on to kitchen areas should be protected against being gnawed through by installation of metal kicking plates.
5. Drains and sewer connections should be checked carefully—these are frequent entry passages for rats.
6. Food should be stored in rodent-proof containers, and waste should be placed in covered bins until collection; daily removal of waste should be arranged if at all possible.

Most of the above measures should be carried out by carpenters or other noncooks. But this should be supplemented by self-help efforts on the part of the kitchen staff. Inspections should be made by the chef at regular intervals. If rodent infestation is indicated, skilled professional exterminators should be called in.

Cockroaches

Cockroaches live in crevices inside buildings or in dark, covered areas outside. They journey into the building to obtain food. There are three major kinds of domestic cockroaches in the United States. See figure 5-4. The *German cockroach* is a yellowish brown insect, growing to about 12 millimeters (0.5 inches) long and having large wings. It commonly infests large buildings, especially those warmed by central heating. The *oriental cockroach* grows to 25 millimeters (1 inch) and is a shiny, dark brown color. The male has wings that cover two-thirds of its abdomen, but the female has very short ones. This type is less frequently found than the German cockroach in modern buildings but is often encountered in kitchens and bakeries of older construction. The *American cockroach* is reddish-brown in color, with a margin of yellow on the thoracic shield. It grows to about 38 millimeters (1.5 inches) in length, and both sexes have large wings.

5-4. Three common species of cockroaches in the United States. From Richardson and Nicodemus, *Sanitation for Foodservice Workers*, 3rd edition.

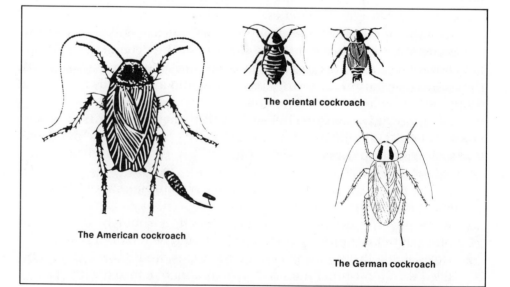

The oriental cockroach

The American cockroach

The German cockroach

Their flat bodies enable roaches to lie concealed in cracks and crevices during the day, from which they emerge at night to feed. They eat almost anything (wool, leather, book covers, as well as human food) and leave their smell wherever they go. Because of their size, their activity at night, and their fetid smell, cockroaches are generally easy to detect. While it is possible for cockroaches to act as carriers and transmitters of infectious bacteria such as Shigella and Salmonella, they are far less dangerous in this respect than the housefly. It is, however, important to eradicate them because of their smell, their corruption of food by nibbling, and their ability to elicit general revulsion. As in the case of rodents, it is best to entrust their extermination to experts. Complete eradication is otherwise difficult to achieve because the eggs are usually well protected in their remote hideouts. Even if all the adults are killed, a new generation can emerge when the eggs finish incubating.

Flies

The various types of housefly are all easily recognizable, and they all readily spread disease. Flies walk on food, regurgitate digestive juices on it, defecate on it and lay eggs on it. Films recording these repulsive habits are seldom forgotten by people who view them, and they therefore make effective training aids.

Flies already within an establishment can be killed by means of insecticide strips or spraying with residual insecticides (insecticides that remain effective on windows and walls over a period). To prevent their entry, screen doors and screened windows should be used; exhaust fans can be directed to force air out of doors that are frequently opened. Food can also be protected by flyproofing larders and covering food. It is even more important, though, to control breeding. This is relatively difficult, but it can be done with scrupulous cleanliness, not only in the kitchen and its departments but in the area outside the establishment, particularly near garbage cans and trash bins. These should stand on hard, washable bases, since earth and soft ground regularly contaminated by rubbish and food waste provide an ideal environment for fly-breeding.

Even with thorough and dedicated preventive measures, some flies will inevitably penetrate the kitchen from breeding grounds away from and out of the control of the establishment. Insecticides and mechanical fly-killing methods should suffice to control such invasions. Persistent entry by flies, however, should receive expert attention in addition to the routine antifly measures taken by the kitchen staff.

Ants, Wasps, and Bees

Ants from outdoors do, on occasion, invade food storage and may carry with them disease germs. They are particularly attracted to sugar products. Complete cleanliness and effective storage of such foods under cover are therefore vital. Barrier insecticides of the powder type can be used to keep ants out. If nests are inside the building, however, destroying them is the only certain method of complete eradication. This may be difficult to achieve because the nests are often inaccessible, so again the problem should be turned over to a professional exterminator.

Wasps and bees are not so much hazards to the customers' health as nuisances to employees. Generally, they can be kept out by the same "proofing" techniques used against flies. Where serious invasions by wasps or bees take place, however, it is advisable to obtain assistance in destroying the entire nest or colony.

Other Insect Pests

A vast range of insect pests can invade foodstuffs. All are less common than those named above, however, because of measures already taken at docks, warehouses, and by packers before commodities are distributed to shops and caterers. If pests such as weevils in flour are present, though, they will soon reveal themselves, and appropriate clearing out and preventive measures may then be taken.

Insecticides

Although insecticides are important in the fight against insect infestation, a number of precautions must be kept in mind when using them in foodservice establishments. Residual insecticides should not be sprayed on surfaces with which food will come into contact, or the food will become contaminated by the insecticide. Open-air fogging should never be done unless all food and dishes exposed to the insecticide are washed thereafter. Sprays should not be directed anywhere near food because they disperse into the air in all directions. If food contaminated with insecticide is eaten, serious illness and even death may result.

Disinfectants in Kitchen Hygiene

In pursuing the goals of clean food, a clean kitchen, and clean equipment, the chef and the kitchen staff will rely on both traditional and new cleaning methods. Hot soap and water and the scrubbing brush, together with elbow grease, will go far in ensuring cleanliness of utensils and apparatuses. But it is often necessary to consider the use of modern chemical disinfectants as well. Very hot water (above 80°C or 176°F) is an effective sterilizing agent in locations where it can be used easily. Commercially available units for steam-cleaning are increasingly common in foodservice establishments.

Chefs should not accept unquestioningly the claims made by manufacturers of name-brand products sold for cleaning. In particular, they should learn to distinguish between detergents that are only effective for general cleaning purposes and true sterilizing agents that kill all infectious bacteria. Where preparations of either type are used, it is important to make sure that the proper concentration of solution is employed. The chef would certainly be wise to seek expert advice when in doubt.

Qualities of a Good Disinfectant

A good chemical disinfectant should:

Act rapidly on as many types of microorganisms as possible

Have an effective degree of penetration (this will vary according to surface tension)

Be active and efficient in low concentration (important because of the cost factor)

Be active in the presence of organic matter

Be stable for storage purposes

Be of a price permitting reasonable use

Types of Disinfectant

Types of chemical disinfectants commonly encountered in foodservice establishments are discussed in the following paragraphs.

Oxidizing Agents. Some disinfectants destroy bacteria by oxidizing them and their spores. These are effective, but they are also unstable and hence cause storage problems. Their effectiveness is significantly inhibited by the presence of organic matter as is found in the solid debris left after washing-up. Disinfectants of this type include sodium hypochlorite, potassium permanganate, hydrogen peroxide, and various halogens (such as chlorine in drinking water).

Chemical Agents—Hydrolysis. Such chemical disinfectants are not today considered very practical because they are either strong acids or strong alkalis, highly corrosive and generally difficult and unpleasant to use.

Derivatives of Coal Tar. These are effective disinfectants which are reasonably pleasant to use. They include carbolic acid, Lysol, and some alcohols.

Quarternary Ammonium Compounds. There has been a considerable increase in the use of this type of disinfectant in modern detergents that also emulsify grease.

Other Types. In addition to the foregoing, some of the traditional methods of preserving foods may also be regarded as disinfectants. Essential oils such as clove oil are active when pure, but they only slow down bacterial growth rather than destroying it. The salts of heavy metals also act as disinfectants, but their effectiveness is due, in part, to the toxic effect of the metal—for example, the mercury in mercuric chloride. Formalin is well-known as a preservative and disinfectant. Strong brines and syrups also have a preservative value and slow up or arrest the process of decomposition caused by bacterial activity. Finally, there are many modern drugs such as antibiotics that can be viewed as disinfectants.

Effectiveness of Disinfectants

The effectiveness of a disinfectant varies and may be improved by heating it (hot Lysol, for example, is much more effective than cold) or by lowering the surface tension of whatever is to be disinfected. This can be achieved by using detergent either beforehand or mixed with the disinfectant. By emulsifying surrounding grease, the detergent affords the disinfectant an opportunity to reach its objective and to work to maximum efficacy. Conversely, the efficacy of disinfectants is impaired by grease or any organic matter that provides bacteria with a protective barrier. For example, food soil, fragments of cloth such as wool, cotton, or silk, mucus, flakes of shed skin, blood, and wood act as barriers, making it difficult for the chemical disinfectant to reach and destroy the bacteria. Stronger chemical disinfectants may kill bacteria more effectively, but if they are too concentrated, they may irritate or burn the user's skin, especially among users with sensitive skin. Finally, no cleanser can remain effective after an unsanitary employee handles dishes and utensils that were previously washed and sanitized.

Recipe for Employee Hygiene

Yield:
A conscientious staff motivated by personal pride and by concern for customer welfare to maintain high standards of personal cleanliness

Behavioral Ingredients:
A daily bath or shower
A daily change of clothes
Handwashing after restroom use
Clean, neat, and restrained hair
Careful handling of dishes, utensils, and food
Using each spoon only once for taste sampling
When sick or infected, staying away from food

Method:
Use formal training sessions, pep talks, reminders, slogans, and wall posters to get these points across. No one wins when disease spreads.

Introduction to Safety

More accidents (many of them fatal) occur in the home than outside it. Domestic accidents often involve the old and infirm or the very young; however, many are not age-related but have to do with carelessness in cooking or in using electricity, gas, machinery, or sharp tools. Accidents of the kind that occur during cooking at home also occur in professional kitchens. Risks in caterers' kitchens are increased by the heightened tempo and volume of work and by the abundance of large and complicated machinery.

Reducing such risks and preventing accidents is humane and also makes good busines sense—because every accident or injury costs money, both directly and in terms of lost time. Furthermore, observance of safety standards is the law under the Occupational Safety and Health Act (OSHA) of 1970. Even if an accident does not occur, a foodservice establishment can be fined for failure to meet safety standards. An OSHA compliance inspector can visit at any time without giving prior notice and is empowered to levy fines for violations. Severe or persistently uncorrected violations can bring steep fines or even imprisonment.

Although OSHA provides for enforcement and penalties, it stresses self-regulation and aims to involve both employers and employees in recognizing the importance of safety. In focusing attention on personal and collective responsibility, the act chiefly outlines what employers must do. But it stresses, too, that employees must be aware of their responsibilities for their own safety, for that of their coworkers, and for that of the general public.

Safety Policy Document Drafting

One way to help reduce accidents is to prepare a safety policy statement that relates specifically to the operation at hand. This safety document should cover activities and possible hazards in all the kitchen sections, as well as in other areas of the establishment. It should be accessible to all employees.

Goals

The safety policy document should be prefaced by a brief statement regarding the health and safety of employees at work. For example:

> [name of company]'s policy aims to create a safe and healthy working environment. The company seeks to involve all employees and secure their active support in achieving the objective of safe working conditions. The policy's objectives include:
> 1. Compliance with the Occupational Safety and Health Act of 1970 and other relevant legislation to achieve high standards of safety, health, and welfare.
> 2. Maintenance of a safe and healthy work environment.
> 3. Protection of both employees and the public from work hazards.
> 4. Training, instruction, and supervision of employees to ensure safe work methods and procedures.
> 5. Promotion of safety awareness among employees.
> 6. Encouragement of cooperation between staff and management in all safety matters.

Arrangements

After the preface should follow details of arrangements for implementing the policy, including ways in which responsibilities may be assigned. These details will vary from one establishment to another, since they must take into account the particular circumstances of each different operation. In a large company, details may well differ from one branch of the establishment to another. Rules, regulations, and codes of practice must deal with the particular hazards at each location and with those encountered almost everywhere.

The name and business address of the person responsible for implementing the policy in the particular workplace must be included in this second part of the policy statement. (The executive chef may well be assigned responsibility for the kitchen and ancillary departments).

Examples of further details to be included are:

[name of person] is responsible for ensuring that working conditions and work areas comply with the Occupational Safety and Health Act and other relevant statutory provisions.

Structural faults in the building should be reported to [name of person].

[name of person] is responsible for acquainting staff with fire procedures, organizing regular fire drills, and taking necessary precautions for storing flammable materials in order to minimize fire risks.

[name of person] is responsible for seeing that entrances and exits are not obstructed and for ensuring that staff and public have adequate means of escape from the premises in the event of fire or other hazard.

Accidents involving personal injury to staff or public should be promptly notified to [name of person].

[name of person] is responsible for training staff in necessary safety procedures.

[name of person] is responsible for organizing first aid and maintaining first aid kits.

Recipe for a Good Safety Document

Yield:
A comprehensible, helpful statement of the establishment's policies for improving employee safety

Ingredients:
A statement of safety goals
    The name of the person to contact regarding:
        Structural building faults
        Fire safety and prevention
        Personal injuries
        First aid
        Safety training
Safety rules, regulations, and work procedures
A list of other relevant safety manuals

Method:
Write in clear, easy-to-understand language. Post prominently and explain to all new employees. Try to involve all employees in the implementation of the safety program.

Relevant points regarding common kitchen hazards, accidents, preventive measures, and first aid from the text that follows hereafter can be incorporated into the "rules, regulations, and code of practice" portion of the safety statement. Other measures of safety regarding a particular operation must also be added. In addition, operator's and safety manuals published by the manufacturers of kitchen equipment and utensils should be made available. There is no need for the written policy statement to include detailed rules for, say, handling knives or dealing with wet floors, but the statement could refer to whatever relevant additional rules, codes, or manuals are available.

Human Relations in Safety

Employers cannot transfer their own responsibility for safety to their employees, but it is sensible for managers to involve employees in the safety process. One way is to create a safety committee with elected or appointed employee representatives. The safety committee should help draw up, revise, and implement the establishment's safety policy document. Involved and informed employees are much more likely to spot and call to management's attention unsafe conditions and unsafe actions of coworkers.

There is a well-established link between accidents (involving equipment damage and breakage as well as injuries) and staff morale and satisfaction. This is not meant to suggest that deliberate sabotage is likely under conditions of stress, anxiety, or poor staff/employer relationships, but to point out that such conditions invariably have a distracting effect that can be a factor in causing accidents. Employee involvement in safety programs, however, can prevent many of these negative morale factors from developing and can blunt their effect of stimulating accidents. Furthermore, a good safety committee can help identify individuals who are genuinely accident-prone and thus pose a serious threat to themselves and others. Such individuals should be referred to counselling and/or be reassigned.

Incentive awards may also achieve good results in engendering employee interest in safety, particularly over the long run. And safety posters should be prominently displayed, especially in places staff members frequently pass and near particular danger spots.

Basic Causes of Accidents

Accidents are usually caused by inattention, thoughtlessness, or bad planning relating to three general factors:

Excessive haste

Use of heat and hot equipment

Use of machinery

When kitchen activity reaches its peak at meal service times, speed is often considered a virtue. Rushing and frantic haste, however, often reduce real progress and increase accidents. Correct handling and use of tools, on the other hand, both increase efficiency and speed and reduce the possibility of mishap. Food preparation and cooking, therefore, must proceed in a controlled manner, in spite of pressures to speed up. If control is lost, accidents are much more likely to arise. The kitchen atmosphere should therefore be orderly and calm, with staff working efficiently and safely as well as expeditiously.

Heating equipment and power-driven equipment are associated with two different kinds of accidents. First, lack of familiarity with equipment and absence of skill in using it can result, for example, in fat fires on stoves, in cut fingers, and in maimed hands from using cutting machines. Second, operators who are skillful but overly familiar and overconfident with equipment may become negligent. Only too familiar are stories of cooks who safely used bread-slicing machines for years, only to cut off the tip of a finger one day.

Such dangers are increased under poor physical conditions such as inadequate ventilation, inadequate lighting, or dirty surroundings. For example, an overheated kitchen can dull alertness and increase the possibility of an accident.

Other factors than those just mentioned can also be responsible for accidents.

Structural Faults

Accidents due to structural faults in kitchens, in related departments, and in connecting corridors are common. For example, faulty floors can cause trips and falls—falls that are particularly serious to a worker who is carrying vessels containing foods and liquids. A frequent cause is deteriorated floor covering, such as broken or displaced tiles, gutters, or gulley covers. Grease or wetness on the floor and improperly placed objects such as crates, boxes, and brooms can also cause slipping and tripping. Nonporous (or semiporous) floor materials such as tiles are best for safe walking. Porous floors (or floors that start nonporous but degenerate through wear) are best avoided. Sealing, either to counteract porosity or to give a quick gloss, is not generally effective in busy kitchen areas. Traffic can break up the seal and the resultant powder can become yet another hazard. (It is worth noting that suitable safety shoes help to reduce not only slipping and tripping but also injury from objects falling onto the feet).

Structural defects of walls and ceilings are usually less threatening, but faulty doors, unfamiliar projections from walls, and window damage that affects lighting can all cause accidents, as can stairs that are slick, of different heights, loose, or otherwise defective. Kitchens are often entirely lit by artificial means. Illumination needs, as measured by lighting experts, should be fulfilled at all times because workers must always be able to see what they are doing. Good lighting is especially important when using fire, knives, and power-driven machinery.

To minimize structural risks, adopt a policy of regular inspection so that unnecessary physical hazards can be located and removed. Use a check list for regular safety inspection practiced on a daily, weekly, or monthly basis as appropriate.

Equipment and Activities

Equipment and activities in the kitchen and its related departments can also endanger workers. Such risks should be identified and controlled. Care in the following areas is especially important:

Equipment:
Food machinery—choppers, mixers, mincers, slicers
Beverage pantry equipment—coffee urns, boilers
Other electrical equipment—fans
Fire extinguishers
Activities:
Knife, chopper, and other sharp tool usage
Handling hot objects; moving food or equipment trolleys
Lifting or moving heavy objects
Spilling grease, water and other materials onto the floor
Climbing—using ladder, mounting boxes

Fire

Few things are as frightening and serious as fires, and yet fire risks are great within the kitchen because cooking involves using intense heat. Stoves, grates, furnaces, heaters, hot ashes, smoking materials, burning rubbish, and sparks are among the dangers. Electrical machinery and cables abound in the kitchen, and possible wiring faults add to the fire risk. Careless work-practices and a failure to take elementary precautions can turn a kitchen into a fire trap. Excessive heat, an open flame, or a spark can ignite frying fats, collected grease, spilled oil, food in ovens, loose clothes, or other cloth and paper articles.

To prevent fires, buildings and equipment should be designed for fire safety. Oven canopies, ducts, and other places where grease collects should be kept clean. Equipment should be operated according to manufacturers' instructions. Deep fat fryers should not contain oil or fat above one-third of capacity, and they should have easily closable lids. Fire exits should be clearly marked.

If a fire begins, it is vital to deal with it promptly and completely, before it reaches a life-threatening stage. The kitchen should have its own smoke detectors, fire alarms, and extinguishers. Since the chef and the kitchen staff are the first line of defense, they should all be drilled on proper action to take in the event of fire, in accordance with the safety plan. Such procedures should be approved by the local fire marshall and should include instruction on the use of appropriate fire-fighting equipment. Fire drill training and information should be down-to-earth. In the case of workers with little or no ability to read English, fire procedures, instructions, and warnings should be provided in their language as well as in English.

There are three types of fire common to kitchens. Class A fires are produced by the simple combustion of wood, paper, cloth, and so on.

Class B fires occur in flammable liquids such as oil and grease. Class C fires originate in live electrical equipment. Three elements keep a fire going: heat, fuel, and oxygen. Fire control, therefore, must aim to eliminate or contain one or more of these fire-sustaining elements.

For example, a simple combustion fire (Class A) is extinguished by lowering the fire's temperature and cutting off its supply of free oxygen with water or foam. Class B fires in flammable liquids must be smothered with foam, carbon dioxide, or dry chemicals. Class C fires, the most dangerous, must be extinguished by nonconducting agents such as carbon dioxide and dry chemicals.

Choosing the wrong fire-fighting apparatus or extinguishing agent can cause as much damage to kitchen equipment as the fire itself. Under certain conditions, it can even make the fire worse, thereby increasing the human danger. Water, for instance, is an excellent extinguisher for Class A fires, but it can spread burning oil and conduct electricity, potentially making Class B and Class C fires worse. For such fires, carbon dioxide or dry chemicals should be used.

Recipe for Fire-Fighting Equipment

Yield:
The proper choice of extinguishing equipment for a given fire

Ingredients:
For Class A fires (ordinary combustion)—foam, soda acid, water, or multipurpose dry chemical extinguishers
For Class B fires (flammable liquids)—foam, carbon dioxide, or dry chemical extinguishers
For Class C fires (electrical equipment)—carbon dioxide or dry chemical extinguishers

Method:
Have the right kind of equipment and enough of it to face the kinds of fires your kitchen is likely to have. The multipurpose dry chemical extinguisher is the only one that handles all types of fires, but its use in the kitchen is not recommended because the chemicals it contains can contaminate food.

Portable extinguishers should be located near doors or at other easily accessible locations near potentially hazardous areas. They should never be installed in a corner, in the middle of a corridor, or in any other hard-to-reach spot. Extinguishers should contrast with their background so as to be easy to see (for example, red containers against a white wall).

An extinguisher should be light enough to be carried by members of the kitchen staff, and its size should be adequate to fight any fire likely to occur in the course of kitchen operations. If larger extinguishers are required, mounting them on trolleys that can be easily wheeled to the point of use may be the best choice. Built-in extinguishers like sprinkler systems should have nozzles in any ductwork where cleaning cannot completely eliminate all grease.

The recommended medium for fighting Class B and Class C fires is carbon dioxide (CO_2) gas. It provides safe, nontoxic protection by smothering flames without tainting food or damaging expensive equipment. Upon expulsion, the compressed gas expands 450 times and reaches into every crevice. After the fire is extinguished, CO_2 quickly disappears, leaving no trace and no mess to clean up. The only drawback of CO_2 occurs if the user "blasts" the fire with it, thereby spreading the burning material. All-purpose dry powders are effective in fighting all three kinds of fire, but they are not recommended for kitchen use because they contaminate food.

Maintenance and recharging regulations vary. Each type of extinguisher has its own special requirements. They should be checked after each use in addition to either an annual or a semiannual check, depending upon manufacturer's suggested practice. A brief inspection of nozzles and other movable parts every month or so is advisable in order to detect tampering or inadvertent damage.

General Accidents

Many kitchen perils are due to human error rather than to faulty structures or equipment. For example, lack of foresight results in such dangerous situations as a person climbing onto an unsteady pile of boxes to reach an otherwise inaccessible object, attempting to lift too heavy a load, running in corridors, bumping into others, leaving saucepan handles projecting from the stove, leaving saucepan handles exposed directly over burners so that they become hot, and so on. Accidents with slicing, mincing, whisking, beating, and bread-cutting machines are almost invariably due to the operator's failure to observe the manufacturers' instructions and/or to carry out the establishment's safety precautions. Such general accidents can be prevented by proper instruction and intelligent anticipation of the consequences of any action.

Safety Regulations and Code of Practice

In 1970 the Williams-Steiger Occupational Safety and Health Act created the Occupational Safety and Health Administration (OSHA) to develop and administer safety regulations. There is clearly a need for this law. Even with it, in 1976 alone, 590,000 illnesses and injuries were reported among service industry workers, including over 500 deaths. However, OSHA has been criticized for being too prolific in its production of regulations: thousands of pages—enough volumes to fill an office bookcase—have been issued to cover safety in various workplaces. Many managers complain of incomprehensible or petty rules and of compliance procedures that require too much paperwork. In any event, OSHA is the law, affecting every business that has one or more employees (in addition to the owners). OSHA inspectors can make un-

Posting and recording (1903.2, 1904.2,5)
- failure to post OSHA poster
- failure to maintain log of injuries
- failure to post year-end summary

Floor and stairways (1910.22,23)
- wet and slippery from drippage, seepage, or splash
- uncovered or unguarded holes
- protruding pipe ends, nails or other obstructions
- litter or items which should not be on floors
- improper or inadequate stairway railings and guards
- lack of protection at floor openings

Aisleways (1910.22)
- not clear of obstructions
- insufficient clearance for carts or traffic

Exits (1910.36 & 37)
- insufficient exits for fire or emergency
- exits locked or blocked
- emergency exits not marked and not illuminated

Ladders (1910.25 & 26)
- broken (and not tagged "dangerous for use")
- unsafe construction

Electrical (1910.309)
- Failure to ground grinders, slicers, and other electrical equipment
- frayed or spliced electrical cords and broken plugs
- circuit breakers and switches not protected

Mechanical equipment (1910.221,252)
- unguarded floor fan (when blade is less than 2.1 m/7 ft. from floor it must be guarded)
- unguarded cutting, chopping. and grinding equipment
- unguarded compressor belts
- improper storage of compressed gas

Fire equipment (1910.157)
- untested fire extinguishers (hydrostatic test every 5 years)
- fire extinguishers not inspected (recorded on tag within 1 year)
- empty extinguisher (not recharged)
- extinguisher hidden or obstructed

Medical and first-aid (1910.151)
- first-aid contents incomplete
- no first-aid kit
- first-aid kit not approved by physician
- no trained first-aid attendant on duty (required in 24-hour operation)
(In absence of an infirmary, clinic or hospital in near vicinity to the workplace, a person or persons shall be adequately trained to render first aid.)

Employee health and comfort (1910.141)
- lack of adequate hand-washing facilities with towels and cleansing agent
- failure to provide covered receptacle in toilet room used by women
- unclean, poorly illuminated, poorly ventilated toilets, lavatories, and dressing rooms
- rooms not clean, orderly, and in sanitary condition

5-5. Most frequent deficiencies cited in foodservice and food-processing operations. From Knight and Kotschevar, *Quantity Food Production, Planning and Management.*

announced inspections at any time, issuing citations for violations and levying fines. If the managers refuse to correct violations, they can receive larger fines. And if the offenses are serious enough, even imprisonment can result.

Particular relevant portions of OSHA regulations, such as those listed in figure 5-5, could be included in the establishment's safety plan and discussed during staff training. People are less likely to be careless, to engage in dangerous horseplay, to fail to dress properly, or to fail to report accidents if they know the applicable regulations. In addition to avoiding the safety lapses listed in figure 5-5, here are some more reminders:

Falls and Collisions

1. Watch where you are going, especially when approaching blind corners or when carrying trays. Walk; do not run.
2. Wear low-heeled shoes that are in good condition. Do not wear shoes with open toes or soft uppers on the job. Keep shoe laces tied.
3. Maintain floors properly. Use nonslip paint or abrasive cloth on consistently wet areas. Determine the causes of leaks and grease spots and correct these promptly. Remove floor spillage immediately. If the floor remains wet afterward, sprinkle it with sand or salt.
4. Use a stool or ladder, but never a box, crate, or chair, to reach high places.
5. Stack trays and trolleys so you can see where you are going. Never overload them.
6. Use bright lights in all passages and storerooms. Never grope around in the dark.
7. Avoid cross traffic. Use "IN" and "OUT" doors. Be cautious of swing doors.
8. Mark overhanging or projecting hazards with alternating stripes of yellow and black and/or with warning notices to attract attention.
9. In storerooms, stack items neatly and control stack heights to eliminate toppling. Arrange heavier items on lower shelves. Watch out for broken crates, protruding wires, and sharp splinters. Remove crates as soon as they are empty.

Cuts

1. Do not attempt to open cans with a knife or tool other than a can opener.
2. Do not sever box wire with knives or tools other than a wire cutter.
3. Do not attempt to slice frozen food—especially meat, from which a knife easily slips.
4. Provide a safe, convenient place for keeping knives and sharp-edged tools. Never place these in a sink or loose in a drawer. Wash and store them immediately after using.
5. Handle knives carefully. Keep hands dry to prevent slipping. Carry knives point down. Keep knives clean and sharp at all times. Make no attempt to catch a falling knife. Pass knives to another person by holding the back of the blade and offering the handle. Always cut on a cutting board with a downward movement. Never cut toward the other hand or toward the body.
6. Handle broken dishes, bottles, and so forth with caution. Discard them immediately into a trash container. Beware of reaching into such containers with bare hands.

Injuries from Machines

1. Manufacturers' instructions and other safety warnings should be clearly displayed in an obvious position adjoining the machine. It is preferable to keep them under glass or clear tape to prevent

fading and damage. General maintenance of electrical machinery is important, as is awareness of the location of safety switches and how to use them.

2. Safety guards should ALWAYS be in position.

3. Always use a wood or plastic stick or plunger to push meat or other food into mincing and grinding machines. A metal object such as an ice pick can cause great damage to the machine. Under no circumstances use hands or fingers; they can easily get caught.

4. Do not try to dislodge material adhering to the sides of a mixing machine's bowl either with hands or with instruments while the machine is in motion.

Electrical Accidents and Shocks

1. Machines with electrical motors should be grounded. It is extremely dangerous to run any machine in a kitchen on a two-prong plug, especially in wet areas.

2. Check all wall plugs to ensure that they are of the grounded type and are not overloaded. Overloading of plugs is a common cause of fire.

3. All electrical cords should be off the floor to eliminate the hazard of tripping.

4. Identify electrical switch panels and keep them clear at all times. Every power-driven machine should have a switch within arm's length of the operator.

5. Turn off an electrical machine immediately after use.

6. Disconnect electrical slicing, chopping, and grinding machines whenever they are being cleaned.

7. Never use or tamper with any equipment that is not working correctly. Do not handle worn or frayed cords. Attach an "Out of Order" sign immediately.

8. Be sure your hands and the floor on which you are standing are dry before touching any electrical equipment.

9. Identify danger areas, fuse boxes, and electrical outlets by painting red, bright orange, or black and yellow stripes.

Sprains

1. Never attempt to lift or carry heavy loads—use trolleys or carts.

2. Practice proper lifting habits. Crouch, do not bend; lift with the legs, not the back.

3. Carry loads on your shoulder, when you must carry.

4. Arrange equipment to eliminate unnecessary lifting or carrying.

5. Never lift heavy articles over your head or above head level.

Gas Equipment Hazards

1. Taps and leads on gas equipment must be regularly checked, and burners must be kept clean so that no obstruction is caused by dirt. Most accidents with gas are caused through carelessness in leaving burners on or in failing to report defects in the taps, leads, or burners.

2. Check that oven pilot lights are in working order; faulty pilots can have explosive results.

3. When gas is smelled or when for some other reason a leak is suspected:
   a. Turn off flames and electrical devices and extinguish smoking materials.
   b. Open windows and doors to disperse the gas.
   c. Check to see if the pilot-light jet has been left on unlit. If not, turn off the supply, at the meter if possible.
   d. Call the local gas utility service.
   e. Evacuate the immediate area.

Burns and Scalds

1. Do not try to lift or carry large containers full of hot food or liquid by yourself.

2. Do not overcrowd the range. See that pans are securely placed. Do not allow pan handles to project into traffic flow or in any other direction where they can be knocked off. Report loose handles and leaking pots so that they can be repaired or replaced.

3. Oven cloths, pot holders, rubbers, and so forth must be absolutely dry when handling hot equipment. Do not use personal clothing such as aprons for this purpose. Lift pan lids and covers with care to avoid having steam burn your hands or face. Use proper tools when removing pans from the oven so as to protect the hands. These tools and oven cloths should always be readily available so that workers are never tempted to use their hands to save time.

4. Avoid splashing when adding hot liquid to food. Never overfill, or even completely fill, kettles and pans. Pour hot water or stock over food rather than dropping food into hot liquids. Avoid overheating fats and oils.

5. Identify equipment likely to cause burns (for example, steam pipes and boilers) by marking the dangerous portions of these with a bright red or orange.

6. Check for utensil defects such as loose taps on stockpots that can cause the utensils to be turned on inadvertently by someone brushing against them, potentially causing scalded feet. Valves and steam joints in steam-heated equipment may become defective and allow the escape of hot steam, if not kept in good repair and checked periodically.

7. Never throw smoldering matches into a waste basket.

8. If clothes catch on fire, stand or lie still, and smother the flames with a fire blanket.

Poisoning and Allergies

1. Clearly label all supplies, especially nonedible or poisonous ones. Make sure the latter have warning labels that are understood by all employees.

2. Keep detergents, poisons, and the like separated from food supplies to prevent serious mistakes.

3. Keep a supply of rubber gloves for those working with detergents or other materials that might cause skin allergies.

Reporting Accidents

Accidents involving staff and equipment can become the subject of insurance claims, compensation demands, and litigation in the courts. In the event of an accident, therefore, the chef should immediately prepare an accurate written report of the circumstances and pass it on to higher management.

Notification of Accident

Among other items, the accident report should include:

The name of the person involved and/or the machine damaged

The date and time of the accident

Where the accident occurred

The cause and nature of the injury

The name of the supervisor in charge

The names of any witnesses

If necessary, the chef should attach a confidential note giving supplementary information about the accident and why it occurred. Blank forms should be prepared in advance for this purpose.

Accident Records

There is a statutory requirement under OSHA to keep a log of all injuries and illnesses (OSHA Form 100), except those requiring only first aid. If a fatality results, or if five or more employees are hospitalized in a single incident, then an OSHA office must be notified within 48 hours. In addition, the employer should prepare supplemental records about each injury (OSHA Form 101) and an annual summary (OSHA Form 102) whether accidents occurred or not. These records should be kept for five years.

In addition to the standard forms for most routine cases, special rules govern more serious situations.

Fatal Accident Procedure

Give top priority to suitable first aid; secure medical assistance to prevent a fatality (or another fatality) from occurring as a result of failure to treat injury. In other words, look after the living first. When you are sure that a fatality has occurred:

1. Phone the local coroner's office and OSHA.
2. Inform the next of kin.
3. Try to normalize the situation quickly; other accidents often occur as a result of the first accident because of emotional distress, distraction, and so forth.
4. Do not move anything until an authorized official permits it, even if leaving the area untouched causes inconvenience—unless not

moving things poses a genuine danger to others. In such a case, the exact prior location of anything that is moved must be recorded, preferably with photographs from different angles.

5. Record as many details as possible of the scene before and after the accident. Take eye-witness evidence as soon as possible.

First Aid

Despite all precautions, accidents occur. Cuts, burns, falls, and other personal mishaps must be anticipated even in the best-ordered kitchen. Since improper treatment or neglect of a minor kitchen injury can lead to major problems, all staff should be familiar with accident reporting procedures and the rudiments of first aid.

First aid kits must be conveniently located, fully stocked and maintained, and checked frequently by a chef or other responsible person. All who work in the kitchen must be informed of where first aid kits are located, who among the staff have superior first aid skills, and how further medical attention may be best and most quickly summoned. Therefore, with or near the kit should be displayed the phone numbers of doctor, local hospital, and ambulance service. In addition to items such as bandages and medicine, a concise first aid manual should be included in the kit.

The following are hints on how to deal with common kitchen mishaps.

Initial Response
Following an accident:
1. Do not move the patient (unless the patient's present location poses further danger).
2. Diagnose the situation by observing the accident scene and the signs and symptoms the patient displays.
3. Priorities: treat first any breathing difficulties; then any bleeding; and only then other injuries and shock.

Shock
In many cases, the injured person will suffer from shock, either immediately or a few minutes after the accident, perhaps during or just after treatment. Shock symptoms include cool or cold skin, turning pale, fainting, and a slow pulse. If these signs appear, loosen the patient's clothing and ensure plenty of fresh air (open a window and avoid crowding). Wrap the patient in a blanket to keep warm, but avoid overheating. If a patient has a head injury, is bleeding, or is unconscious, do not attempt to administer food or drink. If the shock is simply emotional, tea or coffee may be given. If necessary, send for medical help.

Electric Shock
Ensure that the current is switched off and treat the victim for shock.

Falls

Do not let the person move until it is certain that nothing is broken. This can usually be observed through unnatural movements or positions of limbs or by gently passing the hand over the bone area of the body. If a back injury is suspected, do not move the person until medical assistance arrives. The patient's limbs may be moved to a more comfortable position, but be sure not to move the back. If in doubt, keep the patient completely still.

Damage to the head should be treated with great care, and in all cases the patient should be taken to a hospital as soon as possible, particularly if there are symptoms of dizziness or if the patient loses consciousness at any time.

Fire

If clothing catches fire, smother flames with a rug or blanket and douse them with water. Treat the patient for shock. Obtain medical assistance.

Burns and Scalds

For fingers, hands, or arms, immerse the burned area in cold or ice water—but not so cold as to compound any shock suffered. If clothing is affected, cut it off rather than trying to undress the part in the usual way. If treatment is swift enough, blisters may be avoided, but do not break any that occur. If the burned area is extremely painful, use cold water or ice compresses on the affected part until all heat sensation is lost from the burn or scald; this can take from 10 to 15 minutes even for a small burn. Then cover the affected part with sterile dressing. For extensive burns—ones covering more than two to three square centimeters (about ½ square inch)—or for deep burns from red-hot metal, frying oil, boiling water, or electricity, always seek medical help. In a severe case, administer no solids or liquids and promptly call the ambulance.

Cuts

When possible, first scrub your hands. If the wound area is dirty, wash it with running water and gently clean the surrounding skin. Place a sterile dressing on top, and exert pressure to stop bleeding. Cover this dressing with bandages. If bleeding continues, add more pads and bandages. Call for medical help as soon as possible if the blood flow cannot be stopped. Raise the bleeding part—if possible, above the level of the heart—and apply light compression to close the lesion until help arrives. Do not use a tourniquet unless you are medically qualified; improper use can increase damage or even lead to loss of the limb.

Immobilize the injured part by using a sling or by tying an uninjured leg to the injured one. Keep the victim warm; remove to a hospital as quickly as possible. In the case of a severed part, such as a finger, pick it up and pack it in ice for possible surgical reattachment.

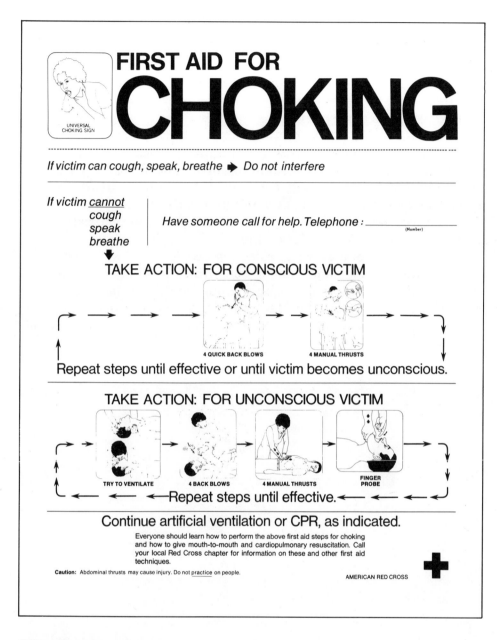

5-6. First aid for choking. Courtesy of the American Red Cross.

Other Treatments

There are many other emergency treatments that kitchen staff should be familiar with. These include cardiopulmonary resuscitation (CPR)—to be used if a person is not breathing—treatment of broken bones and sprains from falls, dealing with foreign bodies in the eyes, and treatment of such other problems as fainting, insect stings, poison ingestion, and choking (see figure 5-6).

Safety Training

Accident prevention and staff response to mishaps should be discussed in introductory sessions for new members of the kitchen staff.

There should also be ongoing, on-the-job training programs and refresher sessions. In addition to meeting legal requirements, such training is essential to prevent suffering. Cuts, slips, burns, and other injuries hurt; a few painful encounters will persuade kitchen workers to use knives and other tools and equipment properly, even if lists of rules and exhortations alone do not.

To be effective, safety training must be simple, direct, and practical. Deal with the basics—how to recognize problems, what steps to take, what equipment to use, and so forth. Visual aids such as film strips and movies have a better impact than talk alone. Effectively designed posters can even be left up on a permanent basis.

The well-ordered kitchen, free from undue haste, anxieties, and physical neglect, will not only be a more pleasant place in which to work, but a much safer one as well. Protecting people, buildings, and equipment against damage and mishap constitutes good business practice because time lost through illness or injury and work impeded by the breakdown of equipment results in actual financial losses. Therefore, measures to ensure welfare are to the advantage of the employer as well as to workers.

6. Nutrition

Because chefs of good restaurants offer such a wide range of foods (all of which presumably are nutritious) and because they cannot compel their clientele to select and eat the right balance of foods, they may be tempted to ignore the whole topic of nutrition. But chefs who recognize their responsibilities to the public are eager to know more about the commodities they use, about how cooking affects foods' nutritional content, and about the dietary effects different foods have. A good chef can aid proper diet by ensuring, insofar as is possible, that the foods leaving the kitchen retain most of their original nutritional value and that all have an appealing look and taste so that customers will actually eat them. This will help prevent customers from gorging on "junk" food while ignoring highly nutritious items—something that becomes critically important in schools, hospitals, and other institutions where usually only one foodservice operation is available.

Importance of a Balanced Diet

The science of nutrition is still young. Biomedical research workers are still discovering new facts about food and discarding or amending old ideas and theories about diet and about the effects of cooking on nutritional content. Nevertheless, certain basic principles are clear. The human body is composed of chemical compounds. Food and drink provide the raw material for those compounds, and a healthy structure depends on the provision of proper combinations of these to work with. Good nutrition is especially important to growing children, who are building their bodies from the foods they consume. But it is also important at every other stage of life; the body is constantly shedding old materials and rebuilding with new ones. A balanced diet of good food not only sustains life and health but adds to the higher pleasures of living.

The chef does not have to worry about the latest theoretical developments in the science of nutrition, but the basic body of knowledge in this field should be familiar so that the chef can plan balanced menus and cook the dishes on them in a way that conserves their nutritive properties. Such knowledge is well-established scientifically and quite simple to understand. Selecting fresh foods in season, offering a wide variety of dishes, and ensuring that food is well-cooked, is served when newly cooked, with other items on the menu will comport with most of the important rules of nutrition.

The Major Nutrient Groups

Food is composed of several different categories of substances, each of which plays a part in meeting the needs of the body and enabling it to function. These different types of components are called *nutrients*.

Proteins

Proteins supply nitrogen, an element essential both for growth and for repair of body tissues. Proteins also function as enzymes and as hormones in regulating body functions. They may also supply energy, but only if the body does not have available enough calories from other sources. No other nutrient can substitute for protein and supply the body with protein's particular nutritional value. Hence, all diets must contain some protein, whether it is from plant or animal sources.

All proteins are composed of chemical building blocks known as amino acids. There are twenty-two of these, some of which must be included in a person's diet and some of which need not be because the body can produce them itself. The main sources of protein are meat (including game and poultry), fish (including shellfish), milk, cheese, and eggs. These animal proteins are said to have a high biological value, which means they contain all of the essential amino acids. Secondary sources include legumes such as peas, beans, and lentils, as well as cereals and nuts. These vegetable proteins are said to have a lower biological value, for they do not contain all the essential amino acids. However, since each plant protein contains a different group of the essential amino acids, a mix of two or three such foods (for example, legumes *and* cereals) can provide all of them.

Proteins are the most important substances found in living material and are the very basis of life. Protein foods are the most expensive foods, but usually are extremely appetizing and give a feeling of satisfaction that is generally absent after a meal of carbohydrates alone. Because animal proteins are especially expensive, it is important to remember that proteins obtained from both plants and animals should be mixed in the diet. See figures 6-1 and 6-2.

Carbohydrates

Carbohydrates provide energy for work and bodily warmth. They include sugars contained in such foods as jams, jellies, syrup, honey, dried fruits, candy, and table sugar itself, and starches in foods such as flour, bread, oatmeal, cereals, fruits, vegetables, potatoes, rice, spaghetti (and other pastas), peas, beans, and lentils. See figure 6-3.

The usual measure of food energy is the kilocalorie or Calorie, spelled with a capital *C* (which is equivalent to 1,000 calories). The Calorie provides enough energy to raise the temperature of 1,000 grams of water (2.2 pounds) by 1° C. The body has been likened to a machine

Item	Weight in grams (ounces)	Approx. portion/measure
Meat and Fish Group		
Bacon	194 (6.8)	7 slices
Cod	198 (7)	1½ portions
Lamb	182 (6.4)	2 cutlets
Beef stewing steak	122 (4.3)	1 large portion
Liver	119 (4.2)	1 large portion
(all raw foods)		
Dairy Group		
Cheese (cheddar)	97 (3.4)	6 cubes 25 millimeters (1 inch)
Eggs (fresh)	225 (7.9)	4 eggs
Milk (whole)	748 (26)	3 glasses
Cereal Group		
Bread (wholewheat)	257 (9)	5 thick slices
Bread (white)	309 (11)	5 thick slices
Oatmeal	204 (7)	1⅜ cups
Rice	398 (14)	2½ cups
Cookies	441 (15)	40 biscuits
Biscuits, cream crackers	305 (11)	33 biscuits
Vegetable Group		
Cabbage	1,147 (40)	
Carrots	3,670 (128)	
Cauliflower	1,690 (59)	
Potato (mature)	1,494 (52)	12 large potatoes
(all uncooked)		
Fruit Group		
Apples	9,880 (346)	50–80
Apricots (dried)	515 (18)	40–50
Bananas	3,144 (110)	30–50 } halves
Oranges	4,014 (140)	16–27

6-1. Amounts of various foods containing approximately one-third of the daily protein requirements of a moderately active adult male.

in which food is the fuel allowing the machine to work. A person who does not get enough Calories begins to feel weak and loses weight; stored Calories (in the form of fat) begin to be used up. A person who gets too many Calories begins to put on weight by building fat. The bodily requirements for Calories vary according to the weight, size, age, state of health and activity level of the individual. The assessment of diets for particular categories of people requires expert knowledge normally outside the scope of the kitchen craftsman. Figure 6-4 shows the different amounts of food required to produce 100 Calories of food energy. Figure 6-5 shows the approximate number of Calories and other nutrients that different people need daily. For each age and sex category, wide variations in daily Calorie requirements are normal.

6-2. Percentage of protein in various foods.

Commodity	Protein, %	Commodity	Protein, %
Fish Group		*Meat Group*	
Herring	16.8	Bacon (raw)	14.4
Salmon	20.3	Beefsteak (raw)	20.2
Sardines (canned in oil)	23.7	Ham (cooked)	24.3
		Lamb (lean cut, raw)	15.9
		Pork chops (grilled)	28.5
Legumes			
Peas (frozen, raw)	5.8		
Lentils (dry)	23.8	*Dairy and Farm Group*	
Peanuts (roasted)	28.1	Cheese (cheddar)	25.4
		Eggs (fresh)	12.3
Cereals		Milk (fresh)	3.3
Flour (white)	10.0		
Oatmeal	12.1		

6-3. Percentage of carbohydrates in various foods.

Commodity	Carbohydrates %	Commodity	Carbohydrates %
Bread (wholewheat)	54.3	Peas (frozen)	10.6
Cornflakes	85.4	Potatoes (raw)	18.0
Flour, white	80.0	Honey	76.4
Oatmeal	72.8	Jam	69.2
Rice	86.8	Sugar	105.0

6-4. One hundred–calorie portions of various foods.

Item	Weight in grams (ounces) of edible portion	Approx. measure
Dairy Foods, Fat, and Oil		
Butter	13.7 (0.47)	1 tablespoon
Cheese (cheddar)	24.4 (0.86)	1 in. cube
Cream (heavy)	22.5 (0.79)	1¾ tablespoons
Egg	68.0 (2.4)	1 very large
Lard	11.0 (0.39)	⅔ tablespoon
Margarine	13.6 (0.48)	1 tablespoon
Milk (fresh)	150.3 (5.3)	1 teacup
Olive oil	11.1 (0.39)	1 tablespoon
Cereal		
Bread (white)	39.7 (1.4)	1 slice
Cookies	19.8 (0.7)	2 small wafers
Biscuits, cream crackers	21.3 (0.75)	3–4 biscuits
		continued . . .

Item	Weight in grams (ounces) of edible portion	Approx. measure
Cornflakes	26.9 (0.95)	½ cup
Cornmeal	28.4 (1.0)	4 level tablespoons
Flour (white)	28.4 (1.0)	4 level tablespoons
Spaghetti	28.4 (1.0)	4½ tablespoons
Oatmeal	24.9 (0.88)	3½ tablespoons
Rice	28.4 (1.0)	4 tablespoons
Meat and Fish		
Bacon (raw)	22.7 (0.8)	2 slices
Cod (raw)	133.2 (4.7)	1 steak, ¾ in.
Herring (raw)	42.5 (1.5)	½ herring
Beefsteak (raw)	59.5 (2.1)	¼ portion
Vegetables, Fresh		
Cabbage (raw)	473.4 (16.7)	½ cabbage
Carrots (mature, raw)	473.4 (16.7)	5–6 carrots, medium
Lettuce	1417.5 (50.0)	12–16
Onion	396.9 (14.0)	4
Potatoes (mature, raw)	127.6 (4.5)	1 medium
Turnips	567.0 (20.0)	4 medium
Tomatoes (fresh)	944.1 (33.3)	10 medium
Legumes		
Peas (fresh)	158.8 (5.6)	3 tablespoons
Green beans	39.7 (1.4)	4 tablespoons
Fruit and Nuts		
Apples (cooking)	280.7 (9.9)	2
Apples (eating)	232.5 (8.2)	3 small/medium
Apricots (dried)	56.7 (2.0)	4–5 halves
Banana	127.6 (4.5)	1 large
Orange	294.8 (10.4)	2 large
Peanuts (roasted)	22.7 (0.6)	1½ tablespoons
Prunes (dried)	62.4 (2.2)	5
Sugar, Preserves, Alcohols		
Marmalade	39.7 (1.4)	3 tablespoons
Milk chocolate	17.0 (0.6)	small slab
Sugar	25.5 (0.9)	2 tablespoons
Honey	34.0 (1.2)	3 tablespoons
Beer	312 (11.0)	½ pint
Spirits (70° proof)	45 (1.6)	—
Wine (red)	142 (5.0)	2 glasses

	Age (years)	Weight (kg)	Weight (lb)	Height (cm)	Height (in)	Protein (g)	Fat-Soluble Vitamins Vitamin A (μg RE)	Vitamin D (μg)	Vitamin E (mg α-TE)
Infants	0.0–0.5	6	13	60	24	kg × 2.2	420	10	3
	0.5–1.0	9	20	71	28	kg × 2.0	400	10	3
Children	1–3	13	29	90	35	23	400	10	5
	4–6	20	44	112	44	30	500	10	6
	7–10	28	62	132	52	34	700	10	7
Males	11–14	45	99	157	62	45	1000	10	8
	15–18	66	145	176	69	56	1000	10	10
	19–22	70	154	177	70	56	1000	7.5	10
	23–50	70	154	178	70	56	1000	5	10
	51+	70	154	178	70	56	1000	5	10
Females	11–14	46	101	157	62	46	800	10	8
	15–18	55	120	163	64	46	800	10	8
	19–22	55	120	163	64	44	800	7.5	8
	23–50	55	120	163	64	44	800	5	8
	51+	55	120	163	64	44	800	5	8
Pregnant						+30	+200	+5	+2
Lactating						+20	+400	+5	+3

	Age (years)	Weight (kg)	Weight (lb)	Height (cm)	Height (in)	Water-Soluble Vitamins Vitamin C (mg)	Thiamin (mg)	Riboflavin (mg)	Niacin (mg NE)	Vitamin B-6 (mg)	Folacin (μg)	Vitamin B-12 (μg)
Infants	0.0–0.5	6	13	60	24	35	0.3	0.4	3	0.3	30	0.5
	0.5–1.0	9	20	71	28	35	0.5	0.6	8	0.6	45	1.5
Children	1–3	13	29	90	35	45	0.7	0.8	9	0.9	100	2.0
	4–6	20	44	112	44	45	0.9	1.0	11	1.3	200	2.5
	7–10	28	62	132	52	45	1.2	1.4	16	1.6	300	3.0
Males	11–14	45	99	157	62	50	1.4	1.6	18	1.8	400	3.0
	15–18	66	145	176	69	60	1.4	1.7	18	2.0	400	3.0
	19–22	70	154	177	70	60	1.5	1.7	19	2.2	400	3.0
	23–50	70	154	178	70	60	1.4	1.6	18	2.2	400	3.0
	51+	70	154	178	70	60	1.2	1.4	16	2.2	400	3.0
Females	11–14	46	101	157	62	50	1.1	1.3	15	1.8	400	3.0
	15–18	55	120	163	64	60	1.1	1.3	14	2.0	400	3.0
	19–22	55	120	163	64	60	1.1	1.3	14	2.0	400	3.0
	23–50	55	120	163	64	60	1.0	1.2	13	2.0	400	3.0
	51+	55	120	163	64	60	1.0	1.2	13	2.0	400	3.0
Pregnant						+20	+0.4	+0.3	+2	+0.6	+400	+1.0
Lactating						+40	+0.5	+0.5	+5	+0.5	+100	+1.0

	Age (years)	Weight (kg)	Weight (lb)	Height (cm)	Height (in)	Calcium (mg)	Phosphorus (mg)	Minerals Magnesium (mg)	Iron (mg)	Zinc (mg)	Iodine (µg)
Infants	0.0–0.5	6	13	60	24	360	240	50	10	3	40
	0.5–1.0	9	20	71	28	540	360	70	15	5	50
Children	1–3	13	29	90	35	800	800	150	15	10	70
	4–6	20	44	112	44	800	800	200	10	10	90
	7–10	28	62	132	52	800	800	250	10	10	120
Males	11–14	45	99	157	62	1200	1200	350	18	15	150
	15–18	66	145	176	69	1200	1200	400	18	15	150
	19–22	70	154	177	70	800	800	350	10	15	150
	23–50	70	154	178	70	800	800	350	10	15	150
	51 +	70	154	178	70	800	800	350	10	15	150
Females	11–14	46	101	157	62	1200	1200	300	18	15	150
	15–18	55	120	163	64	1200	1200	300	18	15	150
	19–22	55	120	163	64	800	800	300	18	15	150
	23–50	55	120	163	64	800	800	300	18	15	150
	51 +	55	120	163	64	800	800	300	10	15	150
Pregnant						+400	+400	+150	*	+5	+25
Lactating						+400	+400	+150	*	+10	+50

*The increased requirement during pregnancy cannot be met by the iron content of habitual American diets nor by the existing iron stores of many women; therefore the use of 30–60 mg of supplemental iron is recommended. Iron needs during lactation are not substantially different from those of nonpregnant women, but continued supplementation of the mother for 2–3 months after parturition is advisable in order to replenish stores depleted by pregnancy.

6-5. Recommended daily allowances for good nutrition. These allowances are intended to provide for individual variations among most normal persons as they live in the United States under usual environmental stresses. Diets should be based on a variety of common foods in order to provide other nutrients for which human requirements have been less well defined. From Dunn, *Fundamentals of Nutrition*, prepared by the Food and Nutrition Board, National Academy of Sciences—National Research Center, 1980.

Fats

Fats or lipids have a dual role. They provide the most concentrated source of energy of all nutrients and in addition provide the essential fatty acids needed for maintaining health. Apart from animal fat, plant oils and dairy products are the main sources of lipids. For indications of how much fat is available in different foods, see figure 6-6.

Like carbohydrates, fats provide Calories that enable the body to function and to maintain its temperature. But fats provide far more Calories ounce for ounce than carbohydrates do. One ounce of fat typically yields 263 Calories, while carbohydrates and protein both yield about 116 Calories per ounce.

Nutritionists have not decided about the human body's daily fat requirements, but people generally do not find their diet palatable if it contains less than about 20% fat. The diet should not contain more

Commodity	Percentage of fat	Commodity	Percentage of fat
Butter	81	Salmon (canned)	8
Pan drippings	99	Sardines (canned in oil)	14
Lard	99	Cheese (cheddar)	34.5
Margarine	81.5	Egg (fresh)	11
Bacon (raw)	41	Almonds	54
Beefsteak (raw)	20	Coconut (desiccated)	62
Ham (cooked)	19	Peanuts (roasted)	49
Lamb (raw)	30	Flour (white)	0.9
Pork (raw)	30	Oatmeal	9
Herring	19		

6-6. Percentage of fats in various foods.

than about 35% fat, however. Because fats are the most slowly digested of all foods, eating too much can be nauseating. Moreover, since some forms of heart disease are associated with increased levels of cholesterol in the blood, and since this is influenced by the amount and kind of fat in the diet, it would be unwise for people susceptible to heart disease to consume very much animal fat. On the other hand, the consumption of vegetable and fish oils, which contain much more polyunsaturated fatty acids than do animal fats, has been associated with lower levels of cholesterol in the blood.

Vitamins

Vitamins are essential elements in foods, despite being present in relatively tiny amounts, because they regulate various bodily processes. Their importance in the diet is most dramatically revealed when they are absent or reduced to a drastically low level. Vitamin C, for example, is found in fresh fruits and vegetables, which were lacking on long voyages in the early days of sailing ships. Scurvy was almost inevitable under these circumstances. The antidote to scurvy was found to lie in citrus fruits such as oranges and lemons, even before the study and naming of vitamins really got under way.

Today, deficiency diseases resulting from a shortage of certain vitamins are still unfortunately common in underdeveloped and poor areas of the world; in this country, however, such deficiency diseases are rare and occur mainly in poverty regions and among individuals who live alone and neglect their diets. Even when people are not so deprived as to get serious deficiency diseases, they may get so little of certain vitamins as to exhibit abnormal symptoms. Such people may eat an insufficient quantity of the right foods not through lack of means, but through lack of knowledge or self-control. This is characteristic of those who prepare ill-balanced meals and use poor preparation, cooking, serving, and storing methods. Such sloppy methods reduce or destroy the potency of many vitamins (and minerals) in foods. It is particularly these aspects of loss that the chef should know about in order to guard effectively against them.

The main vitamins, their sources, and their functions are described in the paragraphs below.

Vitamin A. This is an element necessary for the promotion of growth. It is also known to have an effect on the health and efficiency of the eyes, particularly with respect to night vision. It is formed in the body by the breaking down of a vegetable substance called carotene. This is a yellow pigment (coloring substance) found in plants, especially the leaves. Sometimes all the carotene taken in by an animal is converted into vitamin A, but if excess carotene exists, some may not be converted. Then both the vitamin and the extra carotene may accumulate in the liver, blood, fat, and other tissues below the skin. Cows do not turn all the carotene they get from grass into vitamin A, its natural color indicating the amount of carotene it contains. Since the human body can also convert carotene, we may regard foods that contain carotene as sources of vitamin A. Food sources include fish livers and oils, poultry and animal livers, egg yolk, butter, milk, cheese, animal fat, green leafy vegetables, carrots, and tomatoes.

Vitamin B Complex. This is really a whole group of vitamins including thiamine, niacin, and riboflavin. Diseases resulting from deficiencies include beri-beri and pellagra. While serious forms of these diseases are rare, partial shortages may cause such symptoms as loss of appetite, stomach disorders, digestive difficulties, and general weakness and fatigue. Yeast, yeast extract, wheat germ, whole grain flour and bread, and whole cereal are especially good sources of the B vitamins. Various vitamins of this group may also be found in such foods as egg yolk, milk, meat, and vegetables.

Vitamin C. This vitamin is necessary not only to prevent fully developed cases of scurvy, but also to prevent symptoms such as a tendency to bleeding of the gums, which may impair dental health. This vitamin is of importance also in the healing of wounds and in resistance to respiratory infections. Rich sources include citrus fruits (such as oranges, lemons, and grapefruit), other fruits (such as raspberries, strawberries, and blackberries), uncooked vegetables (such as turnips, carrots, and tomatoes), green vegetables, and potatoes.

Vitamin D. Vitamin D is important for growth. It particularly affects the body's ability to absorb and make use of calcium in the development of bones and teeth. Foods containing vitamin D include butter, enriched margarine, cheese, milk, eggs, and fish.

Vitamin E. This vitamin acts as an antioxidant, which means that it inhibits the chemical breakdown of important substances such as unsaturated fatty acids. It is abundant in vegetable oils, green leafy vegetables, whole grains, eggs, and peanuts.

Vitamin K. This vitamin is essential to enable blood to clot and prevent excess bleeding following a cut. Although it can be produced by the body itself, useful additional sources are leafy vegetables, egg yolks, and grain products.

It would be a mistake for the chef to focus only on the richest sources of certain vitamins and then try to introduce these onto the menu. It is more practical to provide a vitamin by means of foods that may contain fairly small amounts of the vitamin, but that people normally eat in substantial, regular quantities. Potatoes, for example, contain far less vitamin C per ounce than blackberries, but potatoes are a much more useful source of the vitamin because of their more regular acceptance into a diet.

Minerals

In addition to the protective vitamins, another type of food constituent is present in only small amounts, but is extremely important to the maintenance of health. These elements—the minerals—build and repair body tissues and regulate body processes. They include iron, calcium, iodine, and other elements, some of which are found only in trace amounts. Iodine is found in dairy products, in green vegetables, and (in smaller amounts) in meat and fish. Eggs, oatmeal, potatoes, carrots, and so forth, also contain some iodine. Calcium can be found in milk, in other dairy products, in shellfish, and in egg yolk. Good sources of iron are whole grain flour and meat, especially liver.

The absorption and utilization of iron by the body appears to depend on the presence of other minerals such as copper and manganese, just as phosphorus is required for calcium use. Other minerals needed, at least in trace amounts, include magnesium, potassium, sodium, zinc, cobalt, sulfur, chlorine, fluorine, molybdenum, chromium, and selenium. No single food provides all of these, of course, so a good mixed diet is necessary. A shortage of minerals can be just as serious as a shortage of one of the vitamins.

The chef does not have to know how these minerals are used by the body or what precise function each performs, but the chef should know the importance of certain minerals to special groups of consumers. For example, children need extra calcium for growing teeth and bones, while the elderly need adequate potassium to ensure proper mental functioning. The chef should also know how to use cooking methods that retain the mineral content of food. Dieticians are expert in such matters; the chef should work closely with them to ensure that the food is as nutritious as possible.

Nutrient Loss in Cooking

Cooking causes many physical and chemical changes in food which usually improve its acceptability to the consumer by making it more digestible and palatable and by improving its flavor. Keeping quality is also increased, and if thoroughly cooked, food will be rendered safe from preexisting bacteria.

In bad cooking, however, definite nutritive losses may occur and the food's value may decrease. As far as protein foods (meat, fish, poultry, eggs, and milk) are concerned, there is little danger of the protein being lost or its value destroyed in cooking. However, an unappetizing presentation might lead to rejection of the dish by the prospective eater. This is true also of fats, sugars, and starches.

The danger of decreased food value through poor selection, poor methods of preparation, faulty cooking, or incorrect service primarily affects vitamins; to a lesser extent, it also affects minerals. Vitamins B and C are the most likely to be lost because they are water-soluble—that is, they dissolve in water or fluids (such as stock) that contain water. Vitamins A, D, E, and K are fat-soluble—that is, they dissolve in heated animal, vegetable, or mineral oils and other fats. Because cooking oils are less likely to be thrown away than cooking water, the chef should pay special attention to vitamins B and C.

Vitamin C Losses

Water-soluble vitamin C is not only capable of being leached out in water, but also can be destroyed by heat and various other elements in water or in the atmosphere. Iron, if not protected, rusts in the presence of air and water; similarly vitamin C can undergo chemical alteration during storage and transportation, as well as by the actual processes of preparation and cooking. The process of destruction in this way is, of course, hastened if the foods are cut too far in advance of need, thus exposing more surfaces to the atmosphere. Bruising and damaging have similar harmful consequences.

In dealing with vitamin C–containing foods such as green leafy vegetables and potatoes, therefore, the following points should be kept in mind:

1. Select vegetables that are as freshly gathered as possible and that are not bruised or damaged.
2. Buy the correct amounts for current use, avoiding storage in the vegetable storage area, no matter how satisfactory its condition.
3. Ensure that the vegetable storage area is clean, cool, dry, and well-ventilated.
4. Do not prepare vegetables too far in advance. Particularly avoid the premature shredding or cutting of vegetables such as cabbage. Avoid washing and soaking such vegetables once they have been cut and shredded. This applies both to vegetables and fruits that are to be cooked and to those that are to be used fresh, especially tomatoes and citrus fruits.
5. Cook in the minimum quantity of boiling water necessary. Where possible, use the cooking fluid in a dish rather than throwing it away. Steaming, instead of boiling, is a preferable procedure for cooking vegetables, as it helps retain vitamins, color, and flavor better than boiling does.
6. Cook as rapidly as possible. Warm temperatures speed the destruction of nutrients, but boiling temperatures halt the activity of many vitamin-destroying elements.
7. Keep in mind that bicarbonate of soda aids the destruction of vita-

min C, and avoid it when possible (it helps achieve better color and thus promotes readier acceptance of the vegetables in some instances).

8. Serve vegetables as quickly as possible after cooking since hot-plate or *bain-marie* storage is particularly destructive of vitamin C. Cooking vegetables at staggered times, therefore, helps preserve their nutritive content as well as their flavor. Left-over vegetables are likely to have little or no vitamin C remaining.

Vitamin B Losses

Vitamin B is also water-soluble, but foods rich in it are usually cooked differently from those containing vitamin C. Wholemeal grains and yeast are more often baked than boiled in water. In fact, because yeast is so rich in vitamins of the B complex, it is greatly to be preferred as a leavening agent over chemical-raising agents and baking sodas that have a deleterious effect upon B vitamins. Cooking meat with fat (roasting, grilling, or frying) rather than with water avoids the loss of vitamin B by leaching into cooking fluids that are later discarded. On the other hand, the higher temperatures that are reached using fat and oil cooking methods can destroy vitamin B.

To minimize the loss of B vitamins, therefore:

1. Select whole grain breads, or milled flour products that are enriched with vitamins (milling removes those originally present).
2. Whenever possible, use yeast as a leavener rather than baking soda.
3. Put the fluids in which meat with vitamin B has been cooked to use—for example, in soups and gravies.

Fat-Soluble Vitamin Losses

Fat-soluble vitamins (A, D, E, and K) are fairly resistant to loss in cooking. However, carotene, a chemical source of vitamin A, can be lost from vegetables such as carrots by slicing them and then steeping them in water.

Fat-soluble vitamins will, of course, dissolve in mineral or vegetable oil. One of the undesirable results of using mineral oil in diets, in salad dressings and the like, is that it dissolves such vitamins and prevents their absorption, since mineral oil passes through the body unassimilated (which is why it can be used as a laxative).

Mineral Losses

The chief loss of minerals occurs when they are dissolved in cooking fluids that are not subsequently used. It is important, therefore, to use the smallest possible amount of water for cooking purposes (for example, in the boiling of vegetables) and to make every effort to use it in the diet.

Conclusion

In addition to the major groups of nutrients, there are other important elements in food, including food pigments, organic flavors, water, and fiber. The loss of any of these can harm food's taste and appearance. For example, carrots with a dark brownish color and overcooked, dry pieces of meat are not especially appetizing. Fiber, the indigestible material in whole cereals and some fruits and vegetables, is not a nutrient, but it does play an important role in maintaining the regularity and health of the bowels.

Without being a nutrition expert, the chef should know enough to handle and prepare foods without harming their healthful properties. Similarly, customers do not need to calculate their exact intake of each nutrient. If they maintain a balanced diet, and if the foods are adequately prepared, the customers will be in no danger of malnutrition. Chefs can help by making all of their foods so appetizing that customers eat an adequate amount of the various kinds. Food that is rich in nutrients fulfills no purpose if it ends up in the garbage can. Therefore, the intelligent chef will seek to study and understand the tastes of the type of customer that is to be served. The chef must endeavor to satisfy these demands and at the same time reconcile them with the demands of good nutrition.

Recipe for a Balanced Diet

Yield:
A diet that will provide the nutrition required to maintain health and well-being

Ingredients:
Protein, for bodily growth and repair
Carbohydrates and fats, for energy
Vitamins, to regulate bodily processes
Minerals, to build strong bones, teeth, and other parts

Method:
To obtain all of the above nutrients every day, an adult should consume two servings of milk, cheese, or other milk products; two servings of meat, legumes, eggs, or nuts; four servings of fruits or vegetables; and four servings of cereal grains or flour products.

Part II.

The Kitchen and Management

7. Kitchen Organization Emergence and Development

Introduction to the *Partie* System

[handwritten note: Chain of comand]

Partie is a French word meaning "part (of a whole) or section." A *partie* system is one in which an operation's space, equipment, and jobs are divided up into sections. The *partie* system for chefs evolved in the Escoffier era from an analysis of the tasks needed for production and then a grouping of those tasks so as to maximize production speed and efficiency. The original system lasted up to the 1930s and was designed primarily for large restaurants, especially those in major hotels providing extensive *à la carte* and *table d'hôte* menus in the classic French tradition. As the task of the professional kitchen came to involve serving more customers in more and different ways, its organization inevitably became more complex. Highly elaborate dishes required highly specialized experts rather than general chefs who must handle all types of cookery at once.

Modern restaurants and other foodservice systems with quite different styles and sizes of menus cannot adopt the original *partie* system in its entirety, but they can apply the same basic principles of organizing to their own production systems. Such a systems analysis approach should take into account the type of menu and style of service desired, the people (staff and customers) involved, and the physical resources (equipment and layout) of the kitchens to be used. It must organize all of these for efficient meal production. The quantity and quality of work skills required will be determined by the menu; the aim is to assign skilled work to the most skilled individuals so that their abilities are fully used. Repetitive jobs, such as those on the grill or griddle, may be broken down into simplified elements and assigned to staff with lesser or no skills. Many jobs may be considered for "deskilling" in this way.

Each type of operation will naturally need its own unique organization for best results. The organizational charts used in this chapter to describe the *partie* system are therefore for illustration purposes only. They should not be implemented without extensive revision adapting them to precise actual purposes and needs. Nevertheless, the way in which traditional luxury hotel kitchens originally developed their staffing is worth considering in order to grasp the principles of their approach. Such historical knowledge also gives insight into the various customs of the kitchen that have evolved over the years.

Basic Divisions of Kitchen Work

Even in the earliest times and in the simplest kitchens catering to the public, cooks probably divided the work of preparing and cooking so as to minimize effort. The broad features of a kitchen organization soon began to emerge in divisions such as:

> The storage of commodities, both perishable and nonperishable
> The preparation of meat, fish, and poultry (larder work)
> The preparation and cooking of pastries and desserts (the pastry)
> The preparation of vegetables
> The assembly and cooking of prepared foods (the general stove section)

In small kitchens today, this basic arrangement can to some extent be contracted and simplified. As kitchens increase in size and volume of work, this basic arrangement can be expanded as needed.

Historical Overview

Carême was typical of the great chefs who served royalty and nobility rather than a larger public. After him, the organizational pattern that developed in the kitchens of the large private clubs of London was emulated in much of Europe and North America, especially at the modern hotels that began to develop near the end of the nineteenth century. The great writer-chefs of this period, however, tended to write with a view to the domestic cook of the private house. Most of them left behind little information about how to organize work on a large scale. But the greatest chef of the Victorian era, Alexis Soyer, did include kitchen organization in his book, *The Gastronomic Regenerator*, written and published in the middle of the nineteenth century when the author was at the height of his fame. In fact, this book, subtitled *A Simplified and Entirely New System of Cookery*, included, in Soyer's words, "correct and minute plans how kitchens of every size, from the kitchen of a royal palace to that of the humble cottage, are to be constructed and furnished."

Soyer's kitchen plan provided for a larder department with specialized subsections for each type of meat, a separate pastry and confectionary room, and an L-shaped kitchen with different sections for roasting, cooking, and so on. The exact details of Soyer's designs are unimportant now because they were based on methods such as open-fire roasting and physical constraints such as nonrefrigerated storage that are now obsolete. But the principle of designing the physical layout of the kitchen to use one's available methods to best advantage remains.

After Soyer came Escoffier, the first famous chef to use his cooking talents in a large modern hotel, where they would benefit the broader public. This presented for the first time the challenge (which still exists) of how to serve a wide variety of freshly prepared, excellent dishes to a large number of people. Escoffier met this challenge by adding the principle of task organization to that of kitchen layout, thus perfecting the *partie* system. Escoffier studied the food and cookery work behind the recipes and allocated tasks to different specialists so as to help produce even the most complex dishes regularly, efficiently, and swiftly. This sometimes meant breaking down processes and allocating different tasks to different sections for the production of single dishes. Veal escalope, for example, might be cut by the butcher, flattened and breadcrumbed by the larder cook, sautéed in butter by the sauce cook, and then assembled by the chef, using appropriate garnishes prepared in other corners of the kitchen.

The *partie* system today, however, is simpler than it was in Escoffier's time because of several historical developments:

The introduction of machinery to do work previously done by people

Changing public tastes toward simpler menus and meals

Economic factors that encourage the reduction of expensive labor and the simplification of recipes and service

The processing of food by freezing, canning, and dehydration, which eliminates a great deal of basic preparation work

The *partie* system will undergo still more change as automation, method study, and work simplification are increasingly applied within the kitchen. Understanding the *partie* system will remain useful, however, because further improvements are more likely to be conceived by those who know both the traditional system and new technological breakthroughs. This ensures progress rather than haphazard changes which can hurt, or at least fail to help, productivity.

Adaptation and Summarization

The essence of the *partie* system is the division of work into sections; each section or *partie* is controlled by a *chef de partie*, who might be regarded as the section foreman as well as a craft specialist. All the *parties* come under the control of the *chef de cuisine*, who is aided by one or more *sous chefs*. In large establishments, a *sous chef* has no *partie* duties, although in smaller ones, a *sous chef* may also serve as an important *chef de partie*. The chain of responsibility and the organization of a large kitchen under the *parti* system is illustrated in figure 7-1. In the largest hotels and restaurants, about a dozen principal *parties* are established under the *chef de cuisine* and his *sous chefs*. The team of cooks and all their assistants under the *partie* system is comonly called the "brigade."

Adaptations Due to Size

Only a few of the top luxury hotels still carry a brigade of cooks divided into *parties* that include every section that will be referred to in the next chapter. As hotels and restaurants have become more widespread, smaller, and more specialized, varied adaptations of the *partie* system have taken place (figures 7-2 and 7-3) and new but related systems have developed. Common variations include:

The *garde manger*—either alone or with a small staff—handling all the different tasks relating to meat, poultry, and fish

Joining together two or more kitchen *parties*—for example, soup preparation and vegetable cookery

Having a broad three-part division into larder work, pastry work, and the main kitchen work (even here, in very small establishments, there is often intermingling of the branches of work)

The smallest establishments—those employing one chef and one or perhaps two assistant cooks—cannot be regarded as operating even an adaptation of the *partie* system because they lack sufficient people to apportion the tasks in a meaningful way. Each person in such small establishments must therefore be prepared to do almost the full range of tasks.

7-1. Arrangement of large kitchen brigade. From Fuller, *Professional Kitchen Management*.

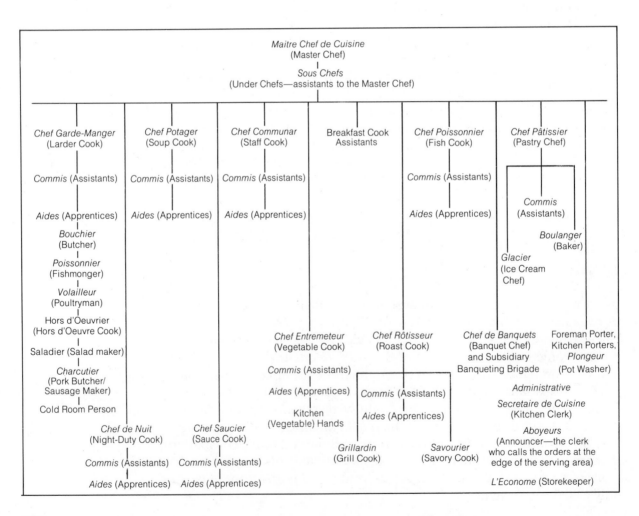

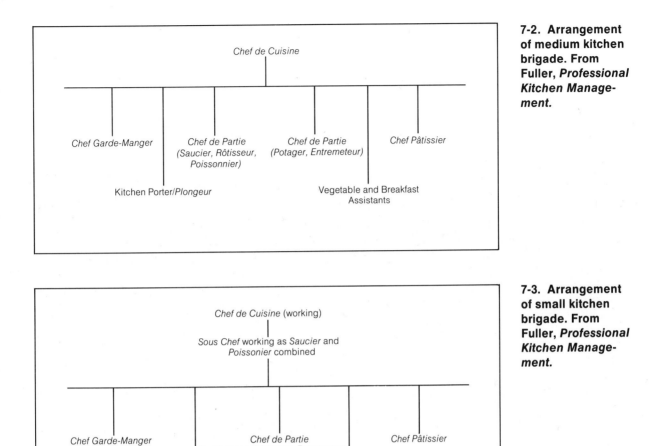

7-2. Arrangement of medium kitchen brigade. From Fuller, *Professional Kitchen Management.*

7-3. Arrangement of small kitchen brigade. From Fuller, *Professional Kitchen Management.*

*Recipe for Organizing a Meaningful **Partie** System*

Yield:
An effective division of space, equipment, and people to perform the job in the most productive way

Ingredients:
Understanding of the establishment's goals regarding menu size and style of service
Knowledge of the type of clientele to be served
Knowledge of the work skills possessed by individual employees
A detailed list of all equipment items and work areas
Understanding of the work procedures required to produce the items offered on the menu

Method:
Lay out the equipment so that it can be used efficiently, preventing unnecessary motion and effort. Items used for related procedures should be kept together, and different groups of items should be kept in separate areas. Assign responsibility for each work procedure to the person(s) with the most skill in doing it.

Adaptations Due to Modern Trends

Apart from simplification of the *partie* system in response to size limitations, other factors increasingly affect the organization of the kitchen. For example, the widespread purchasing of already prepared foods such as portion-controlled cutlets and frozen vegetables greatly reduces and streamlines the food preparation workload. Whereas a good staff ratio in a conventional system is one employee per twenty meals, it is one employee per thirty-five to forty meals in some of the frozen meal systems. The development of microwave ovens and other modern kitchen equipment has also promoted significant progress. New and better apparatuses require continual changes in the way kitchens are operated. The best future adaptations in kitchen organization will be brought about by those who make a careful study of the work procedures involved in light of new facilities, products, and techniques.

8. Kitchen Organization: Staff and Responsibilities

The staff categories and duties defined in the *partie* system described in this chapter were developed in the past and survive today only in a few larger hotels and restaurants. Even in these few places, they have been radically revised. Nevertheless, the *partie* system operated by Escoffier has so affected present-day chefs that a detailed discussion is valuable; it remains an integral part of the culinary craft's tradition and illustrates the enduring principles involved in determining task grouping. It can also serve as a starting point for meaningful future reorganization.

The basis of the old *partie* system and its modern counterparts is the degree of specialization that must exist among an establishment's cooks. In a large foodservice establishment, the operation as a whole runs more smoothly when each person has clearly defined tasks to perform and when these are all coordinated by a supervisor.

Chefs

In the classic *partie* system, chefs belong to a clearcut hierarchy much like that of a military organization.

Chef de Cuisine (Head Chef)

The *chef de cuisine*—who is frequently referred to in these pages as "the chef"—is in command of the kitchen and is second in status only to the overall manager of the establishment. In a large establishment, the *chef de cuisine* is more a departmental manager than a working craftsman—a person selected more for organizing and executive abilities than for culinary skills, though obviously these should be present, too. Nevertheless, the principal functions of the person in this position are to plan, organize, and supervise the work of the kitchens. To accomplish these functions, the *chef de cuisine* must have considerable freedom to operate in a personalized way.

The menu is planned in accordance with higher management's costing and catering policies, and it becomes the "blueprint" for the kitchen's activities. The *chef de cuisine* bears major responsibility for staff selection and dismissal, in conjunction with the personnel department. Because of the complexity of the operation, it is essential to help subordinates develop their skills and art to the fullest extent possible.

In smaller establishments, the head chef may be directly responsible for purchasing food supplies. Even in larger ones, where specialist buyers make purchases, the *chef de cuisine* has responsibility for planning what must be ordered and must also be concerned with the condition of the physical plant and equipment of the kitchen.

It is clear, therefore, that in addition to craft skills and technical knowledge acquired as a result of technical training, apprenticeship, and experience, the *chef de cuisine* must acquire managerial qualities and administrative knowledge; a full understanding of gastronomy, so that the menus and dishes planned and executed will accord with aesthetic as well as commercial considerations; an awareness of (or even an ability to stimulate) modern developments in equipment manufacturing and food processing; and merchandising skills and even showmanship, in order to be an expert at meal presentation.

The executive responsibilities of the *chef de cuisine* can be considered under the principal headings of:

Food and food costs (through menu planning and ordering)

Kitchen staff

Kitchen plant and equipment

All three must be coordinated to produce good food efficiently and economically.

Sous-Chef

The *sous-chef,* or "under chef," is the principal assistant of the *chef de cuisine.* If the *chef de cuisine* is considered the commander, the *sous-chef* is the executive officer, or second-in-command. In large establishments, *sous-chefs* have no sectional or *partie* responsibility, but aid the chef in general administration, in supervising the work of preparing food, and in overseeing its service. Where a very large kitchen operation is involved, there may be more than one *sous-chef.* The position of *sous-chef* is, of course, regarded as an intermediate step between control of a *partie* and complete control of a kitchen. In smaller organizations, one of the principal *chefs de partie* such as the *chef saucier* (sauce cook) or *chef garde-manger* (larder cook) may act as *sous-chef.*

The *sous-chef* in an establishment that has only one will stand in for the *chef de cuisine* when the latter is off-duty and, more importantly, will tend to act as the direct supervisor of practical kitchen activities when the chef is engaged in office work—for example, menu planning, record checking, or similar administrative duties. The *sous chef* usually has the authority to make staff changes during the working day to relieve work pressure. The position requires a person who is something of a disciplinarian, who can keep people industrious, who knows how to be both firm and understanding, and who knows how to do all the tasks subordinates perform.

Additional *sous chefs* are needed when the kitchen staff is large enough, particularly when there are separate restaurants or other food-service operations within the same establishment. In such cases there may be four or even six *sous chefs*—one for each major operation.

Chefs de Partie

A *chef de partie* is a working cook in charge of a clearly defined section of activity within the kitchen. As mentioned above, a *chef de partie* of one of the more important sections, particularly the sauce or the larder, may have the status and duties of a *sous-chef* in addition to sectional responsibilities.

The work of the various *parties* differs in type and magnitude, but there are certain features comon to each. All *chefs de partie* may be regarded as supervisors or foremen of their sections as well as being skillful in their particular areas of cookery. They must, for example, plan and organize their work and staff; normally, they must also prepare daily requisitions for supplies, which usually require review and approval by the *chef de cuisine* or the appropriate *sous-chef*. To accomplish these tasks, the *chef de partie* needs only the menu as a blueprint, and then estimates of the number of customers and of the likely demand for the various items. Once the supplies have been ordered, the *chef de partie* will allocate the work to be done; subordinates include a *commis* (assistant), and one or more apprentices. Though much of this work may fall into a pattern or regular routine, it still remains necessary for a *chef de partie* to cultivate some qualities of a supervisor in order to plan and organize the practical work of the section successfully. This responsibility and task varies in difficulty, of course, according to the size of the particular *partie*.

As an artisan of full standing, the *chef de partie* will invariably have an apprentice or trainee of some kind who is learning craft skills. This benefits not only the trainee and the establishment, but the industry in general; it should be regarded as an important responsibility.

The principal *chefs de partie* are as follows:

Chef Saucier (*Sauce Cook*). Even if the role does not involve doubling as a *sous-chef*, the *chef saucier* is still regarded as only slightly lower in status—and is rivaled among *chefs de parties* only by the *chef garde-manger* (larder cook) and perhaps by the *chef pâtissier* (pastry cook). The reason for the *chef saucier*'s importance is that the duties to be fulfilled are very complex and play a vital role in meeting the requirements of the menu.

The required work comprises cooking, garnishing, and dishing all meat, poultry, and game dishes, with the exception of those that are simply grilled or roasted (these are cooked by the *chef rôtisseur*). The *sauce partie* is normally responsible for at least one of the *plats du jour* or specialties of the day. The work of the *chef saucier* thus involves quite a bit more than the preparation of sauces, important though that may be. (Actually, the *chef saucier* does not prepare every sauce in any case because the *chef poissonnier* (fish cook), for example, makes the sauces and garnishes for fish.)

The *chef saucier* is not only the preparer of the sauce section's foods, but the assembler of food prepared and sometimes cooked by others. For example, when entrées require Italian pastas or vegetables as garnishes on the same dish, these will be sent to the *chef saucier* by the *chef entremetteur*, and the *chef saucier* may receive tournedos already cut and dressed from the larder or *boucherie*. The work of all the parties in the kitchen is similarly interrelated, but the *chef saucier* has the greatest portion of such assembly work. Since the range of possible entrées is enormous, the work of the *saucier* necessarily covers a wide and varied field. This in turn necessitates a substantial degree of training, experience, skill, and artistry in the *chef saucier*. Many know enough to be able to abandon the recipe book and operate by memory alone, at least for their commonly prepared dishes.

Chef Garde-Manger *(Larder Cook)*. The *chef garde-manger* is in charge of the larder, the place where the raw materials of cookery are prepared and dressed. The general work of the *garde-manger* can be divided into two parts: the items for which the *garde-manger* is solely responsible; and the items the *garde-manger* produces to be cooked and worked on by other parties.

The *garde-manger*'s own dishes include those commonly found on a cold table—for example, cold cuts and cold fish dishes. Sandwiches, too, are the responsibility of the *garde-manger*, except for some of the specialty hot or toasted sandwiches such as club sandwiches (ordinarily dealt with by the *chef rôtisseur*). The salad maker, who is responsible for the preparatory work and assembling of salads, usually works in the *garde-manger*'s section. Salad dressings and other dressings and sauces for cold foods are also undertaken by the *chef garde-manger*.

The *garde-manger* is normally accommodated adjacent to but not separated from the main kitchen, with its own cooking facilities (which may, in some circumstances, be within the main kitchen itself). In the larger establishments, larder work is often broken into subsections, each related to another of the parties with which the *garde-manger* works. Smaller establishments do not need subdivisions of the larder, but the wide range of duties of the *chef garde-manger* explains why this position in the kitchen brigade enjoys a status comparable to that of the *chef saucier*. The principal subsections and their heads, if needed, are as follows:

In the professional kitchen, there may be enough work to justify a fulltime *boucher* or butcher; usually, however, the *chef garde-manger* or one or more assistants can handle the limited cutting and dressing of meat required. Nowadays, the work of this subsection and of the subsections that follow has been reduced by meat suppliers who normally provide meat butchered to order. A *charcutier* (pork butcher and sausage maker) is rare in modern professional kitchens because suppliers usually provide these services also. The *volailler* (or poulterer), if needed, is responsible for plucking, cleaning, and dressing not only poultry, but game birds and rabbits. The work of the hotel *poissonnier* (or fishmonger) includes skinning, filleting, and portioning fish and shellfish. Where the workload justifies it, the preparation of hors d'oeuvres of all kinds is organized separately by an *hors-d'oeuvrier* (hors d'oeuvre cook). The range of dishes prepared by this subsection can be great, involving many varieties of vegetable salads as well as meat and fish side dishes.

Chef Potager *(Soup Cook)*. Reviewing the remaining *parties* in a sequence similar to that of the courses on a menu brings forward first the *chef potager*. This *chef de partie* is responsible for preparing all soups for the establishment and for making all accompanying garnishes. Because the *chef potager* prepares for the earliest course of lunch and dinner, the job's hours sometimes begin (and end) a little earlier than do those of the other cooks.

The work of the *potager* is important because soup frequently creates the first gastronomic impression of the whole meal. The position requires the ability to produce a wide repertory of soups, including consommés (clear soups), cream soups, purées, broths, bisques (shellfish soups), and many specialty and national soups. Consommés alone can be composed with different flavorings and can be garnished in hundreds of ways.

The foods used by the *chef potager* can be supplied by other *parties* —for example, garnishes may come from the *garde-manger* and stock for fish soups from the *chef poissonnier*—but a substantial amount of garnish preparation for the soup corner itself still remains, requiring skillful use of the knife and of other culinary tools. Particularly prominent is the need for producing vegetable adornments in a wide variety of shapes and sizes.

As for all cooks, a cultivated palate is an important attribute of a *potager*, because the adjustment of seasonings and the finishing of a soup requires personal judgment as well as technical skill. This *chef de partie*, like the *saucier*, works normally in a section of the main kitchen.

Chef Poissonnier (*Fish Cook*). The *chef poissonnier* is responsible for most of the cooking, garnishing, and sauce-making for the fish courses of a menu, including freshwater fish, saltwater fish, and shellfish such as crabs, crayfish, shrimps, scallops, lobsters, and mussels. However, there are exceptions: deep-fried fish are normally handled separately by an assistant cook; fish grilling may be done by the grill cook or by a subordinate in that section; and raw oysters are ordinarily served direct from either the fishmonger or the *garde-manger* (only when cooked are they dished direct from the *chef poissonnier*'s corner).

The *chef poissonnier*'s *partie* works, as is the case with the *saucier's partie*, on a stove section in the main kitchen. The prior preparation of fish for this *partie*'s cooking is undertaken either by the establishment's fishmonger (one possible role of the *chef garde-manger*) or by an outside fish supplier. This means that cleaning, scaling, gutting, skinning, filleting, portioning, and breadcrumbing are carried out not by the *chef poissonnier* but by someone else beforehand. It sometimes is arranged, however, that an assistant *poissonnier* be detached some of the time to assist in these preparatory functions. The subordinate engaged in egg and crumbing work, for example, is called the *panadier* in a French system.

Chef Rôtisseur (*Roast Cook*). The work of the *rôtisseur's partie* has changed more, perhaps, than that of any other section. Roasting with a spit over an open fire has largely been replaced by oven roasting, which is virtually the same as baking. Spit roasting has recently been revived with special electrical heating equipment, but its use is normally limited to certain appropriate foodstuffs, such as chicken.

While the methods and equipment for roasting have changed, the duties of the roast cook have remained similar. Foods to be roasted still cover a wide range of poultry, game, and meat. In large establishments, the joints, poultry, and game to be cooked are given basic preparatory treatment in the larder, by the butcher or poulterer, rather than by the *rôtisseur*. However, this *partie* is responsible for several other processes in addition to roasting, including all deep-frying (such as of french-fried potatoes). In fact, the *rôtisseur* may have an assistant, the *friturier* (frying cook), for the task. The *chef rôtisseur* is also responsible for savoury items such as Welsh rarebit, for hot sandwiches of the club sandwich type, and for all stock for the gravies that accompany roasts.

Dishes prepared by the roast cook are not as complex as many completed by the *saucier* or *poissonnier*, yet the chef of this *partie* needs many skills, such as how to gauge the correct cooking of roasted items of varying sizes and kinds. This section of the kitchen also tends to be most demanding physically. In large establishments, heavily loaded roasting trays can only be handled comfortably and safely by a person of strength. Adding to the physical demands is that this section is located in the main stove area, where many items of heating equipment are grouped together, making it one of the hottest in the kitchen.

Larger establishments may have additional specialists in this *partie*. For example, a *chef trancheur* (carver) may be under the control of the *rôtisseur*. The *trancheur* normally is skilled only in carving, not in cooking, and may operate at the hot service counter behind the scenes, at a buffet table in the dining room, or by patrolling the restaurant with a heated cart. In some establishments, the work of the grill cook is simply undertaken by a subordinate of the *chef rôtisseur*. A separate *grillardin* (grill cook), if needed, may deal with savouries and combine the functions of the *grillardin* with those of the *savourier* (savoury cook). The *grillardin*, therefore, is a semiskilled specialty cook or assistant rather than a full *chef de partie* of experience. The specific skill required is to be able to deal with traditional charcoal grills, or more modern grills using electricity or gas, with care, experience, and judgment.

Chef Entremetteur (*Vegetable, Egg, and Noodle Cook*). The *entremetteur* in the kitchen brigade is concerned mainly with cooking vegetables, but also with preparing eggs (especially omelets), pasta, rice, and other starchy dishes. When these are served as separate courses, they are cooked and assembled in the *chef entremetteur*'s own corner. Other responsibilities may include passing vegetable garnishes to another *partie* for completion of a dish there, and sending items such as cooked spaghetti and rice to another chef as garnish for other dishes—for example, noodles to accompany Hungarian goulash. The *chef entremetteur* also cooks pancakes, usually with batter supplied by the *chef pâtissier*.

Important though these items are, they are not more significant than the vegetables prepared and cooked as accompaniments to the main meat, poultry, and game dishes. The proper cooking, flavoring, assembling, garnishing, and service of vegetables is of great importance to the culinary reputation of an establishment. Yet because of the nature of the commodities to be cooked by the *entremetteur,* the amount of food handled in this section usually is greater than that handled by any other. Cooking vegetables well in large quantities demands not only great experience and skill, but also a familiarity with a wide repertoire of methods (as is the case for other *parties*).

To facilitate vegetable cookery, the portion required for the *table d'hote* meals is often organized separately from the *à la carte* vegetable service. The peeling and cleaning, trimming, and other basic treatments of vegetables can be tedious and time-consuming, but modern processing methods such as deep freezing, dehydrating, and canning are reducing much of this workload in the kitchen.

Chef Pâtissier (*Pastry Cook*). The *chef pâtissier* in a large and important establishment has a status different from, but certainly not less than, the *chef saucier* and the *chef garde-manger.* The *chef pâtissier* is responsible for all hot and cold sweets such as pastry, pudding, and ice cream. The work of this section is normally separated from the main body of the kitchen, and its area is self-sufficient—with its own cold storage, specialist machinery, equipment for making ice cream, and baking and cooking facilities. Hardly any hotels and restaurants nowadays operate their own bakery with a full-time *boulanger* (baker). Where baking is normally restricted to a limited quantity of bread and rolls, the work is likely to be in the hands of one of the *chef pâtissier*'s subordinates.

However regrettable it may seem to gourmets, the art of making various kinds of ice cream is also disappearing from all but the most exclusive hotels and restaurants. Such work formerly was in the hands of a *chef glacier* in the *pâtisserie,* but now ice cream is usually purchased from outside or made by machine from a standard mix. Desserts based on ice cream, sherbet and so on, regardless of the source of these, are still prepared and assembled in the *pâtisserie.* This includes specialty dishes such as peach melba, as well as the traditional ones such as sundaes and banana splits.

Other arts of the *pâtisserie* that were developed to satisfy a wealthy and leisured clientele of the past included work with pulled and colored sugars in the shapes of flower baskets and other objects to serve as decorative centerpieces, as well as shaped chocolates and sculpted blocks of ice. Today these arts are practiced by a dwindling number of chefs, and more often as a personal craft or hobby than as a commercial venture.

Rather than being concentrated on a few exotic sweets, the work of the department is now devoted to producing a considerable volume of less spectacular pies, cakes, fruit salads, and so forth. But this still requires great skill and experience. The *chef pâtissier,* therefore, must have specialty skills as well as the ability to coordinate and organize the work of a number of subordinates.

Chef Tournant (*Relief Cook*). The *chef tournant* is simply the *chef de partie*'s replacement—for any *partie*—when the latter is away on business, for training, or on vacation. Some *chefs de partie* choose an experienced *commis* (assistant) for this position, because this person has fresh memories of all the *parties* gained during apprenticeship. For a *commis*, the opportunity to serve occasionally as *chef tournant* also provides good experience for a future appointment as a *chef de partie*. As a result, the *chef tournant* is often a young, "up and coming" cook. Occasionally, however, the appointment may go to an older, more experienced person as a prelude to appointment as a *sous-chef*; this would provide a useful variety of experience for a *chef de partie* who had been specializing in a single *partie* for a long time.

Chef de Garde (*Duty Cook*). The term *chef de garde* means simply the "chef on guard"—that is, the duty cook in charge when the *chef de cuisine* and most of the kitchen staff are off-duty. This happens in the late evening after dinner or during the between-meal break in establishments in which the split-shift system is practiced. The *chef de garde* role may be undertaken by any *chef de partie* or experienced assistant in the kitchen. During the period of duty, the *chef de garde* remains behind with a small number of assistants to continue any work that cannot be delayed until the remainder of the staff returns to work. In large establishments, separate *chefs* or *commis de garde* remain in the *pâtisserie* and in the *garde-manger*, as well as in the main section of the kitchen. Each may oversee the affairs of more than one of the kitchen *parties*.

Chef de Nuit (*Night-Duty cook*). The *chef de nuit* is similarly a chef whose duty is to take over when the main kitchen staff has gone. A separate *chef de nuit* may be retained in the *garde-manger*, but normally one person suffices for the whole kitchen. The *chef de nuit* remains on duty all night at establishments that stay open that long. Otherwise, this person leaves when orders for late meals have ceased.

Chef des Banquets (*Banquet Chef*). In the largest establishments, completely separate arrangements may be provided for banquets and meals for special functions, with the *chef des banquets* in charge. The *chef des banquets'* responsibility includes overseeing the assembly and service of the banquet, but not necessarily all of the cooking.

Breakfast Cook. The traditional *chefs de partie* normally appear with their *commis* in time to prepare lunch. The cooking and service of breakfast in hotels is commonly entrusted to a specialty cook whose range is limited to the needs of breakfast. This person does not rank as a full *chef de partie* but nevertheless needs to possess good skills within the limited field.

Breakfast meats are ordinarily prepared in advance by a subordinate of the *chef garde-manger*. Similarly, the preparation of fruit compotes and fruit salads is a matter for assistants in the *pâtisserie*. The breakfast cook and helpers are left with the relatively simple task of assembling and cooking breakfast dishes—for example, bacon and the various forms of eggs. The pastry chef might also be involved in breakfast preparation of breads, pastries, and the like.

Chef Communar (*Staff Cook*). In many small establishments, food for the hotel and restaurant staff is prepared by the same *chefs de partie* who cook for customers. But in larger houses, a separate section of the kitchen, or even a completely separate kitchen, may be allocated for producing staff meals. Either way, the *chef communar*, operating under the *chef de cuisine*, is in charge.

Staff meals ordinarily imply meals provided for "rank and file" wage-earning staff, such as uniformed staff, chambermaids, waiters, and lower-grade clerical staff. The *chef communar*'s staff prepares and cooks meals principally for this type of employee. Catering of this nature should be influenced by nutritional and aesthetic factors. The establishment's managers should regard it as a personnel-management feature that contributes significantly to staff well-being, morale, and efficiency.

In contrast to workers fed at staff meals, supervisory and executive staff at the level of department manager and above are often given dining facilities in the restaurant itself, or even in their own quarters, from the regular *table d'hôte* menus. In the case of more junior executives, some restrictions on the selection of higher-cost items on the menus may be imposed.

Staff

Working under the direction of the various chefs are a number of subordinate personnel of different types.

Cooking Artisans

Commis (*Assistants*). The chef of each *partie* is assisted by one or more trained cooks who have not yet reached full chef status. These assistants or *commis* have presumably completed their apprenticeship training, but are still in the process of gaining experience before taking full *partie* responsibilities. Nevertheless, the first *commis*, as the senior assistant in each section is called, should be capable of taking charge when the section's *chef de partie* is off. As second in command, the first *commis* should take considerable responsibility under the *partie* chef even when the latter is there.

Apprentices. Each *partie* has apprentices or trainees who, while learning, are also helping in the practical day-to-day work of food preparation and cookery.

The first two types of personnel subordinate to chefs are concerned with craft work only. Unskilled operations are largely undertaken by porters, kitchen hands, vegetable preparers, and the other workers.

Noncooking Kitchen Staff

In addition to the various chefs and artisan cooks, other functionaries are on the kitchen staff in the *partie* system. Some staff members of this kind work in the main kitchen itself and others in departments surrounding it.

Secretaire de Cuisine (*Kitchen Clerk*). The number of clerks employed in a hotel or restaurant kitchen depends on its size and volume

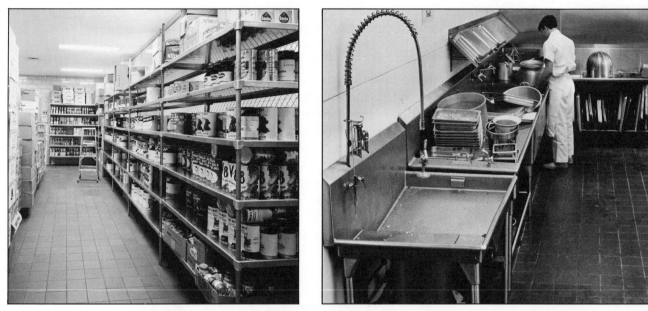

8-1. Stored foods should be kept off the floor and arranged so that foods stored first will be used first. From Richardson and Nicodemus, *Sanitation for Foodservice Workers,* 3rd edition.

8-2. Excellent pot-washing facilities. Note roomy drainboard on left for dirty pots. Next two compartments are for rinse and final rinse. Slanted draining shelf, open at left end, allows water to drain into washing sink. From Richardson and Nicodemus, *Sanitation for Foodservice Workers,* 3rd edition.

of trade. Clerks supervise the checking system at the serving line and at the line for customer payment. They handle shipping and receiving of goods such as meat, fish, poultry, and pastry. One kitchen clerk is likely to be attached to the *chef de cuisine* as a personal assistant for office matters the chef must manage.

Assembleur (*Expediter*). The *assembleur* or barker is stationed at the edge of the serving area during the time of meal service. On receipt of the written orders from the waiters, he calls out the orders to the different *parties*, by loudspeaker if necessary. In smaller places, the kitchen clerk or even a *sous-chef* may fill this role. The *assembleur* needs not only a clear voice, but some culinary knowledge. Part of the job involves recognizing kitchen terms and (later) the items themselves when the time comes to check the order prepared by the kitchen.

Économe (*Storekeeper*). The storekeeper is responsible for receiving, recording, and allocating storage. In addition to being familiar with the normal range of grocery items, the storekeeper in some establishments must be familiar with foods from all parts of the world. Experience in the arrangement and storage of grocery items to avoid spoilage and deterioration is also necessary. See figure 8-1. Personal integrity is a vital factor in the character of a storekeeper and his assistants, if any.

Cold and Perishable Storage Attendant. In establishments doing considerable trade, the placement of meat, poultry, and so forth in refrigerated storage and of fruits and bulk butter in cool storage is likely to be separated from the main storage operation and placed under the control of a separate functionary. This type of storage attendant may well be a kitchen porter who has received on-the-job training in the care and arrangement of perishable foods needing cold storage.

Kitchen Porters. The unskilled work involved in the operation of a large kitchen is considerable and involves the employment and organization of a staff often more numerous than the *chefs de partie* and their *commis.* Responsible for the greatest part of this unskilled work are kitchen porters. The head porter, who is responsible directly to the head chef, acts as a foreman over most of the others. But some kitchen porters are assigned to *parties,* where each is directed by the appropriate *chef de partie.* Apart from obvious duties such as carrying kitchen loads and cleaning, porters assist in vegetable preparation and in unskilled kitchen work of all kinds.

Scullery Person. The cleaning of metal kitchen vessels and implements is separate from that for plates and table silver. The latter are dealt with by the silver cleaner (*argentier*) who usually comes under the control of the maître d'hôtel. The former are cleaned by the kitchen scullery worker (or *plongeur*). Keeping these metal vessels scoured in a busy establishment is both a full-time job and a heavy one. See figure 8-2.

Kitchen Hands. In addition to having a number of kitchen porters, large kitchens employ unskilled or semiskilled workers called *kitchen hands.* They are attached to *parties* or to the various storage and vegetable rooms for tasks such as making pats of butter, replenishing hors d'oeuvres trays, peeling vegetables, and preparing fruit salad. They may also assist at the serving line, particularly at breakfast.

Recipe for a Complete Kitchen Staff

Yield:
A complete staff to handle all forms of kitchen work

Ingredients:
A *chef de cuisine* in charge
A *sous-chef* for second-in-command
A *chef de partie* to head each section
Members of the cooking staff, including assistants and apprentices
Members of the noncooking staff such as kitchen porters, clerks, storekeepers, assemblers, and cleaners

Method:
Hire competent people—just as many as are required for the job at hand.

Conclusion

Jobs change as new demand, new-style menus, and new technology affect the kitchen. In modern operations, some tasks may be regrouped and others may disappear. Ethnic and exotic specialty restaurants, for example, require new staffing concepts and different designations for sectional cooks to deal with language barriers, special areas of cooking emphasis, and so on. And in different countries, even when everyone speaks the same language, task groupings and job titles differ. The International Labor office in Geneva, Switzerland, is a useful source of information on job descriptions in the hotel industry throughout the world. Despite present and future variations, knowing how the great kitchens of the past operated to provide classic French service should long be of value in devising new approaches to new needs.

9. Layout and Design

People in management often complain that kitchens seem to be added to hotels, hospitals, and other institutions as an afterthought without receiving sufficient attention during early planning. A kitchen plan or layout should be determined on the basis of catering policy when the establishment's overall plan is first being developed. This policy is affected by many factors, including the type of food to be served, the establishment's location, the type of customer anticipated, seasonal pressures, and the possibility of expansion.

In determining kitchen layout (as well as in organizing subsequent work within it), the fundamental intention remains constant no matter what specific features the operation has: to receive a variety of commodities and convert them into meals in such a way that food and service are acceptable and attractive, within limitations of economy, time, and quantity. All aspects of foodservice planning hinge on this basic combination of considerations. Subsidiary details should not be introduced so early that basic issues are obscured. Premature preoccupation with detail can result in poor design, subsequent operating confusion, and failure to achieve aims.

When planning, allowances should be made for future developments such as new equipment, new organizational concepts, and continuing inflation in labor, food, and fuel costs. Future trends stemming from today's economic problems include:

Greater mechanization (for example, the use of conveyor belts in place of busing carts)

Development of new cooking appliances and methods (for example, cook-freeze or cook-chill systems that help smooth out the work load by allowing earlier food preparation and longer food holding)

Simpler operations (for example, through the use of convenience or pre-prepared foods, or through labor-saving approaches such as self-serve buffets)

Use of new commodities (for example, soy and other vegetable proteins)

Reduced size of food production areas (kitchens), concurrent with more frequent preparation of food in smaller quantities for immediate service, reducing the need for hot storage equipment (using pre-prepared food reduces the need for vegetable preparation areas and equipment, as well)

Development of specialty dishes or forms of service that give distinctive character to an establishment

Decisions about catering policy and the basic kitchen plan should be reflected in the menu. The menu then serves as a blueprint for all details regarding kitchen design and appliance selection.

Information Required

Before kitchen planning can begin, answers to various questions about catering policy are needed. For example:

1. What types of meals will be offered?
2. How many persons will be served?
3. When will these meals be required? Will the main meal be A.M. or P.M.—that is, will it be a lunch or dinner service or daylong and/or nightlong?
4. What will be the extent of beverage service requirements—that is, how much tea and coffee for lounge as well as restaurant will be required?
5. Is allowance to be made for special functions?
6. To what extent will "convenience" foods be used?
7. What area of floor space is available?
8. What is the position of windows, ventilation, drainage, water supply, and so on?
9. What type of service is proposed—self-service, cafeteria, or waiter/waitress service?

Area Required

Kitchens are sometimes designed in a reduced size in order to provide more space and increased seating in the restaurant. This reduction does not necessarily increase a restaurant's trade, however, because cramped kitchens lead to delays and other faults in service that discourage customers from returning. A reduction in kitchen size must, therefore, be accompanied by plans to maintain (or even increase) productivity while still presenting a satisfactory workplace for employees.

Calculating in advance the kitchen area needed is difficult for many reasons. Generally speaking, as the number of patrons increases, the kitchen area needed *per person* tends to decrease; but information about numbers alone is not sufficient. Knowledge of peak loads (based on experience or intelligent forecasting) is essential. In addition, the nature of the establishment plays a role. The dining room (including tables and passageways) at a coffee shop may have as little as 0.93 square meters (10 square feet) of space per person, while a luxury hotel restaurant may have 1.67 square meters (18 square feet) of space per person. Some experts believe that kitchen space per customer should be about one-half that of the dining room. See figures 9-1 and 9-2. Very small places serving less than fifty people may need about 0.84 to 0.93

Numbers eating in busiest period	Kitchen area desirable per customer
100	0.46–0.84 sq m (5–9 sq ft)
100 to 250	0.37–0.56 sq m (4–6 sq ft)
250 to 500	0.37–0.46 sq m (4–5 sq ft)
500 to 1000	0.28–0.37 sq m (3–4 sq ft)
Over 1000	0.23–0.28 sq m (2.5–3 sq ft)

Note: Area reductions may be made when for example, convenience foods are fully exploited. The lower figures relate to such simpler operations, and the higher for more complete catering.

9-1. Approximate indication of kitchen requirements. From Fuller, *Professional Kitchen Management*.

Total meals per day	Restaurant area in		Kitchen area in		Total catering floor space in	
	sq m	sq ft	sq m	sq ft	sq m	sq ft
100	34.83	375	13.93	150	48.77	525
250	51.02	560	19.97	215	72.00	775
500	88.25	950	27.87	300	116.12	1,250
1,000	139.35	1,500	45.45	500	185.80	2,000

Seating capacity	Restaurant area in		Kitchen area in		Estimated possible number of meals per hour
	sq m	sq ft	sq m	sq ft	
50	63.03	700	27.87	300	75
75	92.90	1,000	37.16	400	115
100	116.12	1,250	46.45	500	150
125	162.58	1,750	69.67	750	190
200	255.48	2,750	116.12	1,250	300

9-2. Possible areas, on a daily basis, of catering capacity. From Fuller, *Professional Kitchen Management*.

Number eating	Kitchen space	
	sq m	sq ft
150	51.10	550
250	74.32	800
450	125.40	1,350
600	160.00	1,730

9-3. Approximate kitchen space required in non-profit institutions. Adapted from Fuller, *Professional Kitchen Management*.

square meters (9 or 10 square feet) of kitchen space per person. Areas designed as school lunchrooms or industrial service kitchens are more generous than those commonly used in profit-making establishments because the possibility of staggering meals in the former is less. See figure 9-3. Since the workload has higher peaks, the available space must be greater.

Of the total area of a kitchen, between 15% and 25% is likely to be required for storage, according to the nature of the operation and the supplies it uses. The remaining space goes to food preparation, cooking, and serving.

Calculating the various areas needed by a particular establishment does not yield exact results, of course, because each establishment has unique needs and limitations. The rules of thumb provided here are only rough estimates. Architects and kitchen engineers must calculate space requirements based on each operation's scope.

Planning

Teamwork and the Chef's Role

As in other details, initial planning of catering areas is not a job for one person alone. It normally involves a project planning team that includes the owner-manager, the chef or maitre d'hotel, design consultants, and kitchen engineers, all of whose activities are coordinated by the architect.

A chef may never have a decisive voice in determining the space allotted to the kitchen's activities. Despite being on the planning team, the chef may be unable to give advice that is followed by the others. Nevertheless, the chef should have an interest in the whole kitchen concept and should be prepared to provide information on culinary matters in the planning, construction, and equipping of the kitchen. If the chef's input is not relevant, accurate, or articulate, the rest of the team cannot fairly be blamed for all design mistakes that follow. The chef must work hard to build and present a sound case to avert design mistakes before they are implemented. Wisdom after the event is no substitute for intelligent anticipation by a trained and experienced person.

Work and Method Study

A layout is based on a good work-flow from the receipt of raw materials to the final serving of dishes to guests. Overfamiliarity with traditional processing sometimes inhibits creative thinking; a detached, analytical view is helpful, and a work-study specialist can provide it. Even a small operation can probably afford to engage a part-time consultant. When possible, chefs should be trained to practice work-study techniques. These may include using a process chart (which breaks work into small parts called elements), films of spatial movements of workers within their work areas, and string diagrams that indicate work pathways. Above all, the planner must ask questions: What is done? Why is it done? What should be done? Similar questions about the where, when, how, and why of every task should be asked. Can a particular task be eliminated or combined with another? Can its sequence of movements be changed or simplified? Chefs should try to anticipate procedural bottlenecks and other barriers to efficiency, and then should prevent these by using work-study and work-simplification procedures when planning or altering kitchens.

Flow of Work

Intelligent placement of preparation machinery, sinks, and work benches (figure 9-4) can reduce the total daily "kitchen mileage" covered by the food and cut down on unnecessary traveling by the staff. A perfect kitchen from this point of view is one in which raw and cooked material undergo minimum movement and never cover the same route twice. Therefore, if each section or *partie* has been satisfactorily planned—individually and in combination—the layout must comply as nearly as possible with the flow chart in figure 9-5. To obtain a continuous flow of goods from section to section as illustrated, the design of each section must be considered carefully to ensure that paths do not cross and that staff members do not have to backtrack needlessly because of poor planning.

This may seem simple, but in many cases the task involves streamlining an existing old kitchen or laying out a new kitchen within existing premises. Many difficulties can arise in the course of developing a work-flow system, and often the best that can be made of limited opportunities is a distinctly imperfect system. Kitchen planners, engineers, and caterers frequently find that area allocation is done first and that their detail work must follow. But they should at least consider in detail the arrangement of necessary equipment in the kitchen—before final decisions about area utilization are reached.

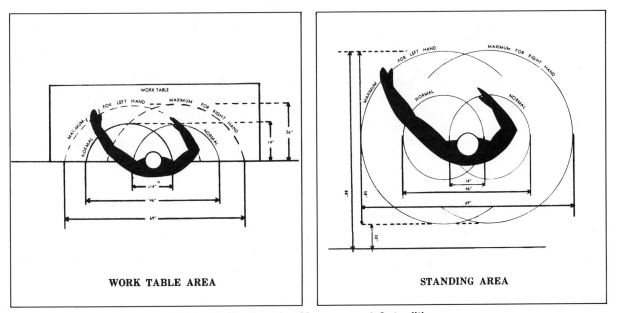

9-4. **Work table areas. From Eshback, *Foodservice Management,* 3rd edition.**

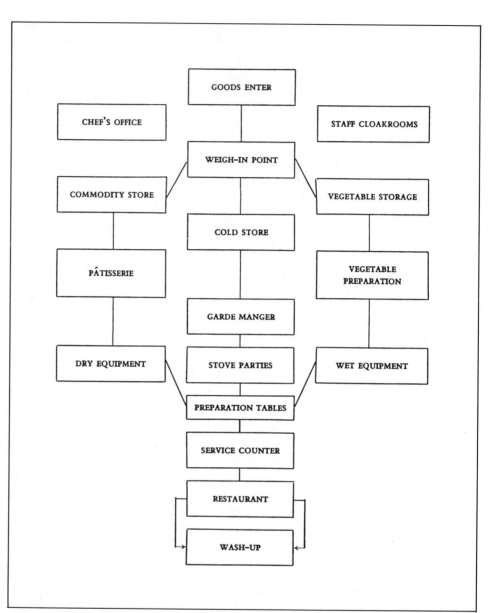

9-5. Work flow diagram. A well-planned layout depends largely on the following requirements, which, if properly provided for, establish good basic kitchen conditions: incoming supplies and raw materials (checking and weighing); food storage; food preparation; cooking; serving area arrangements; pan-washing arrangements; crockery and cutlery wash-up. From Fuller, *Professional Kitchen Management.*

Areas of Consideration

Traffic Lanes and Work Aisles

Adequate and properly devised traffic lanes and work aisles are indispensible to achieving a satisfactory work-flow—one with minimum path-crossing and backtracking. The main traffic flow should avoid work aisles, which should if possible be at right angles to main traffic lines. See figure 9-6. Distances between key points such as receiving areas, storerooms, preparation tables, cooking areas, and the serving line should be as short as is practicable. Aisles should be wide enough to accommodate the volume and type of traffic they will sustain. Examples of necessary widths are given in figure 9-7.

Passages and Ancillary Offices and Facilities

Passages to and from the kitchen must be unobstructed, with adequate space for the entry of goods, the exit of containers, and the easy movement of staff members. Space must also be allowed for such staff facilities as lavatories, offices, a staff dining room, and a cloakroom for kitchen employees. Each of these areas should be located near the work areas in order to facilitate supervision and communication between sections, as well as to encourage staff usage.

Goods Receiving Facilities

External space is needed for delivery van parking. At the entry point for goods, sufficient space should be reserved to allow goods to be received and checked and hand trucks and/or trolleys to be parked. There must also be space to accommodate receiving equipment such as weighing machines, checking tables, and desks—as well as room for temporarily holding delivered goods prior to storage. For smaller kitchens, a separate space within the goods reception area should be provided for waste bins and empty containers. In larger kitchens, a separate room for refuse and waste may be required. Having a tiled floor with a central drain facilitates daily cleaning of lower walls and floor.

Storage

The storage space a kitchen requires depends on the nature of the supplies (their types, quantities, and frequency of delivery) and containers (sacks, cartons, and so on) to be stored. Different areas must be provided for dry goods and for refrigerated ones. All storage areas should be close to the receiving point and on the same floor level with it to facilitate the use of trolleys and carts.

Storage Space Allocation. Total storage for food and equipment should generally not exceed one-quarter of the kitchen area. The dry goods storage area alone is seldom more than a room representing 10% to 13% of the total kitchen area. A rule of thumb is to set aside 0.20 square meters (2 square feet) of vegetable storage and 0.37 square meters (4 square feet) of commodity or dry goods storage per person accommodated in the dining room. This would be enough space to handle a 5-day supply of perishables and a 2-week supply of dry and frozen produce. Another way of looking at storage requirements is that storage space per meal should be about 0.46 square meters (5 square feet) on the average, with a minimum of about 0.28 square meters (3 square feet) for large operations and a maximum of 0.65 square meters (7 square feet) for small ones.

While large-scale or bulk buying can lower purchase prices per

9-6. The flow of food. From Eshback, *Foodservice Management,* 3rd edition.

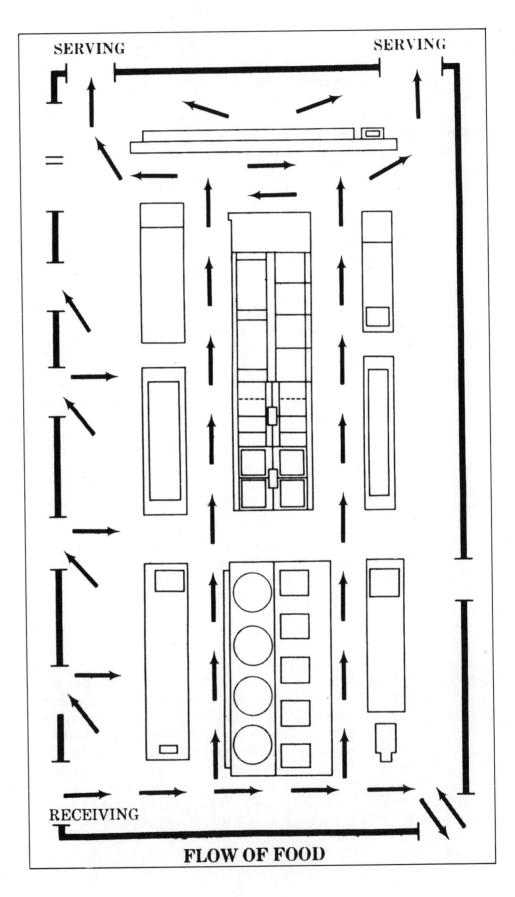

SERVING

SERVING

RECEIVING

FLOW OF FOOD

- 750 mm (30 in) width allows two persons to pass
- 600 mm (24 in) width plus cart width for one person to pass one cart
- 1.5 m (60 in) width for one cart to pass two persons working back to back
- 1.5 m (60 in) minimum for main traffic lane
- 900 mm (36 in) minimum clearance between equipment and work tables
- 1 to 1.20 m (3.5 to 4 ft) minimum in front of cooking equipment (to which food is conveyed by cart)

9-7. Work aisle and traffic lane widths. From Fuller, *Professional Kitchen Management*.

unit, buying in smaller quantities and holding minimum stocks may reduce costs in installing and maintaining more specialized storage equipment. Small caterers in more remote locations, however, might find it hard to persuade suppliers to deliver to them with sufficient frequency to make the small-quantities approach feasible. Caterers who lower or eliminate food preparation through increased use of convenience foods usually need to increase the area of refrigerated storage they maintain. Accurate forecasting of actual requirements can help reduce the amount of storage space that is set aside unnecessarily.

Storage Trends. Precise guidance about amounts of storage space required cannot be given because so much depends on delivery frequency, on the establishment's food purchasing policy, on its proximity to suppliers, on shelving arrangements, and on storeroom design. There are several general trends, however, in force today:

Increased storage at −18°C (0°F) for quick-frozen items such as:

uncooked foods (fish, meat, poultry, vegetables, fruit, and frozen desserts)

prepared or cooked foods (confectionery and baked goods, ready-cooked individual items, and completely cooked meals)

Increased storage provision for dehydrated, dried, canned, plastic-wrapped, and ready-mixed products (soups and sauces, vegetables, fruits, potatoes, confectionery, and pie fillings)

Reduced storage provision for vegetables, fruit, meat, poultry, and fish at chill temperatures—those between −7°C and 1°C (between 19°F and 34°F)

Storage Temperatures. Storage temperatures (without refrigeration) recommended for dry goods and fruit and vegetable storage are approximately 5° to 21°C (41° to 70°F) for dry goods; 18° to 24°C (64° to 75°F) for ripening fruits and vegetables; 10°C (50°F) for potatoes; and 9°C (48° F) for other vegetables. These temperatures should be maintained by natural ventilation or by air conditioning in warm weather.

Vegetable Storage. Vegetables should be stored and prepared in an area separate from the kitchen so that soil brought in with them does not come into contact with other foods. Vegetables packed close together in warm, unventilated corners will deteriorate rapidly. They will last much longer if stored on raised platforms with slats or on open mesh racks so that they are kept as cool and as exposed to circulating air as possible. Galvanized tubing is preferable to wooden shelves. Racks or bins should be mounted at least 230 millimeters (9 inches) above the floor and fitted at the bottom with removable dust collection trays. In the adjacent vegetable section should be included an electrically operated peeling machine, a tank, a sink, and preparation tables.

Dry Storage. A dry storage area should accommodate such grocery items as canned and packaged goods, together with unpackaged or bulk-stored sugar, flour, dry cereals, and legumes. Conveniently arranged, adjustable shelving allows maximum space utilization. Shelving equipped with wire trays (metal is superior to wood) allows complete aeration of food. Having shelves mounted on wheeled stands makes transporting supplies to the kitchen easy. Shelves should be at least 230 millimeters (9 inches) above the floor for ease of cleaning. All benchwork and shelving should be mounted at least 100 millimeters (4 inches) away from the wall for the same reason. The dry storeroom should be equipped with both platform and table-model weighing scales for checking receipts and issues of daily supplies. These scales should be positioned at the entrance of the storage area for convenience. The most frequently handled goods should also be placed near the entrance. Dry stores should be protected against vermin of all kinds. The storeroom should be lockable, well-ventilated, and long and narrow rather than square, in order to economize on floor space.

Equipment, Cleaning, and other Storage Rooms. In addition to commodity storage *(l'econome)* and the vegetable store, adequate provision must be made for storing spare utensils and equipment, cleaning material, and empty returnable containers.

Bread Storage. A bread storeroom should be well-ventilated and provided with shelves of open construction to permit maximum exposure of the goods to air circulation. Shelves should be arranged for bread to be stacked methodically, with new deliveries going to the rear so that older loaves are used first. An adequate amount of shelving is important; bread should not be stacked too high or too close.

Larder Storage. Slate, tile, or marble shelving, which gives a cold and easy-to-clean surface, is desirable for larder storage. Leftover perishable foods should be kept in refrigerated storage for maximum safety.

Refrigerated Storage. Because catering operations vary so much, the amount of refrigerated storage a kitchen requires will be different for each individual establishment. For example, using convenience foods minimizes larder and preparation space requirements, but increases the need for refrigerated space. Forecasting actual food requirements within a clear operational policy is vital to calculating exact refrigerator needs and the types of apparatus required. See figure 9-8 for general standards. Walk-in units become feasible at quantities above 300 to 400 meals served daily; their capacity ranges upward from a minimum of about 112 cubic feet (3.17 cubic meters). In these, aisles should be 900 millimeters (36 inches) wide if trolleys or wheeled racks are not used, but 1.25 meters (4 feet 2 inches) if they are. Because of these aisles, only about half the space in a walk-in refrigerator is usable.

Reach-in units require less floor space and most of the inside capacity can be used for actual storage. As a general guide, about 20.52 kilograms (45 pounds) of encased frozen food and 15.96 to 18.24 kilograms (35 to 40 pounds) of refrigerated food can be accommodated per cubic foot of storage space.

In terms of refrigerator temperatures, there are two basic zones: $-20°C$ ($-4°F$) for frozen foods, and $0°C$ ($32°F$) to $4°C$ ($39°F$) for chilled foods. See figure 9-9. Other aspects of refrigeration to consider are ice-making, display cases (whether enclosed or open), chilled drinks, and blast freezing and rapid chilling (for cook-freeze and cook-chill catering systems respectively). Because of its high moisture content and the danger of other foods becoming flavor-tainted, fish cannot be successfully stored in a normal refrigerated room. Special fish storage cabinets should be kept at $0°C$ ($32°F$) and provided with high humidity to prevent drying out.

Standard-Size Modular Food Containers. Whenever possible, the same container should be serviceable for more than one purpose. Containers of uniformly standard size are available for multiple purposes— for example, storage (including cold storage), cooking, and placing directly into a service counter. Figure 9-10 illustrates the efficiency of this flexible approach. There are many advantages to such a system. Standard containers provide:

> An uncomplicated flow of food from one section to another in the proper operational sequence
>
> Increased stacking space within smaller areas
>
> Simplified kitchen layout and work methods, leading to shorter working paths and consequent savings in staff time and effort
>
> Universal use of transport and storage units

Such standard containers come in many sizes. The British 500-millimeter by 325-millimeter size, for example, can be used for fast-food service, snacks, and light meals in institutions such as hospitals and schools. The 600-millimeter to 700-millimeter modules are designed as medium weight equipment and fit fryers, griddles, boiling rings, ovens, hot cupboards, and *bain-maries.* The 700-millimeter to 800-millimeter modules fulfill the same functions, but can handle larger food loads.

**Recommended Minimum Refrigeration Space
for Average Full-Menu Restaurant,
Not Including Beverage Cooling or Frozen Foods**

Number of meals served daily	Recommended capacity
75 to 150	20 cu ft
150 to 250	45 cu ft
250 to 350	60 cu ft
350 to 500	90 cu ft

SOURCE: Ohio Department of Health.

Test Final

9-8. Space needed. From Knight and Kotschevar, *Quantity Food Production, Planning and Management.*

9-9. Refrigerated storage temperatures. From Fuller, *Professional Kitchen Management.*

General cold room	4°C (39°F)	Milk and dairy produce	4°C (39°F)
Fresh meat	1°C (34°F)	Ice cream	−10°C (0°F)
Frozen meat	−7°C (19°F)	Deep freezer	−21°C (−5°F)
Wet fish	0°C (32°F)	Blast freezer	−34°C (−30°F)

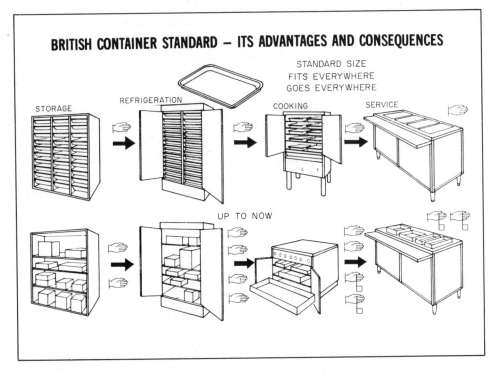

BRITISH CONTAINER STANDARD — ITS ADVANTAGES AND CONSEQUENCES

9-10. British container standard, its advantages and consequences. Reproduced by permission of British Standards Institution; from Fuller, *Professional Kitchen Management.*

The Kitchen's Task: Preparing, Cooking, and Keeping Ready

Kitchens must have facilities for handling food at every stage, from preparation tables and cooking ovens to holding vessels. Different types of food should have different preparation areas. Cooking equipment should be sited close to the appropriate preparation point; boiling pans should be close to vegetable preparation, pastry ovens should be close to pastry preparation, and so on. Arrangements for holding prepared foods ready for serving must ensure that hot foods are kept hot and cold foods cold.

Vegetable, Fish, Meat, and Poultry Preparation

If quick-frozen and/or dehydrated vegetables are fully exploited, vegetable washing and cleaning areas can be limited to those needed for salad preparation only. Peelers and sinks for potatoes may be required in some operations but the availability of "instant" dried potatoes and quick-frozen potatoes may satisfy the demands of some establishments.

Most types of meat, fish, and poultry can be obtained in ready-to-cook forms. Taking advantage of these renders trimming and dressing space unnecessary, allowing preparation areas to be restricted to simple washing facilities and a work bench. For items that are purchased already portioned, breaded, and so forth, no preparation area is needed.

Apparatus Requirements

Cooking and serving high-quality food in large quantities, and on a strict time schedule, is an exacting task, even under the most favorable conditions. By the correct choice, disposition, and use of cooking equipment, purely physical strain can be eased. Moreover, the favorable environment of an adequately equipped kitchen leaves greater scope for exercising skill, maintaining quality, and controlling costs.

Economical cooking of any dish depends on the use of an apparatus designed for its purpose and deployed to meet actual conditions. In a new kitchen, it is important to guard against putting in too much equipment. The ideal is to prepare, cook, and serve food with the minimum number of appliances that will do the job well. This keeps down both initial capital outlays and operating costs.

In improving an old kitchen, it is important to bear in mind the capacities of existing appliances and particularly the uses to which they are put. In many cases, smaller but more efficient equipment is preferable to the equipment already in place.

Types of Cookery and Categories of Apparatus

Whatever commodities are used, equipment must be provided for the different cookery processes. These include:

Roasting and baking
Boiling
Grilling and toasting
Steaming (vegetables, fish, puddings)
Deep frying (fish, french fries)
Shallow and griddle frying
Soup, stew and stock making
Plate and food holding in hot cupboards
Beverage making (tea, coffee, other hot drinks, and milk)
Heating water for culinary purposes

The apparatuses required naturally reflect the types of cookery being planned. Important items of equipment likely to be considered are:

Ranges or cookers
Roasting, general-purpose, and pastry ovens
Forced-air convection, bakers', and microwave ovens
Boiling tables
Bains-marie and hot cupboards
Steaming ovens, pressure steamers, and convection steamers

Shallow tilting frypans or skillets
Boiling pans and vegetable boiling pans
Water-boiling apparatuses
Deep fryers, pressure fryers, and oil-filtering appliances
Grills/toasters/salamanders
Stockpot stands

In deciding on the type and size of a needed apparatus, the chef in a good restaurant or hotel kitchen may have to make provision for *à la carte* or specialty restaurant menus in addition to coffee shop or *table d'hôte* service. Additional equipment may also be necessary to deal with special dishes. Furthermore, in restaurants that cater for parties and banquets, allowance must be made for equipment to deal with unusually large loads. Consequently, it is essential to know the cooking capacity of an item before buying it. Before final selection of equipment, it is advisable to visit other catering establishments where cooking equipment has recently been installed, so that first-hand up-to-date knowledge can be obtained.

There are many recent trends which may continue in the future:
More wheel-mounted kitchen equipment
More cantilevered equipment, which is recognized as having advantages in accessibility, convenience, hygiene, and strength
Less equipment for quantity preparation of fresh vegetables; more equipment devised for faster cooking of smaller quantities of frozen vegetables
More use of the tilting steam-jacketed boiler than of traditional stewing pans
Greater use of the self-generating steam oven for frequent batch cooking
Ovens with improved temperature control, and increased use of forced convection ovens, which give speedier cooking and more even temperature
More microwave ovens, which permit high-speed cooking and reheating

Equipment Placement

Positioning ranges or cookers is important. One efficient way is to install stove equipment in a cluster, with a ventilation canopy above. There should be room for a cook at the center of this work "island," and plenty of space around it. *Bains-marie* and stockpot stands should be close to ranges. Boiling tables, steaming ovens, and vegetable boiling pans should also be near the center of the kitchen and easily accessible to workers at vegetable preparation tables. Adequate provision for carts, mobile racks, and other mobile processing apparatuses should be made. The deep fryer should be conveniently sited near the main ranges, but with a separate extract canopy of its own.

Generally, a canopy edge should project beyond the cooking equipment by at least 45 millimeters (18 inches) on the side where equipment doors open and 305 millimeters (12 inches) on the other sides. It should be mounted 2 meters (6 feet 9 inches) above floor level. Canopies should be fitted with a small gutter around the bottom to deal with any condensation caused before the canopy heats up. This condensation gutter need not be connected to a drain because evaporation is rapid.

Canopies are usually made of one of three materials: metal, glass, or plastic. Whatever the material of construction, they should be functional, pleasing in appearance, easy to clean, and designed without any horizontal surfaces to collect dust. Metal canopies are best constructed of anodized aluminum, with bulkhead lighting; these are lightweight and easily cleaned. Glass canopies are normally constructed of wired glass with an aluminum section frame. These look attractive, are easy to clean, and allow light to pass through, but they are also heavy. Plastic hoods made of corrugated, transparent plastic sheets and mounted on an aluminum frame are lightweight, easy to clean, and colorful.

Stillrooms should have a coffee-maker or quick boiler, as well as other equipment for providing hot and cold drinks. The stillroom or other special service point may also need quick-service cooking equipment such as a contact grill, toasters, and a griddle plate. Additional hot cupboards in or near the main restaurant may also be needed for hot storage of plates, coffee cups, and other crockery.

Food Preparation Surfaces

Preparation tables topped with stainless steel, laminated plastic, or some other impervious material are easy to clean, and thus hygienic.

Human beings vary in size and reach. Yet table and work surfaces must be sufficiently high for everyone. It is better to err on the side of their being too high rather than too low; shorter employees can always use a stand, but taller employees should not be forced to bend. The best solution is an adjustable table with screw-out legs. Failing that, the table heights which will suit most people are as follows: for light work, average work table heights are 925 to 975 millimeters (37 to 39 inches) for women and 975 to 1,000 millimeters (39 to 41 inches) for men; for heavy work, a height of about 900 millimeters (36 inches) is good.

People can reach about 370 to 500 millimeters (14½ to 20 inches) without stretching. A worktable's width should be between 700 and 750 millimeters (24 to 30 inches). If the table has to accommodate containers or other material at the back, then a 900-millimeter (36-inch) width is okay. About 1.2 to 1.8 meters (4 to 6 feet) of table length is adequate for one person, and 2.4 to 3 meters (8 to 10 feet) suffices for two people working side by side. These figures are all average estimates only and should not be considered definitive.

Cutting Boards

Chefs long preferred wooden cutting boards, but it is now known that these are more easily contaminated than impervious surfaces having no cracks or pores to collect food particles and bacteria. Washing wooden boards at temperatures below about 42°C (108°F) does not kill the bacteria. As a result, butcher's blocks and cutting boards now have synthetic surfaces made of polypropylene, rubber clay compound, synthetic rubber, or some other impervious material. Chefs must select boards according to cost, operational requirements, and their own experience.

Sinks

Ancillary tasks are also important. Arrangements for washing of pans, crockery, and cutlery must be convenient as well as sanitary. There should be adequate racking for washed dishes and space for those awaiting treatment. Mechanized systems with conveyor belts should be used if affordable. Sinks and draining boards should be fitted wherever possible along external walls. More natural light will be available to people working at them if they are placed under windows. The guidelines mentioned previously for worktable heights and widths should also be applied to sinks. Detachable tops for sinks may be useful (especially in vegetable rooms) in providing extra preparation space. In addition to stainless steel sinks for dishwashing, porcelain sinks should be available for ordinary hand-washing.

Flooring

Important requirements for the floor area are:
Ease of cleaning
Good, clean-looking appearance
Nonslip surfaces for foot comfort and safety of kitchen workers
New floor surfaces are continually being developed. Terrazzo and granolithic chips embedded in concrete make good, hard-wearing floors. Glazed, kiln-fired ceramic tiling provides a durable and stain-resistant kitchen floor surface but it is slippery when wet. Asphalt and vinyl tiling provide softer floors, which are easier on the back; moreover, they are not slippery, even when wet. Skirtings and corners, whatever the material used, should be coved to facilitate cleaning. As all kitchens must be equipped with drains, it is important that floors be sloped towards drainage outlets to ensure speedy and efficient flow-away.

Walls

Kitchen walls should be:
Easy to clean
Attractive and hygienic-looking
Able to reflect light
Many wall surfaces—for example, plastics and washable paints—give good results in kitchens. Nevertheless, wall tiling (with either low-gloss or high-gloss finish) should be used up to a height of 1.5 to 1.8 meters (5 to 6 feet) above the floor. Above the tiling, sound-absorption and anticondensation materials are advisable. Where cost is a factor, such special protection may have to be limited to sink and stove areas.

Lighting

Some kitchens are in basements or other locations where there is little natural light. Artificial lighting is almost invariably required. Lighting in kitchens and serving areas is important not only for supporting comfortable and efficient operation, but also for promoting cleanliness and preventing color distortion, which can make food look less appetizing. White bulbs should be used. At 0.91 meters (3 feet) above floor level (the height of tabletops and other equipment tops), at least 20 lumens per square foot is generally thought necessary.

Kitchens that have odd angles and variable heights present special problems. Equipment and fittings may also cast shadows. A thoughtfully planned fluorescent tube installation is likely to be most satisfactory in reducing shadows and in illuminating interiors of cupboards, ovens, and other fittings. Canopies over cooking equipment, especially if made of metal, should have bulkhead light fittings that are watertight. If fluorescent tubes are used, control gear should be externally mounted.

Condensation and grease are commonplace in conventional kitchens; light fittings should therefore be sited and mounted for ease of cleaning. For example, reflector fluorescent tubes designed to throw light in one direction (downward) are affected relatively little by dirt settling on their tops. Particular attention needs to be paid to lighting under canopies and lighting for sinks and worktables. Because of its complexities, lighting is often a matter in which an expert lighting specialist should be consulted.

Ventilation

The efficiency and productivity of the kitchen staff may be hampered or enhanced by the kitchen's levels of heating and ventilation. Kitchen ventilation must be sufficient to maintain comfortable working conditions, prevent condensation, and confine cooking smells to the kitchen.

Color

The color of walls, ceilings, and floors can aid staff efficiency and cleanliness, by increasing light reflection, and can affect staff moods, by providing an encouraging and pleasant workplace. Advice should be sought from an architect, interior designer, or other expert regarding the reflective value of colors and their most effective use.

Different paint manufacturers often use different descriptive names for the same basic shades of color. But the following are rough indications of the percentages of light reflected by various colors:

White, off-white, ivory, and buttermilk—84%
Pale yellow, green, blue, bluish green, and pink—72%
Pale colors such as gray, stone, and greenish yellow—56%
Mushroom and light pinkish-brown—42%
Apple green—30%
Light reds—20%
Strong blues and golden browns—12%
Dark red—9%
Various browns and chocolate—7% to 2%

Strong functional reasons, as well as aesthetic ones, therefore exist for decorating kitchens in pale shades that have a high reflective value (at least 72%). Colors with a reflective value of less than 50% are not suitable for extensive wall areas in kitchens, although they are very useful for emphasis in outlining doorframes or other borders.

Color is also important in creating effects of spaciousness or closeness. The cool colors (blue, green, ivory), for instance, make an area seem larger and airier. The hot colors (red, orange, yellow), on the other hand, make a space seem smaller. Careful use of color gives the decorator an opportunity to "modify" faults that cannot be structurally altered.

Ceilings

On kitchen ceilings, paints that inhibit moisture condensation should be used. Ceilings need no longer be very high to accomplish ventilation purposes because fans and air conditioners are common. Nevertheless, a high ceiling up to about 3 meters (10 feet) can give workers a psychological lift and also aid in lighting. A hemmed-in, oppressive room is to be avoided. On the other hand, higher-ceilinged kitchens are noisier kitchens unless sound-deadening materials are used.

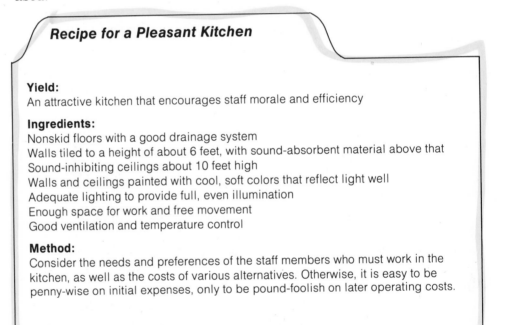

Recipe for a Pleasant Kitchen

Yield:
An attractive kitchen that encourages staff morale and efficiency

Ingredients:
Nonskid floors with a good drainage system
Walls tiled to a height of about 6 feet, with sound-absorbent material above that
Sound-inhibiting ceilings about 10 feet high
Walls and ceilings painted with cool, soft colors that reflect light well
Adequate lighting to provide full, even illumination
Enough space for work and free movement
Good ventilation and temperature control

Method:
Consider the needs and preferences of the staff members who must work in the kitchen, as well as the costs of various alternatives. Otherwise, it is easy to be penny-wise on initial expenses, only to be pound-foolish on later operating costs.

Conclusion

In addition to the general considerations involved with floors, walls, and ceilings, some final points regarding the kitchen are that it should be:

Able to withstand the presence of fire hazards

On the same story-level as its departments (all of which should be at the restaurant or service level)

Exposed to the outside air and light whenever possible

When lighting, wiring, ventilation, plumbing, and hot and cold water services of a kitchen are being planned, appropriate specialists should be consulted at an early stage.

The problems of catering and kitchen management are many, and only experience can teach the caterer how to avoid pitfalls in kitchen planning. But most problems can be anticipated if the human factor is considered alongside the restaurant's policy, menu, and economic constraints.

10. Kitchen Equipment

Tools and equipment are required for receiving, storing, and distributing food; for cleaning, preparing, and trimming; for cooking; for decorating dishes; and for presenting food (including temporary hot storage and portion control). Equipment type and quantity will be determined by:

Market demand (and the menu designed to meet that demand)

Volume of business

The fuels chosen

Rules about equipment needs should not be applied automatically. They can only point out the principles the chef should use when calculating individual needs.

Forecasts of item demand and portion size determine the total amount of food to be purchased and produced. This amount and the type of supplies used (such as convenience or unprocessed foods) then determine total equipment needs (see Figure 10-1). These needs should be met by choosing pieces of equipment that have the right capacities and that use the desired energy sources (gas or electricity). Purchase

MENU ANALYSIS					EQUIPMENT REQUIREMENTS					
MENU ITEMS	PRESENT AND FORECAST PRODUCTION				Heavy equipment (storage, preparation, cooking)	Light equipment	Utensils	Others	Size/model of equipment required	Number of equipment required
	Volume demand	Portion size	Total food load	Other factors						
Breakfast										
Lunch										
Dinner										
Other meals/ Services										

10-1. **Possible format for equipment-needs analysis. From Fuller,** *Professional Kitchen Management.*

cost, operating costs, cooking time, and ease of use (which affects staff efficiency) should also be considered. The example of equipment needs analysis in figure 10-1 can be adapted as necessary.

Fuels

Electricity

It is difficult to plan in advance for the right mix of electric and gas equipment. It may be possible to earn a discount by exclusively using one or the other. But no one can predict the future of supply problems and price increases. The characteristics discussed below are among the advantages claimed for an electric kitchen.

Efficiency. Electricity has high thermal efficiency, which means that more of the energy expended actually goes into heating pots and pans and less is lost into the air. A useful trick to save energy is to turn the electric burner off a few minutes before removing the pan, letting the residual heat in the coil finish the cooking, rather than be wasted. (The same may be done with ovens, whether electric or gas.)

Cleanliness. As there are no products of combustion, cleaner equipment and kitchens may be achieved.

Versatility. Electricity is usable for all kitchen functions requiring energy; for example, it can run refrigeration and cooking, as well as dishwashing, air conditioning, and lighting.

Flexibility. Electricity usually requires lower installation costs than gas and is easily adapted to changing situations.

Exclusivity. Many new and advanced types of catering equipment are available only in electrically operated models—for example, microwave ovens and forced convection ovens.

Safety. All electrical equipment is examined for safety, and approved items get the Underwriters' Laboratories (UL) seal.

The actual installation of electrical equipment is clearly an activity for the specialist. Outlets should be about 23 centimeters (9 inches) from the floor. Adequate provision must be made for a main circuit box with a main circuit breaker, from which the various kitchen circuits branch off.

Gas

There is a wide range of reliable, efficient, and economical gas equipment. Gas itself is a convenient fuel—free of smoke and useful for most purposes. Like electricity, it is brought directly to the point of use, thus minimizing the need for fuel storage and handling. (A small store of bottled gas or solid fuel may be kept on hand for emergencies, however.) Some chefs feel that gas brings pots to a boil faster, but actually electric burners can be equipped with radiant rings to accomplish the same purpose. Another advantage of gas is that it allows continuous adjustment of heat from burners, whereas electrical coils can only be adjusted by segment, each changing the burner's heat incrementally.

Steam

The potential applications of steam are all too frequently overlooked. In addition to cooking, steam may be used for hotplates and cupboards, for dish- and pot-washing equipment, and for other cleaning operations. A good boiler can provide a supply of steam for all these purposes. Solid fuel and oil-fired boilers have been increasingly replaced by gas-fired boilers, which can be automatically controlled, have high efficiency, and operate cleanly. Because fuel is piped directly to the point of use, boilers can be placed in a wide range of positions.

Cost Considerations

Buying cheap, but relatively low-quality equipment may result in increased staff costs, as can a decision to use mostly raw as opposed to mostly pre-prepared foods. Continuing inflation in the cost of energy, as well as of labor and equipment, means that every cost factor should be scrutinized closely. In different times and places, different fuels may appear to be most economical; independent conclusions can be reached for a specific locale by applying equivalent energy values to the local rates per unit of different forms of energy. Use the conversion table in figure 10-2 for this purpose.

1 therm equals	100,000	British thermal units (Btu)
1 therm equals	29.3	(kW) of electricity
1 therm equals	0.27	liters (0.61 gal) of oil
1 therm equals	3.4	kilos (7.5 lb) solid fuel (approx.)
1 therm equals	2.26	kilos (5 lb) bottled gas

10-2. Energy equivalents. From Fuller, *Professional Kitchen Management*.

Rate charges, however, are only a part of total fuel-related costs. In comparing equipment designed to use different fuels, the prospective purchaser should compare overall costs of initial purchase, of maintenance, and of repair, as well as energy efficiency and value depreciation. For example, the initial cost of electric cooking equipment is greater than that of gas appliances, but the operating expenses often are lower, so that the extra capital outlay may be recovered within a reasonable period.

Energy Conservation and Cleanliness Considerations

No matter what type of equipment is chosen and no matter how reasonable energy costs appear, the professional chef should endeavor to conserve energy by using the most efficient cooking methods available. International awareness of the need for energy conservation has

MONTH	HEAT DEG. DAYS	COOL DEG. DAYS	OCCUPANCY HOUSE COUNT	ELECTRICITY KWH	PURCHASED STEAM M (LBS.)	FUEL OIL GALLONS	GAS CU. FT.	TOTAL ENERGY USED MILLIONS OF B.T.U. THIS YEAR	PRIOR YEAR	ENERGY USED PER GUEST DAY M.B.T.U./GUEST DAY THIS YEAR	PRIOR YEAR	ENERGY UTILIZATION INDEX BTU/SQ. FT.
1	2	3	4	5	6	7	8	9	10	11	12	13
JAN.	935		6,556	200,400		33,059	3,561	5,478		835.6		26,380
FEB.	954		6,442	182,400		33,836	3,468	5,530		858.4		26,631
MAR.	135		6,663	198,000		28,421	3,783	4,798		720.1		23,106
APR.	366	19	7,249	190,800		23,337	3,855	4,036		556.8		19,436
MAY	198	35	7,891	235,200		28,978	4,190	5,006		634.4		24,107
JUNE	27	160	7,918	274,800		43,246	4,100	7,209		910.4		34,707
JULY	3	389	7,975	307,200		52,288	4,237	8,630		1082.1		41,559
AUG.		376	10,802	312,000		48,284	4,693	8,067		746.8		38,848
SEPT.	53	117	7,342	264,000		39,048	3,631	6,563		893.9		31,605
OCT.	346		7,824	200,400		19,082	4,084	3,452		441.2		16,624
NOV.	529		6,606	199,200		20,719	3,711	3,685		557.8		17,746
DEC.	807		4,353	202,800		23,368	3,781	4,082		937.1		19,658
TOTALS	4,953	1,096	87,621	2,767,200		393,666	47,094	66,536				320,402

PROPERTY NAME_____ FLOOR AREA _____ YEAR _____

LEGEND

B.T.U. — BRITISH TERMAL UNITS
M.B.T.U. — THOUSANDS OF B.T.U.
K.W.H. — KILOWATT HOURS
M LBS. — THOUSANDS OF POUNDS

10-3. Sample energy consumption form. Reprinted with permission, American Hotel and Motel Association; from Keiser, *Principles and Practices of Management*.

pressured equipment manufacturers into developing more efficient machines. Keeping gas burners clean, for example, wastes less energy. Figure 10-3 shows an example of a filled-in energy consumption form that can help managers keep track of energy use and costs.

Chapter 5 stressed the importance of kitchen hygiene. Increased use of stainless steel has made high standards of cleanliness possible, as has improved equipment design. But equipment positioning is also important. Mobile equipment can be pulled out for easy cleaning of its sides and back, and of the floor beneath. Equipment that can be reached from all sides is another possibility. No matter how positioned, of course, all appliances, whether electric or gas, will in time be dirtied by the ordinary grease of cooking. Cleaning should therefore be carried out routinely. Wipe down cooking surfaces while equipment is still warm, and use a mild abrasive cleaner occasionally. Helpful items for keeping the kitchen clean include dishwashers, waste disposal units, waste compactors, automatic floor scrubbers, and floor dryers.

> ### Recipe for Energy Conservation
>
> **Yield:**
> A kitchen operation that uses fuel energy efficiently, thereby cutting costs and improving profits
>
> **Ingredients:**
> Buy modern equipment that has greater energy efficiency
> Buy equipment small enough that its full capacity is used
> Insulate appliances and water pipes
> Clean and maintain equipment so that it stays in good condition
> Use a thermostat to ensure against excess heating or cooling
> Turn unused items of equipment off
> Keep track of energy use
>
> **Method:**
> Every staff member should realize that fuel energy is a precious but limited and expensive resource. Each should strive to waste as little of it as possible. Incentives for conservation could include bonuses for energy-saving suggestions and for staying within energy-use quotas.

Design

Equipment demands vary according to the nature of the menu. Some of the main types of equipment to consider are discussed below.

Ranges

For many years, the key appliance in foodservice has been the cooking range, which combines an oven on the bottom with a boiling-table on the top. The working surface, where the burners are, should not stand too high. A chef should be able to see into kitchenware without standing on a platform and should not have to raise either arm higher than 45°. The most useful range height is generally about 865 millimeters (34 inches)—about the same as for work table surfaces where heavy work is done.

There are two main types of gas ranges: the open-top range (similar to domestic ranges in design, but larger), and the closed-top or "heavy duty" range. The ovens of either type can be internally or externally heated. Ranges can be built on the unit principle, with units assembled to form a range of the size needed.

Open-Top Range. An open-top range is suitable for smaller restaurant kitchens where the cooking load is lighter. Burners are often arranged under an open hotplate grid, with some larger burners for fast cooking and some smaller ones for sauce making and simmering. Some gas ranges have burners that are all the same size, but also have a flame size that is easily adjustable.

Closed-Top Range. Closed-top ranges are specially designed for heavy continuous work in professional kitchens. The boiling top is solid, thus providing a stable surface for utensils, and has removable rings. Burners located under the solid top can give a core of intense heat—up to 538°C (1,000°F)—at a central spot or "bull's eye," with a gradual reduction of heat toward the edges of the hotplate. Fast cooking can therefore be done at the center, and gentle simmering at the edges. If different heats are needed for the job, they can be obtained by shifting the cookware around as needed. By this means, chefs who must work rapidly during the preparation of sauces, soups, and small boiling processes need not bother with heat taps or control switches.

The working surface on closed-top ranges is generally smaller than that on the open-top type. Approximately 850 millimeters to 870 millimeters (2 feet, 9½ inches to 2 feet 10¼ inches) from the floor is reasonable. The cookware used on closed-top ranges tend to be relatively heavy and tall.

Combination Units. Where space allows, it is a good idea to have both open-top and closed-top ranges in the kitchen, for different types of work. Most manufacturers supply gas units with both open burners and closed burners. There is similarly a wide choice of electric boiling-tops: solid tops with a hot spot in the center (and with heat diminishing as distance from the center is increased), rectangular or round solid tops with heat consistent throughout, and radiant rings for rapid control of heat output. The possible combinations are numerous, and normally each burner has independent controls.

Grills and Ovens

Most range units include an oven; some have a grill as well. Chefs generally prefer to have the grill separate. If it is part of the range, space must be left over the oven to accommodate it. Direct or internally heated ovens are those with a visible flame. This type provides varied temperatures from top to bottom, enabling different foods with different oven temperature requirements to be cooked at the same time. By contrast, in the indirect or externally heated ovens, burners are usually placed beneath a sole-plate, and heat enters the oven through vents in this sole-plate. The constant heat of the indirect oven makes it suitable for large kitchens where the oven is used for one kind of food at a time.

Open-top ranges typically come with internally heated ovens that are fitted with swing doors. This type is most suited for *table d'hôte* service because the side swing doors allow each shelf to be occupied by large dishes. On the other hand, closed-top ranges normally incorporate semiexternally heated or externally heated ovens and are generally fitted with drop-down doors. External heating gives the chef a little more control over oven temperature, which is useful in some kinds of cooking. The externally heated type is most suited for *à la carte* cooking, in which each oven contains one major dish such as a roast or a baked ham.

Special roasting ovens may be needed in large kitchens in addition to these general purpose ovens. Larger gas-heated ovens are manufactured to meet this requirement. They have double doors and a number of shelves and drip pans to catch fat.

Ovens

In addition to ovens that are a built-in part of ranges, large-scale catering requires separate commercial ovens for general-purpose baking and roasting.

Pastry Ovens. Some types of pastry baking require a moist or steamy heat, while others need a drier baking atmosphere. Pastry baking therefore requires special ovens in which both ventilation and temperature can be controlled. The most versatile types have separately heated and ventilated decks or tiers, which allow simultaneous baking under different oven conditions. This system also helps conserve energy, since only the decks required for a given job need to be heated. Both gas-heated pastry ovens and electric convection ovens are available with this separately controlled deck system.

Forced-Air Convection Ovens. Forced-air convection ovens are equipped with a fan or blower that circulates heated air over food at a much greater rate than occurs in a conventional oven. The more efficient heat usage in forced-air ovens permits quicker cooking at lower temperatures, thus saving both energy and time. Forced-air convection ovens are useful for handling frozen food and for doing most kinds of baking, although different models are especially designed for each kind of work. Because they are able to hold more food than a conventional oven does, forced-air ovens can produce more cooked food than regular ovens with minimum space occupancy. See figure 10-4. Ovens may be heated by either gas or electricity. Some models provide for water injection into the cooking area to reduce moisture loss from the food during cooking.

Infrared Ovens. Increased safety consciousness has encouraged the use of infrared ovens. Such ovens only heat objects that are placed in the direct path of the infrared rays—thus ensuring that the oven itself remains cool. See figure 10-5.

Slow-Roast Ovens. Energy conservation encourages slow roasting, which takes longer but works at much lower temperatures. In addition to having relatively low fuel consumption, this type of oven can be used to tenderize less popular, cheaper cuts of meat and can reduce meat's shrinkage, thus allowing more portions per cut and improving the profit ratio.

Microwave Ovens. Microwave ovens use a heat source that is new to cooking. Normal electric current is converted by a magnetron and a wave guide into radio waves, which cause water molecules in food to vibrate at 240 megahertz (MHz). The resulting friction generates the heat that cooks the food. The main advantage of microwave ovens is the speed at which they cook food, which is in minutes or even seconds. They also cook food more-or-less evenly throughout (unless the item is very thick), rather than producing the brown outside and cooler middle that conventional ovens do. Browning can be achieved separately when desired by cooking separately just long enough to achieve that effect or

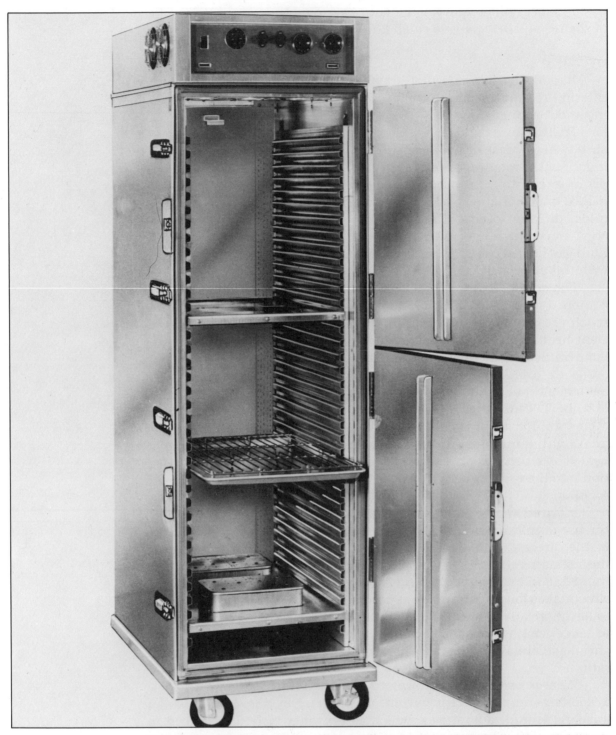

10-4. Mobile convection oven cabinet takes less than 182.9 centimeters (6 feet) of floor space, provides temperature range from 66° to 177°C (150° to 350°F). Recommended for slow cooking, roasting, and baking. From Wilkinson, *The Complete Book of Cooking Equipment*, 2nd edition.

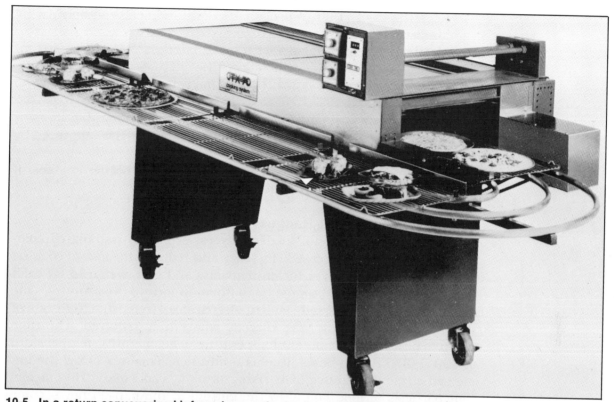

10-5. In a return conveyorized infrared oven, the food moves in a loop around the oven, passing through a heat tunnel at the back. This permits flexible loading or unloading as pans may be taken off or put on at any point on the conveyor outside the heat tunnel. Additional decks or tiers can be added as menu changes require. From Wilkinson, *The Complete Book of Cooking Equipment,* **2nd edition.**

by incorporating conventional radiant heat within the microwave oven.

The rapid heating potential of microwave ovens is recognized in fast-food operations, because dishes can be cooked quickly just prior to their service to the customer. In addition, frozen items can be quickly thawed. Different foods respond to microwaves differently, so it is not always desirable to use microwave ovens for dishes involving a variety of separate foods. Because ice heats up more slowly than water, the power should alternately be switched on and off during the defrosting of frozen food to allow food temperatures to even out during the switch off periods.

Since microwaves have harmful effects on the human body, safety precautions in design and operation are important. Leaking of radio waves is the most significant danger. Therefore, the following rules should be observed:

1. Examine new ovens for possible damage upon delivery.
2. Read and follow manufacturers' operating instructions.
3. Do not attempt to modify or bypass safety locks or controls, nor to slip objects through the door seal or window screen during operation.

4. Keep the oven clean (especially its door and seals) without using abrasives.
5. Metal containers or plates with metal banding cannot be used inside the oven because metal reflects the microwave radiation. If this returns to the wave guide, the magnetron (which is expensive to replace) can fail.
6. Do not operate an empty oven. For testing, use about 0.5 liters or 1 pint of water in a nonmetal container of a material approved by the manufacturer.
7. Have the oven regularly serviced and consult the service engineer if the oven's performance is questionable.

Deep-Frying and Frying Ranges

Design improvements in deep fryers, especially automated computer control, have increased efficiency and reduced the loss of cooking oil. Fryers should be of sufficient capacity and of a design to fry each item (fish, for example) from start to finish in four to five minutes. One advantage of the immersed-element electric deep fryer is its high rate of thermal efficiency. Heat goes directly where it is required. The time taken to heat oil from ambient temperature to an operating temperature of 190°C (375°F) can be as little as 6 minutes. The area below the immersed element (because heat rises) forms a "cool zone." This means that particles of food falling to the bottom of the pan do not become charred. This feature increases the life of oil and also prevents charred particles from being deposited as black spots on the food being fried. Gas-heated deep fryers also include thermostatic control to save fuel and prevent overheating of the fat, and they, too, have "cool zones." Despite its widespread use, the cool zone's efficiency has been questioned, however. One alternative is to use an oil-filtering appliance that removes sediment and charred food.

Whether gas or electric, fryers should have automatic temperature control, pan covers, and fume-extraction devices. Providing ventilation for fryers may require more thought than for other appliances. All surfaces touched by the frying fumes become greasy and require frequent cleaning. While 99°C (210°F) is often used for browning french fries, the closer the oil temperature is kept to 87°C (190°F) for steady frying, the less frequently the oil has to be changed. Though deep fryers are still frequently called deep fat fryers, vegetable oils with a higher heating point than animal fat are now more widely used as frying media.

Pressure Fryer. The pressure fryer found early application in fast food establishments—for example, for the rapid frying of chicken portions. Food is placed in a deep pan of oil, which is heated by electrical immersion heaters. The lid is clamped down so that steam from the food causes inside pressure to build up, which in turn enables the liquid's temperature to be increased. A valve regulates the escape of excess steam but maintains the desired pressure. This process maintains the desired level of contact between the oil and food surfaces, thus improving heat transfer. However, turbulence in the oil can cause batter coatings to shake off, leading the oil to deteriorate more rapidly. Pressure fryers are therefore not suitable for foods that have a high water content, such as unblanched french fries. Operating instructions and safety precautions must be closely followed, including periodic checks of safety valves.

Automated Frying. In fast food operations, high-technology equipment achieves both service speed and consistent high quality. Deep fryers, for example, are often computer-controlled. At the press of a button, a predetermined quantity of frozen french fries, for instance, is lowered into the cooking oil by a basket-lift mechanism. The computer controls the amount of oil in the fryer, the temperature, and the cooking time. When done, it automatically lifts the basket. Such computers free staff members to do other work while the cooking is taking place.

Boiling Pans

A boiling pan is designed to permit all forms of bulk boiling and stewing—for example, of soups, vegetables, or puddings—without fear of burning. The most suitable model is a steam-jacketed boiling pan that makes use of internal pressure. It may be heated by electricity, gas, or steam. Boiling pans are of varying capacity; most are from 45.45 liters (10 gallons) upward. Of particular interest are tilting kettles/boiling pans, which range in size from 13.6 to 400 liters (3 to 86 gallons). A worker can pour one of these by tilting rather than by lifting. The trend to use frozen foods with high-pressure steamers and convection ovens has lessened the need for larger boiling pans. Nowadays, chefs generally prefer to have a large number of smaller pans rather than a smaller number of larger pans.

Bratt Pans

The popularity of the Bratt pan or tilting braising/fry pan (figure 10-6) is founded on its versatility. Available in both gas and electric models, Bratt pans can be used for boiling, stewing, braising, griddling, shallow- or deep-frying, and even roasting in quantity. Their ability to tilt allows an easy pouring action. In large-scale catering, Bratt pans have wide application for all meals and most foods.

Grills and Toasters

Intense radiant heat is required of a grill. The apparatus may be used to grill meat, fish, and vegetables, to toast bread, or to finish or glaze cooked dishes. Electricity is ideal for these purposes because it creates no smell, and food that is placed in close proximity to the source of heat consequently does not acquire a distinctive flavor from the fuel.

Gas-heated grills are available that, by adjustment, will perform any of these operations. Gas-heated grills generally have a Swank-type burner with a ceramic fiber plaque that provides quick heating with high efficiency. Most grills include bottom cooking plates that enable food to be cooked on both sides at once without turning. Bread toasts similarly on continuous rotary toasters; the bread is fed onto a continuously moving power-driven chain and passes between vertical radiant surfaces.

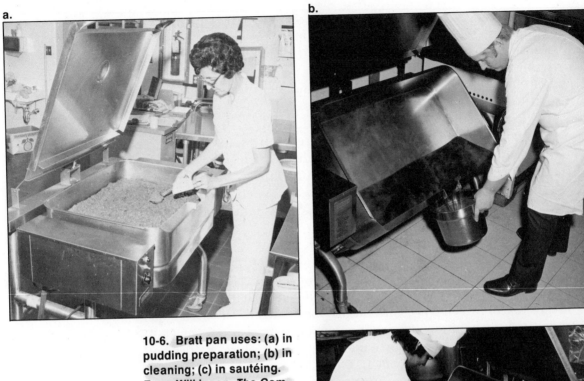

10-6. Bratt pan uses: (a) in pudding preparation; (b) in cleaning; (c) in sautéing. From Wilkinson, *The Complete Book of Cooking Equipment,* 2nd edition.

Chops and steaks can be cooked on grills over a glowing heat fueled by gas. Lava (pumice) blocks are generally used for the fire bed. Ceramic briquettes or plates are also used. Coke is now little used for this purpose, and the popularity of charcoal is waning.

Griddles

An item of equipment becoming increasingly popular is the griddle, either gas or electric. It can perform many of the same functions as the grill, but it cooks only on the bottom side rather than on both sides simultaneously. It is particularly suitable for producing "short-order" items such as bacon and eggs.

Steamers

Steaming ovens have one, two, or three compartments and are fitted with perforated trays or wire baskets for holding the food to be cooked (for example, vegetables or puddings). Some cooks incorrectly assume that the more steam coming from the vent, the faster the steaming process is taking place. All that is necessary is for the oven to be full of steam and at 100°C (212°F). Automatic temperature control ensures both these requirements with a minimum of fuel consumption. Manual control, in comparison, often wastes energy. For steam-oven temperatures to be maintained at 100°C, the steam oven must operate at a slight pressure so that the temperature control can be set just above the boiling point.

Household steamers are used basically at atmospheric pressure or at 0.035 kilograms per square centimeter (0.5 pounds per square inch). But many catering operations use pressure steamers operating at pressures as high as 1.06 kg/cm² (15 pounds per square inch). See Figure 10-7. The pressure in these ovens means fast cooking times—up to 1,200 portions of peas per hour in one model that takes up about 0.55 square meters (6 square feet) of floor space. Electrically operated, these ovens can be fueled by external generators, or the steam can be built up internally by the ovens themselves.

Convection steamers are atmospheric-pressure steamers equipped with the same kind of fan that convection ovens have. Convection steamers operating at atmospheric pressure can cope with large batches of food just as quickly as pressure cookers can, and they can handle relatively fragile foods like tomatoes more gently than pressure steamers can.

Steamer care is important for the equipment's safeness and efficiency. Pressure steamers in particular need safety-locking devices, which help prevent scalding accidents. They also need good seals to ensure that leakage does not reduce efficiency and waste energy.

Hot Cupboards and *Bains-Marie*

Doors of hot cupboards should open easily so that they can be operated by knee when a cook's hands are full. Construction of the hot cupboard should be rigid so that unevenness in the floor does not make the doors bind. Doors must be removable for easy cleaning of the slide channels, where food debris can easily get trapped. Heating should be even throughout the whole cupboard area because hot spots might cause the glazing to crack. Hot cupboards and serving counters can be heated by steam, gas, or electricity. They are obtainable with solid boiling tops or with surfaces containing carving wells and *bains-marie.*

If desired, the *bain-marie* can be obtained as a separate piece of equipment, mounted on legs and fitted with a drain-off tap. Thermostatic controls can be added. When fitted with its own burner and thermostat, the dry *bain-marie* gives service comparable to that of the water-filled type. Dry *bains-marie*, however, tend to dry out food left too long in them. Indirect heating is usually best when food may have to be kept uncovered. Mobile units fitted with braked casters permit ease of cleaning and more flexible arrangements for food distribution. For cafeteria service, *bains-marie* with fitted containers are particularly useful.

Stockpot Stands

Electrically heated and gas-heated stockpot stands are designed to withstand heavy use. Gas stockpot stands are available with an open-top burner. The height of the stand is normally 610 millimeters (24 inches), but some may be available as small as 455 millimeters (18 inches).

Water Boilers and Tea and Coffee Makers

There are three main types of gas and electric water boilers: bulk, expansion, and pressure. Operational demand determines the type selected. A demand for service that is prolonged throughout the day and evening makes necessary the ability to produce boiling water at short notice at any time. A "continuous flow" heater, of either expansion-type or pressure-type can provide this. For service limited to a specific period —for example, during meals, a bulk boiler of adequate capacity suffices. Counter sets consisting of a water boiler with milk and coffee urns are popular. Coffee percolators and glass vacuum coffee makers are also used. In addition, many kinds of electric automatic coffee makers are now available. These are often ideal in restaurant dining areas because of their ability to produce coffee rapidly when required.

Hot Water Washing Up

Either storage or instantaneous water heaters may satisfy the hot water requirements of some kitchens. Storage heaters, as their name implies, have a storage cylinder or tank as an integral part of the apparatus; thermostatic controls keep the stored water at a preselected temperature. The storage heater is normally used for plate washing.

Instantaneous heaters, on the other hand, heat the water as it runs through the appliance. A small instantaneous gas heater, for example, can supply about 2.27 liters (0.5 gallons) per minute at 32.3°C (100°F) —about enough to serve only one lavatory. But a large multipoint model can supply about 6.82 liters (1.5 gallons) per minute. This type, when wall-mounted, takes up no floor space and is relatively inexpensive.

There are now dishwashers for establishments of all sizes; dishwashers range from the undercounter variety to the large automatic belt conveyor type. Most are electrically heated and powered. They require temperatures of between 60°C (140°F) and 71°C (160°F) for initial washing and of about 82°C (180° F) for rinsing. Mechanical washing is required because 77°C (170°F) is necessary for effective sanitizing, and human hands can only stand temperatures of about 49°C (120°F).

Refrigeration and Other Kitchen Tools and Aids

Equipment for refrigeration and deep freeze storage is discussed in chapter 9.

In addition to cooking and refrigeration, other essential kitchen services are needed. Those powered by electricity include: potato-peeling machines, dough mixers, meat and bread slicing machines, dumbwaiters, ventilation equipment, food trolleys, coffee grinders, bread and

10-7. Pressurized steam cooker. This model is designed to thaw frozen food first and then to build pressure for the cooking process. This eliminates any possibility of ice crystals remaining in the center of frozen foods when they come out of the cooker. From Wilkinson, *The Complete Book of Cooking Equipment*, 2nd edition.

butter machines, ice makers, knife cleaners and polishers, silver polishers, dishwashers, waste disposal units, and waste compactors.

Disposable Materials

The use of disposable materials in dining rooms may be more widely noticed than that in kitchen and meal production areas. Nevertheless, aluminum foil, plastic wrap, plastic bags, and foil containers have widespread cooking and catering use. For refuse disposal, plastic bags are especially useful.

Equipment	Installed load (in kW)
1 oven range, 200 liter (7 ft³) (2 solid plates, 2 radiant rings)	17
1 forced convection oven, 200 liter (7 ft³)	12
1 double-pan deep fryer	20
1 high-pressure steaming oven	12
2 grills (2 × 5 kW)	10
Refrigeration (1 × 3,400 liter (120 ft³) chill walk-in cabinet	1
1 × 200 liter (70 ft³) cold (−20°C) reach-in cabinet	1
2 × 1,850 mm (6 ft) hot cupboards (1 × flat top; 1 × *bain-marie* top)	10
Dishwasher, 2,000 pieces/hr	10/19
Waste disposal unit, 0.75 hp	0.5
Coffee set, 36 liter (8 gal) per hr	15
2 mixers (1 × 20 qt; 1 × 12 qt)	1.5

10-8. Possible requirements for electric equipment in a medium-sized hotel serving 200 to 250 guests. From Fuller, *Professional Kitchen Management.*

Sample Installations

Equipment requirements vary widely according to the particular goals and workload of the business. Obviously, much depends on the number of chefs, the type of menu, the number of customers, and so on. Only in standardized units of a restaurant chain or school system will the equipment requirements be known exactly in advance. The following tables therefore provide only general guidelines and must be adjusted in light of individual circumstances.

Figure 10-8 identifies electrical equipment likely to be needed by a hotel kitchen catering for 200 to 250 guests. The items listed should permit a satisfactory *table d'hote* service to be operated. In such an installation, it would be possible to arrange the "wet" and "dry" sections into two separate islands, leaving the outside walls available for storage and for the various preparation sections.

Figure 10-9 identifies comparable needs for a first class hotel kitchen serving about 150 guests per meal, and figure 10-10 does the same for a popular restaurant serving about 100 customers per meal. For establishments dependent mainly on gas energy, the three tables in figure 10-11 identify possible equipment needs for various sorts of kitchens.

Equipment	Installed load (in kW)
1 oven range, 200 liter (7 ft³) 　(2 solid plates; 2 radiant rings)	17
1 forced convection oven, 114 liter (4 ft³)	7
1 double-pan deep fryer	20
2 grills (2 × 5 kW)	10
Refrigeration	
1 × 1,280 liter (43 ft³) reach-in chill cabinet	1.5
1 × 570 liter (20 ft³) reach-in (meat) chill cabinet	1.5
1 × 570 liter (20 ft³) reach-in cold (− 20°C) cabinet	1.5
1 × 1,850 mm (6 ft) hot cupboard 　(flat top with one "gastronorm" *bain-marie* slot)	5
Dishwasher, 900 pieces/hr	9/16
1 × 20 qt mixer	1
Rotary toaster	5.5
Coffee set	9

10-9. Possible requirements for electric equipment in a first class hotel kitchen serving 150 persons per meal. From Fuller, *Professional Kitchen Management.*

Equipment	Installed load (in kW)
*Griddle	6
*Deep fryer	12
Bain-marie	2
*Oven range	8
Microwave oven	2.6
Refrigeration	
1 × 1,280 liter (45 ft³) reach-in cold (− 20°C) cabinet	1
1 × 425 liter (15 ft³) reach-in chill cabinet	1
Dishwasher, 900 piece/hr	9/16
2 automatic coffee makers (2 × 3 kW)	6
1 bulk water boiler	4
Heated plate dispenser	0.5
Service shelf with infrared lights over	2
Bun toaster (4 slot)	1

*Modular equipment suite

10-10. Possible requirements for electric equipment in a restaurant serving 100 persons per meal. From Fuller, *Professional Kitchen Management.*

Possible requirements for gas equipment in a medium-sized hotel serving 200 to 250 guests

two-oven solid-top range
141.5–cu cm (5–cu ft) convection oven
six-burner open-top boiling table
steaming oven
660-mm (26-in) grill
760-mm (30-in) griddle

tilting pan
stockpot stove
large single-pan deep fat fryer
2.43-m (8-ft) hot cupboard with doors both sides
pressure-type water boiler

Possible requirements for gas equipment in a first-class hotel kitchen serving 150 persons per meal

solid-top range
small convection oven
four-burner boiling table
large griddle
660-mm (26-in) grill

stockpot stove
large deep fat fryer
1.83-m (6-ft) hot cupboard with doors both sides
pressure-type water boiler

Popular restaurant kitchen serving 100 per meal

open-top range
small convection oven
four-burner boiling table
large griddle

660-mm (26-in) grill
medium-sized deep fat fryer
expansion-type water boiler

10-11. Gas equipment requirements. From Fuller, *Professional Kitchen Management*.

Safety and Efficiency

When questions or problems arise, equipment manufacturers, dealers, and suppliers, and utility companies can provide advice and service. Some offer a number of publications and films that can be useful for training in equipment operation as well as in cleaning and maintenance.

Underwriters' Laboratories (UL) tests and approves electrical equipment; the American Gas Association does the same for gas equipment. Normally, only items with their seals of approval should be purchased. Chapter 11 and chapter 5 provide further guidance related to the safety and efficiency of catering equipment.

Safety, energy conservation, and efficient operation depend mainly on well-informed and well-motivated staff. Training on the job and in vocational schools and colleges should always include instruction on proper and safe use of all types of kitchen equipment.

11. Maintenance

Maintenance costs are as real as food costs, wages, and other regular expenses. If this is not recognized, serious trouble may result. Preventive maintenance measures are cheapest in the long run, yet too often minor repairs are neglected until they become major ones, with major costs. Appliances that are not well-maintained become inefficient and reduce employees' productivity. When a refrigerator, mixing machine, or slicer is inoperative, resultant damage to efficiency or business in terms of dollars and cents is difficult to measure. Damage and cost undoubtedly do result, nonetheless.

Cleaning, which is mandated by health regulations, is a part of maintenance. So is replacement of worn parts and entire pieces of equipment when necessary: kitchen machinery should be replaced when it becomes too inefficient or costly to keep. Ensuring these and other types of maintenance in the kitchen is primarily the chef's responsibility, although the actual work may be done by a maintenance department within the establishment.

Mechanical Equipment

Maintaining mechanical equipment requires an efficient system of regular checking. This should include frequent checks by the chef and by kitchen assistants so that problems can be spotted early and repaired promptly. It should also include less frequent but more thorough inspections by the maintenance section of the establishment itself or by the manufacturers and/or dealers who have issued maintenance contracts as part of the sale guarantee or rental agreement.

Furthermore, all operators of equipment should be encouraged to report problems as soon as they notice anything wrong—especially with safety devices. This continuing, immediate level of attention is especially important when maintenance services and contracts are infrequent or limited. Once a defect is noticed, however, no one on the cooking staff without specialized training for such work should attempt on-the-spot repairs. Anyone involved with equipment can report breakdowns, but only experts should attempt to repair them.

Maintenance Log Books

One way of ensuring that equipment is kept continually under review by responsible staff is to keep a maintenance log book. In small establishments, the chef may take charge of filling this out. Even in large establishments, however, the chef is responsible for seeing that it gets done. There is no set form for the log book, but the following points are generally useful (see also figure 11-1 for a sample form):

1. Include a complete list of all equipment that has moving parts or parts that can otherwise deteriorate through use.
2. Group these items according to the frequency with which routine and major inspections are planned.
3. Indicate separately the person or persons responsible for carrying out routine inspections and major inspections. The principal person could be a *sous-chef*, head kitchen clerk, or even head porter. But at least once a year, the chef or an appointee should make an additional inspection.
4. Provide a column for each person responsible to initial to indicate that the appropriate inspection has been carried out. In this column, the date of the inspection should also be entered, along with comments about what action (if any) is necessary.
5. An adjacent column should be provided for indicating the date on which action is in fact taken and the precise nature of the job completed.
6. Leave one or more columns open for any special instructions to be particularly noted—for example, instructions regarding the functioning of safety devices or reminders about dates when major overhauls are due.

11-1. Possible layout of a maintenance log book. From Fuller, *Professional Kitchen Management*.

Equipment item	Make and ref. no.	Where sited	Sous chef's quarterly check; date . . .	Initial of sous chef checking	Chef de cuisine's initial

General Repairs Record

The kitchen department contains many things besides mechanical equipment that require supervision and attention. For example, floors, wall tiles, paintwork, plumbing, cupboards and fixtures, and locks and keys all can either aid or impede efficiency and improve or mar working conditions, depending on the level at which they are maintained. Even in the largest establishments with a special maintenance department, the need for repair and maintenance must be noted and recorded immediately by those on the kitchen staff. Figure 11-2 provides a sample form that can be used for this purpose. Such a record should include a description of the work needed, the action taken and its date of occurrence, a comparison of the estimated cost quoted by the repairer and the cost actually incurred, and a record of the firm(s) that may be contacted when repairs are next needed. In addition to this kind of record in sheet form, a card file may be kept for each individual item of important equipment that needs regular servicing. To some people, this may seem an excessive amount of records-keeping, but if it is not done, memory alone will be inadequate to keep maintenance up to date.

Controlling Use and Conserving Energy

Since preventing is better than curing, it is important to control the use (and abuse) of kitchen equipment and facilities. These should be used only by those who have been properly trained and who are specifically designated by the chef. Control of this type may not, strictly

11-2. Simple maintenance record. From Fuller, *Professional Kitchen Management*.

Date	Work to be done	Action taken	Date	Cost estimate	Firm's name	Date completed	Actual cost

speaking, be a form of maintenance, but it certainly contributes to the working life of equipment.

Although energy still accounts for only a small percentage of total meal production costs, fuel prices continue to rise. On grounds of both individual unit economy and a national need to conserve energy, kitchen supervisors are under pressure to control energy costs.

In general, chefs and staff members should frequently check energy-use meters and keep track of how much they are using. Chefs should train subordinates in ways to save energy, and supervise them in practicing these methods. Avoiding wasteful use of heat not only saves on utility bills, but also improves staff working conditions by making possible a cooler workplace. Vigilance in turning off appliances and machinery after use constitutes maintenance because it helps prevent their overheating and overworking, thus lengthening their useful lives.

Older members of the kitchen staff often have a surprising tendency to overestimate the knowledge and aptitude of more recent recruits in using mechanical appliances. Because a technique is familiar to them, they assume it to be familiar to everybody. But the failure to provide initial instruction to new workers can lead not only to accidents causing painful injuries, but also to damage to the equipment itself.

Recipe for Conserving Energy in the Kitchen

Yield:
Individual kitchen operations that each use energy wisely

Ingredients:
Keep ovens and hot cupboards turned off when not needed
Always use the right size oven or steamer for the cooking job at hand
Do not let ovens and ranges get hotter than necessary
Keep lights off when they are not needed, and use only as much wattage as is necessary
Set the thermostat for room-cooling equipment as high as possible, while still allowing people to remain comfortable
When boiling food in a pot, always keep the lid on to minimize heat loss
Keep equipment clean so that it uses energy efficiently
Keep refrigerator and freezer doors closed whenever possible
Defrost freezers as often as needed—ice build-up does not help keep food cold but interferes with the cooling process and wastes energy
Keep an eye on meter readings, energy-use figures, and bills

Method:
Recognize that energy is not free and unlimited; it is a precious resource that must be conserved whenever an operation involves using it.

The *chef de cuisine* is responsible for delegating to competent staff the duty of ensuring that apprentices, kitchen hands, and others who have to use machinery are given proper instructions beforehand. Such on-the-job training combined with simple visual aids or instruction charts can make tasks simple that might otherwise baffle new employees. Also, as further reminders, clear and succinct working instructions together with safety notices should be prominently displayed on mixers, slicers, and all other mechanical devices.

The Maintenance Checklist

The following are suggested objects for periodic inspection and maintenance, grouped by recommended frequency:

Daily
1. Trash and garbage removal
2. Clearance of obstructions from exits (so that emergency doors are operational), passage ways and aisles
3. Accessibility of fire-fighting equipment
4. Cleanliness of toilets and washrooms
4. Proper observance of storage procedures
6. Repair or replacement of any broken tools or equipment (to be noted as needed)

Weekly
1. Proper functioning of electric power leads to equipment (replace at sign of wear or damage)
2. State of guards on mechanical equipment (immediate repair of defects, note possible future weaknesses/breakages)
3. State of flooring even under equipment (repair cracks and breaks, replace tiles)
4. Proper cleaning and disinfecting of grease traps and gulleys (more frequently than weekly, if necessary)
5. State of all safety installations
6. State of any stairs (structural faults, poor lighting, and obstructions to be identified)
7. Recharging of water softening installations

Monthly
1. State of equipment and machinery (thorough check linked with maintenance log or cards)
2. Secureness of floor bolts on machines and equipment (looseness causes vibration damage and possible accidents)
3. Protection being given to equipment by painted surfaces

Quarterly
1. Information on labels of fire extinguishers. Ensure freshness of contents
2. State of kitchen external wall and surrounds

Biannually
State of electrical circuits (replace worn wiring and parts)

Annually
Effective reflection of light by wall surfaces (repaint if low)

In carrying out a maintenance check, the following notes should be kept in mind.

Electrical Equipment. Keep clean and grease free (grease may infiltrate wiring elements and cause a short in the unit).

Refrigerators (Reach-in or Walk-in). Check gaskets. Any necessary replacement should be done immediately, as inefficient gaskets may cause leaks of refrigeration and air and overtax the compressor. Do not allow ice to build up. Defrost periodically. Verify that servicing calls have been made. Ask when valve replacement is likely to be needed.

Motors on equipment. Keep clear of dust and dirt. Clean and oil periodically; base oiling on number of hours operated. Over-oiling is as dangerous as under-oiling. Ensure that switch is off when cleaning.

Gas Equipment. Keep clean (especially burners and oven walls) to reduce hazards and operating costs. The flame should be blue; a yellow-tipped flame indicates an inefficient mix of fuel and oxygen, yielding a less hot flame.

Kitchen Exhausts. Clean and chemically treat ducts at least twice a year. Clean grease filters in hoods. If steam is unavailable, soak overnight in cleaning solution.

Knives and Tools. Grind and reset whenever they seem blunt or ineffective.

Cleanliness

The chef's main responsibilities in the area of maintenance probably lie in ensuring that the kitchen and related sections are clean and in working order. Chapter 5 indicates the importance of scrupulous cleanliness, some of the main dangers of filth, and the remedial action needed. In addition to preventing food poisoning, however, good reasons exist for keeping the kitchen clean.

Danger and Inefficiency. Dirt, in flues and cooker hoods, for example, reduces heat efficiency and raises fuel costs.

Aesthetic Reasons. Food, particularly in hotels and restaurants, is a source of pleasure as well as a biological necessity. Dirt, decay, and bad smells are aesthetically taboo in a kitchen because they directly impair food's taste and appearance.

Professionalism. Dirtiness encourages a slipshod and unprofessional approach to the task of food preparation. Obviously, a kitchen and its subsections cannot function at the peak of their efficiency in a dirty and untidy condition.

Staff Working Conditions. Some of the old, dismal hotels of the past, ill-lit and ill-ventilated, were not only dangerous and distasteful from the point of view of customers, but were drab and dispiriting places to work in. Kitchens must be kept thoroughly clean in order to qualify as pleasant workplaces. In addition to salary and prestige, the atmosphere of the workplace is an important factor in recruiting suitable professional staff.

Cleaning Routines

For all the above reasons, cleanliness is important, but if the *chef de cuisine* is too busy to oversee it personally, a junior *sous-chef*, the head kitchen porter, or even a kitchen clerk should be assigned to assess the tasks to be done, striving to eliminate wasted time, movement, and effort. The methods of work-study can be used to ensure that necessary jobs are accomplished as quickly, efficiently, cheaply, and happily as possible.

General Principles Affecting Cleaning

Each kitchen is unique, but a few general principles should be borne in mind when considering cleaning routines:

1. Only tasks that meet real needs of hygiene and efficiency should be done. These will include cleaning the kitchen facilities (floors, cupboards, and workbenches), as well as the cooking equipment. But it is as important from the point of morale and efficiency to cut out unnecessary "spit and polish" as it is to ensure that necessary work is covered.

2. Before plans for cleaning routines are completed, every effort should be made to correct any faults of layout and work techniques that create unnecessary dirt and disorder and thereby increase the cleaning load.

3. Tasks should be carried out in a regular order and at regular times. Such a rhythmic pattern of work helps to prevent memory lapses on the part of the cleaning workers and also helps supervisors recognize what should or should not be going on at a given time.

4. Cleaning routines should be assigned to specific individuals for specific times, so that everyone knows who is responsible for a given job.

5. Routine washing down and other cleaning should not be done during food preparation times. Of course, schedules must be flexible enough so that unexpected spills and other mishaps can be handled without delay.

6. Work routines for unskilled and semiskilled members of the staff should be outlined on paper and not merely communicated by word of mouth. They can be displayed on a bulletin board in the kitchen or at least kept for reference in the chef's office. Preparing such records helps the chef analyze, assess, and review what needs to be done and the best time to do it. Having work routines in writing also makes transferring jobs from one employee to another easier —especially if the worker receiving assignments is new. Written assignments for unskilled and semiskilled workers helps the supervisor keep track of what remains to be done at a given time, too.

Techniques and Appliances

When preparing cleaning routines, the planner should review the techniques, appliances, and materials to be used. Since labor is usually the most expensive commodity in the kitchen, the purchase of laborsaving devices should be considered. For example, a floor-scrubbing machine may cost less in the long run than continued hand mopping. Work routines should also include clear instructions about the strength and quantity of detergents and other cleansers to use for the various chores. This helps prevent waste and at the same time ensure maximum effectiveness of each product. Finally, cleaning tools like scrub brushes, cloths, squeegees, mops, and buckets must be provided. If they are not kept clean and in good condition, such tools become useless.

Specialized Cleaning

Pots and Pans

The function of the *plongeur* or scullery person is to scour and clean metal cooking vessels. This is hardly an attractive task, and there is usually rapid turnover of employees in this job. Although pot washing can hardly be glamorized, the work area should be made as pleasant as possible. For example, proper ventilation, with adequate floor drainage, suitable duckboards, and conveniently positioned racks for clean and dirty pans, can help improve working conditions. It is also imperative to provide the scullery person with suitable working clothes, with facilities for frequent changes of overalls, and with a waterproof apron for added protection. A good working uniform does much to improve the self-respect of the operator, and it is worth the slight additional laundry expense.

Efficient pan cleaning can probably best be achieved by means of a three-tank technique using very hot water. In the first tank, pans already cleared of loose food debris by preliminary scraping with a rubber, plastic, or wooden spatula are placed to soak. More debris, when softened by soaking, can then be removed by spatula or scraper, and then the pans can be given a major clean in the second tank. The cleaning agents used in this tank depend on the type of metal being treated, as discussed below. In the third tank the clean vessel can be given its final rinse before being placed on the rack to drain and dry.

Methods and materials for cleaning pots and pans vary according to the metal. It is desirable, therefore, to avoid mixing equipment composed of different metals in the same wash. Instead, each type should be washed in a separate batch. (See also the discussion of metals in the kitchen, in Chapter 4).

Copper. Tin-lined copper vessels, after preliminary soaking and scraping, should be immersed in very hot water with a little baking soda. Then, as necessary, they should be scoured with an abrasive cleanser. Green discoloration of the copper can be removed with vinegar and salt. Metal polish can also be used to give brightness to the exterior. It is important that the pots be retinned when the lining begins to wear through.

Aluminum. Since soda chemically attacks aluminum, it is important that aluminum pots should not be left to soak in water to which soda has been added, nor should they be allowed to come into contact with boiling soda-and-water solutions, even briefly. Furthermore, metal scrapers should not be used on aluminum pans because the aluminum is soft and easily scratched. Modern detergents, as well as plain soap and water, are perfectly suitable. Steel wool and mild abrasive powders are useful for thorough cleaning. Ordinary metal polish may be used if a brighter finish is required on the external surface.

Cast Iron. Some iron cooking vessels, such as omelette and pancake pans, should not be wet-washed, but simply wiped clean with clean paper or clean cloth (salt may be used in bad cases). Otherwise, iron vessels do not require special treatment and can be satisfactorily washed in hot water with a little baking soda or with other soaps and detergents, as desired. Abrasive powders and metal scourers may also be used. It is important, however, to dry iron pans thoroughly after cleaning.

Stainless Steel. Stainless steel is easy to clean. Hot water and soap or any of the modern detergents can do the job. Stainless steel should be dried with a clean cloth, since air drying can cause a spotted appearance.

Ovens and Stove Tops

Heavy-duty solid tops of ovens and stoves should be kept wiped clean during the day. An effective way of accomplishing this is by a quick rub with a heavy wad of coarse material while the top is still hot. The cloth should be dry rather than damp, since a damp cloth would send up a cloud of hot steam. (Griddles should similarly be wiped dry rather than washed).

When cold, the exterior of stoves and ovens can be cleaned more thoroughly. Oil and grease should be removed with any reliable cleanser. The interior of ovens should also receive regular attention. Shelves should be removed and the oven thoroughly cleaned with a grease solvent such as soda and hot water.

Graters and Sieves

Graters and sieves have tiny cracks and holes where food can easily become lodged. As a result, they need special checking and attention. Metal graters and wire sieves should be thoroughly washed in hot water immediately after use.

Pastry Brushes

Pastry brushes must be thoroughly washed after use. Stand them in hot water to which soda or detergent has been added, and then clean them thoroughly with a clean swab. It is important to clear brushes all the way to the roots. After thorough rinsing, shake them well and allow them to dry.

Conclusion

As noted in Chapter 5, the greatest care in cleaning equipment is wasted if staff members spread dirt and contamination with their own hands, clothes, and so on. The chef will, of course, delegate routine inspections for cleanliness to responsible aides. But if cleanliness is to be taken really seriously, the chef must show personal commitment to it by conducting occasional cleanliness inspections in person. In addition to inspections, the chef should supervise planning of the kitchen's layout and work procedures to reduce the need for cleaning in the first place. It is better not to create a mess than to be able to clear one up effectively.

Occasionally, the chef's own staff will be unable to perform a particularly difficult cleaning job—for example, on a range canopy or a deep fat fryer. At such times an independent cleaning contractor should be brought in to do the work. For some jobs, regular service contracts may even be preferred.

Recipe for Effective Maintenance

Yield:
A smoothly run operation that minimizes breakdowns and mishaps, but which promptly takes care of them when they occur

Ingredients:
A maintenance logbook to ensure periodic inspection of equipment
A general repairs record to ensure that needed repairs are acknowledged and completed promptly
Use control to prevent unauthorized use or unnecessary overuse of equipment
Training of all equipment users to ensure correct and safe operation
Keep kitchen facilities and equipment clean

Method:
All staff members should be trained to follow proper procedures and should be supervised to ensure that they continue to follow them. All should be encouraged to report any sign of equipment wear or malfunction.

12. Menu Production

A menu informs the customer of the foods available to select from and how much each costs. But it need not be only a dull piece of cardboard. A visually attractive and well-written menu can help build a positive mood before the meal and increase a diner's desire to return in the future.

The menu's significance for the caterer and chef, of course, differs from its significance for the customer. To the foodservice expert, a menu is marketing in action—a major step in merchandising the meal. By means of the menu, the caterer seeks to appeal to a consumer who has been identified through market research and/or previous menu monitoring. The menu is thus a "great silent salesman," a piece of sales literature certain to be read. But a menu also expresses catering policy. As discussed in earlier chapters, decisions the menu embodies affect staffing, selection of equipment, layout, kitchen activities, work schedules, and so on.

Steps in Menu Planning

In many operations the chef still prepares the menu. Some sensible steps to take include:
1. Get a clear idea of the catering policy as expressed by the proprietor or manager. This policy should identify the market to be reached, acceptable price levels, profit constraints, and other pertinent general information.
2. Decide whether to have *à la carte* service, *table d'hôte*, or a blend of both.
3. Decide on the number, variety, and quality standard of dishes. Decide whether or not to have specialty items.
4. Decide to what extent processed and convenience foods will be used.
5. Develop actual figures on costs of meals (to the establishment), based on purchase prices of raw materials, preparation and labor costs, overhead, and so forth.
6. Calculate selling price based on costs, clientele, portion sizes, and the desired profit margin.
7. Pick a style and quality of menu paper, and plan the layout.
8. Monitor the effectiveness of the menu based on actual costs, sales records, and profits.

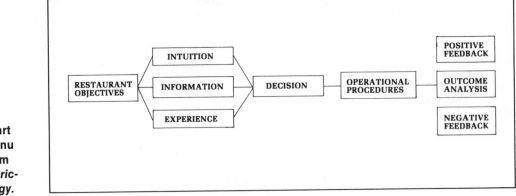

12-1. Flow chart for making menu decisions. From Miller, *Menu Pricing and Strategy.*

9. Solicit suggestions for improvement from key customers and co-workers.

Revise as needed.

See figure 12-1 for an outline of this process in diagrammatic form.

Kinds of Menus

À La Carte, Table d'Hôte, and Modifications

The term *à la carte* means "from the card"—that is, from the menu. The customer composes a meal by choosing from among a selection of independently priced dishes. Naturally, *à la carte* selection by the customer may involve waiting some minutes for the order to be prepared.

The term *table d'hôte* means "the host's (or *hôtelier*'s) table." This is a set menu with fixed prices and much less—if any—choice.

Current modifications of these two traditional types involve measures such as limiting the number of items offered and coordinating different menus used in any one operation (for different rooms and functions) in order to minimize the workload. Restricting the number of items offered to a few highly popular ones minimizes the number of commodities to be purchased, received, and stored. This effects savings of many types.

Selective Menu Plan

One compromise between *table d'hote* and *à la carte* is the selective menu plan, which involves pricing the whole meal by the main menu item only. Then the customer can choose one each from set lists of appetizers, vegetables/salads, desserts, and drinks. These secondary meal elements are not priced separately.

Static Menus

At traditional restaurants, menus change frequently. But at chain steakhouses, fast-food restaurants, and other specialty houses, the menu is basically static or unchanging. Such menus build a good public image and create considerable repeat business. Narrowness of range also enables production and service teams to build up expertise. But, of course, some change occurs even with so-called static menus. Although it occurs less often, new items are occasionally added, and less popular ones are dropped.

Cyclical Menus

Cyclical menus are rotated or repeated in a predetermined pattern. They are more common among institutional foodservice operations than in public restaurants. The cycle's length and the number of times each cycle runs have to be decided by the menu maker. A 6-week (42-day) cycle, for example, requires composing 42 menus. The chef uses one menu each day, in a set, numbered sequence; after the period is up, the meals begin all over again with Menu 1. After three or four cycles, the chef may wish to consider changes. If menu choices are offered, the chef should keep records of which items are most popular and then run them more often in each cycle. The cyclical menu facilitates advance planning of food buying, but makes using leftovers more difficult.

Market Menus

Market menus are particularly responsive to seasons and the availability of fresh produce, specialty seafoods, and so forth. Before completing a menu, the chef should scrutinize the market, look for the best buys available (in terms of freshness, quality, and price), and select dishes that use them. Such menus obviously cannot be completed very long in advance, and they must be changed frequently. They are most common in gourmet operations, but the basic principle can be used in all types of establishments.

Planning Considerations

The steps in menu planning have already been listed. But consideration must be given to other factors, as well.

Customer Profile

The importance of consumer orientation in menu making has already been stressed. Market research is needed to determine consumers' desires and the operation's potential to meet them. Only in this way can customers be attracted and retained. Deluxe hotels traditionally designed menus of such great scope that they embraced all possible kinds of customer. But most modern establishments must aim at select types of people. Trying to please everyone means having an expanded menu, with increased food, labor, and overhead costs. It is better to avoid such problems by pinpointing primary customers and catering mainly to them.

In order to achieve this goal, the planner must avoid two serious pitfalls. First, the planner must discern what customers really want, not just what he or she is inclined at first thought to imagine they want. Very often this first idea is simply the planner's own preference. Second, the planner should not ignore their preferences in an effort to get them to accept what they "should" want. There are times when the caterer may deplore customers' tastes and may be tempted to educate them about good food. However, this can usually best be achieved by preparing, cooking, and serving—as superbly as possible—food that is known and liked by customers; then gradually introducing new items, but only as alternatives to established favorites, which should remain on the menu also. Abrupt and broad-scale assaults on customers' dining habits are seldom successful. Customers are usually just driven to find what they want elsewhere.

Cost and Price Policy

Costing and pricing policies are determined by managers, whose main concern is to produce a viable profit. It was once thought that food costs were virtually the only important factor to consider in menu pricing. Most caterers today, however, recognize the increasing importance of labor costs. Because of this concern, they may make decisions about using processed and pre-portioned foods, which save on labor expenses.

A sales price is established by calculating the cost per portion, using costed recipes (figure 12-2) or some other method, then adding a percentage share of labor and total overhead expenses (as calculated from profit and loss statements), and then adding the desired profit margin in terms of a percentage mark-up. Rounding-off and other price adjustments can reflect an item's popularity and the prices for the same item in competing restaurants. See figure 12-3.

Menu Specification and Portion Control. With management controlling other costs, many chefs primarily concern themselves with food costs. Portion size is the most important factor to consider, especially for expensive meat and fish dishes. But the portion size of even less costly elements must be determined and carefully controlled. Menus must therefore specify portion size, garnish, and service style for each dish. This way, the cooking and service staff and the customers know what to expect. Control of this kind helps maintain the balance between costs and prices.

Price Stability. Customers never like to see prices go up, so chefs should change them as infrequently as possible. Prices of at least some items should be set high enough to handle daily fluctuations in ingredient costs. Of course, when the costs of major commodities go up steeply or consistently, the chef (or other person responsible for setting prices) needs to raise prices. A steady reduction in profits is a definite sign that prices must go up. But other factors also affect the duration of a price. For example, when there is a lot of plate waste of a certain item, the portion size (and accompanying price) can safely be reduced. Dishes that sell poorly can be offered at a discount price or eliminated entirely from the menu.

Supplies: Availability and Season

Food should be bought for a specific culinary purpose, not just because it is on sale. Nevertheless, seasonal gluts of fruits and vegeta-

```
FORM FOR COSTED STANDARDIZED RECIPE

                                        ITEM: CHICKEN FRIED STEAK

                                        PORTION: 50

                                                4 oz. raw weight

                                        GARNISH: Parsley

                                        SERVING PIECE: 12 by 20 pan—
                                                       serve on 8-in. plate
        RECIPE
        ST. LOUIS, ST. LOUIS COMMUNITY COLLEGE
        HOTEL AND MOTEL—RESTAURANT OPERATIONS
```

| INGREDIENTS | QUANTITIES | | COST | |
| | Amount served | | Unit | Total |
		50		
Cube Steak		12-1/2 lb.		
(4/1 lb.)			$1.20/lb.	$15.00
Flour		1-1/2 lb.	$0.12/lb.	$0.18
Egg Mixture		3 cups	$0.15/cup	$0.45
Bread Crumbs		2 lb.	$0.14/lb.	$0.28

METHOD

1. Dip steaks into flour, then into egg mixture, then into bread crumbs. Make sure steak is completely covered with crumbs.
2. Lay steaks on a sheet pan until ready to cook.
3. Cook steaks in 375°F. deep fat fryer for 7 min. or until breading is golden brown.
4. Remove steaks from fryer baskets and place in 12x20 serving pans (25 per pan), overlapping steaks in pan.
5. Keep hot in warmer or low (200°F.) oven for service.
6. Garnish pan with four sprigs of parsley before sending to serving line.

NOTE: Do not bread steaks more than one hour prior to cooking.

Total Cost $15.91

Per 50 4 oz. portions

Per Portion $0.39

12-2. Form for costed standardized recipe. From Miller, *Menu Pricing and Strategy*.

bles create lower prices and ensure that supplies are abundant and fresh. The chef should consider making such purchases (and developing the menu accordingly) also because of gastronomic appeal. Humans are attuned to seasonal changes and come to expect and desire certain items at certain times. Melon, for example, is very popular in the summer. But it would not be so in the winter, no matter how well preserved it was. The wise menu maker, therefore, takes seasonal change into consideration for gastronomic and nutritional reasons, even when factors of cost and availability are not particularly relevant.

Processed Food

The principal effect of using processed foods is to reduce the need for labor, space, storage facilities, and equipment. Less space is needed

Step 1 Calculate the cost per portion.
For example, chicken fried steak is $0.39 (see fig. 12-2).

Step 2 Add other costs in terms of percentages.

Overhead costs = 37.4% ⎫ calculated from the
Labor costs = 17.0% ⎬ profit-and-loss statement
Desired profit = 15.0% ⎭

Total = 69.4%

Step 3 Find the percentage of total cost attributable to food cost.
(Subtract **step 2** sum from 100%)

100.0%
−69.4%

30.6%

Step 4 Divide **step 1** figure by **step 3** remainder to find the selling price.
For example, $0.39 ÷ 30.6% = $0.39 ÷ 0.306 = $1.27

Step 5 Round off, compare to competitors, or make other adjustments.
For example, in this case, $1.25, $1.30, or $1.50 would all be reasonable prices.

12-3. Calculating a selling price. Adapted from Miller, *Menu Pricing and Strategy.*

when processed vegetables, fruit, fish, meat, and poultry are being handled, and consequently the chef's need to allocate preparation work to different sections also diminishes. Instead, the kitchen staff can become increasingly concerned with final cooking and presentation. Chefs who at first deplored processed products because they believed that they reduced the chef's role or made all menus too similar, now recognize that usually only basic chores have been eliminated. The refined skills of cooking, finishing, and garnishing still remain in the hands of the chef. Indeed, they permit even greater care and concentration on the finer points and can help widen the scope of menus.

Capacity of the Staff

It is one thing to compose a menu that reads well and satisfactorily stimulates the gastric juices; it is quite another to translate the menu blueprint into reality. Adapting the menu to the cooking skills available in the staff is better than attempting to create a great menu plan which can't be brought to life. Simple dishes that are well within the competence of the establishment's cooks must always be chosen in preference to pretentious items that are outside the team's experience.

Equipment

In new operations, the selection of equipment should reflect the needs of the menu, which can be developed first. But in many operations, the limitations of kitchen equipment (as of staff) will become major factors in planning a workable menu (or menu revisions).

Thought must be given to avoiding overly heavy loads on the oven at any one time, ensuring that equipment needed for a given dish is available, and so forth. At the same time, existing equipment should be reviewed in light of actual menu requirements. For example, it might be wise to eliminate redundant machinery, resituate equipment, and replace old pieces with equipment better suited to the menu's needs.

Business Balance

In normal food and beverage operations, menu balance is not a simple matter of food aesthetics. It is a business challenge—a competitive exercise in which cost, price, popularity, and other marketing considerations have to be taken into account. The planned profit percentage obviously means nothing if the menu fails to attract consumers. Therefore, the chef's role in helping to compose menus that sell is highly significant.

Gastronomic Balance

In addition to business balance and nutritional balance (see chapter 6), a menu should have gastronomic balance. This refers to balance among the colors, textures, and flavors of foods in a given meal. Besides their aesthetic value, such gastronomic balance and appeal are necessary to realize economic and nutritional balance: if highly nutritious items are presented in appealing combinations, they are more likely to be sold and eaten.

Of course, the criteria for menu balance play a more important role in fixed *table d'hôte* menus; in an *à la carte* operation, the customer selects the meal combination. But even in preparing individual dishes, providing gastronomic balance demands from the chef a wide knowledge of foods in their raw state and a wide repertoire of dishes that can be prepared using them. There is no substitute for artistic "instinct" and experience in putting food components together, but some particular areas of importance can be pointed out.

Color. An experienced menu composer can nonetheless spoil the bill of fare with color monotony. For example, the repeated appearance in a selection of dishes of the color brown can induce boredom in a customer, even though the individual dishes look perfectly good. Agreeable color contrast is not, however, simply a matter of having each item a different color; it involves achieving an appropriate color composition that is pleasing to the eye. For instance, a green vegetable such as peas goes well with the white of potatoes and the orange of carrots. Sometimes, of course, the color of vegetables is changed by cooking. The menu writer must therefore keep in mind the cooking techniques to be used and their effects on the final color combination. Brownish french fries, for example, contrast better with broiled white fish than do white mashed potatoes. As a further help, garnishes can always be used for a final dash of color.

Texture and Flavor. The texture and flavor of foods must also be varied and balanced to be appetizing. No matter how good each individual item is, assembling components of similar consistency and texture can only tend to create boredom for the palate. For example, a dinner of soup, stew, mashed potatoes, and rice pudding would displease most customers. Soft entrées should have hard or crunchy side dishes; conversely, firm entrées should be accompanied by tender or mushy side dishes. Food shapes should also be varied as should flavors. The contrasting flavors of some items seem naturally to go together—for example, roast pork and apple sauce. With other combinations, the chef must use just the right spices or create just the right sauces and gravies to make the different items accentuate each other—for example, roast beef and boiled rice.

Promoting Business with the Menu

The ultimate purpose of the menu planning considerations discussed above is to reconcile the potential of the kitchen and its staff with the satisfaction of customers. A good menu should also have an attractive layout and design and should read well, thus creating appetite and pleasurable anticipation. See figure 12-4. The menu in this way becomes a tangible and effective expression of the establishment's marketing policy.

Recipe for Special Menu Features

Yield:
A marketing menu that promotes, advertises, and informs

Ingredients:
Include house specialties—dishes that make this establishment unique within its territory
Feature local foods—ones known to be highly popular in this area
Tune the menu in to modern trends—add new fads and novelties before the competition does
Include a children's section with junior portions and youth-oriented dishes; sometimes parents are attracted through their children
Emphasize the most popular items, as revealed by sales histories
Add a separate menu for desserts—if pictures and descriptions are included, so much the better

Method:
Study other menus that you admire as marketing triumphs. Then incorporate the best of other people's ideas in your own original blend.

Menu wording is important. A bald statement like "steak and two veg" arouses little interest. While a menu's language should not get too flowery, there can certainly be nothing but good in indicating precisely the entrée's cut, origin, and method of cooking. For example: "Sizzling top sirloin steak, charcoal grilled to your order, accompanied by a tossed garden salad and your choice of potato." Dishes from other countries can usually be listed with their original names. The foreign names will

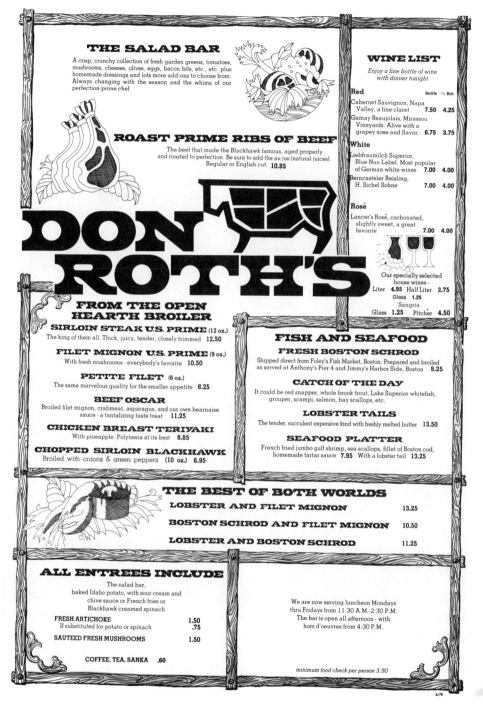

THE SALAD BAR

A crisp, crunchy collection of fresh garden greens, tomatoes, mushrooms, cheeses, olives, eggs, bacon bits, etc., etc. plus homemade dressings and lots more add-ons to choose from. Always changing with the season and the whims of our perfection-prone chef.

ROAST PRIME RIBS OF BEEF

The beef that made the Blackhawk famous, aged properly and roasted to perfection. Be sure to add the au jus (natural juices). Regular or English cut **10.85**

DON ROTH'S

FROM THE OPEN HEARTH BROILER

SIRLOIN STEAK U.S. PRIME (12 oz.)
The king of them all. Thick, juicy, tender, closely trimmed **12.50**

FILET MIGNON U.S. PRIME (9 oz.)
With fresh mushrooms - everybody's favorite **10.50**

PETITE FILET (6 oz.)
The same marvelous quality for the smaller appetite **8.25**

BEEF OSCAR
Broiled filet mignon, crabmeat, asparagus, and our own bearnaise sauce - a tantalizing taste treat **11.25**

CHICKEN BREAST TERIYAKI
With pineapple. Polynesia at its best **6.85**

CHOPPED SIRLOIN BLACKHAWK
Broiled with onions & green peppers (10 oz.) **6.95**

WINE LIST

Enjoy a fine bottle of wine with dinner tonight

	Bottle	½ Bot.
Red		
Cabernet Sauvignon, Napa Valley, a fine claret	7.50	4.25
Gamay Beaujolais, Mirassou Vineyards. Alive with a grapey nose and flavor.	6.75	3.75
White		
Liebfraumilch Superior, Blue Nun Label. Most popular of German white wines	7.00	4.00
Berncasteler Reisling, H. Sichel Sohne	7.00	4.00
Rosé		
Lancer's Rosé, carbonated, slightly sweet, a great favorite	7.00	4.00

Our specially selected house wines -
Liter **4.95** Half Liter **2.75**
Glass **1.25**
Sangria
Glass **1.25** Pitcher **4.50**

FISH AND SEAFOOD

FRESH BOSTON SCHROD
Shipped direct from Foley's Fish Market, Boston. Prepared and broiled as served at Anthony's Pier 4 and Jimmy's Harbor Side, Boston **8.25**

CATCH OF THE DAY
It could be red snapper, whole brook trout, Lake Superior whitefish, grouper, scampi, salmon, bay scallops, etc.

LOBSTER TAILS
The tender, succulent expensive kind with freshly melted butter **13.50**

SEAFOOD PLATTER
French fried jumbo gulf shrimp, sea scallops, fillet of Boston cod, homemade tartar sauce **7.95** With a lobster tail **13.25**

THE BEST OF BOTH WORLDS

LOBSTER AND FILET MIGNON	13.25
BOSTON SCHROD AND FILET MIGNON	10.50
LOBSTER AND BOSTON SCHROD	11.25

ALL ENTREES INCLUDE

The salad bar,
baked Idaho potato, with sour cream and chive sauce or French fries or Blackhawk creamed spinach

FRESH ARTICHOKE	1.50
If substituted for potato or spinach	.75
SAUTEED FRESH MUSHROOMS	1.50
COFFEE, TEA, SANKA	.60

We are now serving luncheon Mondays thru Fridays from 11:30 A.M.-2:30 P.M. The bar is open all afternoon - with hors d'oeuvres from 4:30 P.M.

minimum food check per person 3.50

6/78

12-4. An attractive menu. From Miller, *Menu Pricing and Strategy*.

sound romantic or glamorous, but be sure to add a brief description in English. This literary aspect of menu writing is important in promoting business. Doing it successfully demands good taste, good sense, and discernment. It is no accident that chefs who produce well-written menus are also broadly educated and cultured—in addition to being culinary experts. The best way for beginners to get good ideas is to study the menus of such experts.

Menus and Consumer Protection

While making menu language vivid and specific, the writer must be careful not to exaggerate or mislead. California and some other states have already passed truth-in-menu legislation. The National Restaurant Association and other industry groups have tried to encourage self-regulation in this area in lieu of further government legislation. Their policy is outlined in a statement entitled, "Accuracy in Menu Language Guidelines for the Food Service Industry (AIM)." The basic point is to think of the menu as a legal contract, describing exactly what will be served if an order is placed. Specifically, if the menu mentions any of the following, it must be in accurate terms: quantity, quality, price, geographic point of origin of food, means of preservation (for example, fresh versus frozen juice), means of preparation, and dietary or nutritional claims (for example, salt-free food), etc. For more information, contact:

Environmental Health Administration
District of Columbia Government
415 12th Street, N.W.
Washington, D.C. 20004

Types of Menus

Menus, like mealtimes and like cookery itself, are subject to constant change in response to social and economic pressures. Fashions and fads come and go, and studying past menu practices does not always prepare a menu maker for the future. Nevertheless, the following are some current guidelines for each of the basic types of menu.

Breakfast

The typical American breakfast in a restaurant includes three basic courses: first, juice, fruit, or cereal; second, eggs with bacon, sausage, or ham; and third, toast, pancakes, or waffles—all washed down with coffee or milk. This traditional breakfast has declined somewhat in popularity, however, because of growing inclinations to reduce calories, save time, and save money. Customers are definitely more price-conscious at breakfast than at other meals. Therefore, except on special occasions or for brunch, it is unlikely that breakfast will become any heavier. Indeed, fast food breakfasts resembling sandwiches are gaining in popularity, as are continental breakfasts composed of juice, coffee, rolls, butter, and jam.

Luncheon

Normally luncheon as a meal is lighter than dinner, having fewer or smaller courses, and taking a shorter time. It is usually less expensive, too. In style and pattern, luncheon is not as formal as dinner because it caters primarily to busy shoppers and to workers on a lunch break. The following indicate the possible range of luncheon items: appetizers, soups, sandwiches, pastas, fish and meats, vegetables and salads, desserts, and drinks. Some of these items, such as sandwiches and chef's salads, are usually considered inappropriate offerings for dinner.

Dinner

At some restaurants, the lunch and dinner menus are the same. But traditionally (in contrast to lunch) the evening dinner is regarded as the most important meal of the day. In most hotels and restaurants, therefore, dinner commands a higher price than luncheon. It is a more substantial meal and requires more time for preparation, service, and eating.

Appetizers or hors d'oeuvres are more commonly accepted at the evening meal than during the day. At least for formal dinners, the Escoffier tradition of serving a fine soup as an appetizer is still honored. At dinner time there is also a greater inclination to feature wines as well as cocktails. Naturally, the dinner menu is more extensive than the menu for lunch. Steaks, roasts, and seafood are commonly included as entrées, and this is the time to feature house specialties and foreign dishes. An open salad bar is becoming an increasingly important part of the dinner menu. Relatively exotic desserts are more popular at dinner than at other times.

Supper

Suppers are harder to define than dinners or luncheons. A theater supper, for example, is an intimate little affair after the show, in which a simple assembly of courses suitable for dinner makes up the meal. But to most people, supper implies a kind of early or late dinner of somewhat reduced scope. It offers to the chef or menu composer an interesting exercise in the creation of a subtle yet simple meal. A typical informal supper includes soup, a main meat or fish course with accompanying vegetables, and a simple dessert such as ice cream or fruit.

Special Occasions

No single chapter can deal with all the types of menus possible for functions and special occasions. Even chefs of long experience may occasionally be called upon to create menus along special lines that demand some new approach. Such an occasion may be handled by featuring various foods or by featuring courses of some particular nationality, or by assembling courses to set off a particular range of wines. Whatever the function or occasion, the basic aspects of menu composing remain constant, and the chef who is successful in menu composition from day to day need only apply a little flair and finesse to handle special events. Special events may include buffets (figure 12-5), banquets (figure 12-6), and the British afternoon tea. The latter includes such items as dainty sandwiches (egg, chicken, cheese and tomato, and so forth); breads (with butter, jam, or honey); pastries (scones, doughnuts, cookies, and cakes); and, of course, tea itself.

On occasions such as these, labor-costly artistic creations such as ice carvings and elaborate birthday cakes may justify their extra expense by helping to increase special-event business.

Menu Writing and Layout

The physical production of a menu, including its layout and printing, is of great importance in view of the menu's selling task. Except in rather modest operations, hiring of a professional designer or artist is justified. Even in small establishments, the chef should seek help and advice about these aspects of menu production from the printer. Caterers and chefs should cooperate enthusiastically with management and

12-5. A typical brunch buffet menu and a typical dinner buffet menu. From Waldner and Mitterhauser, *The Professional Chef's Book of Buffets.*

Brunch
Fresh Fruits
Broiled Canadian Bacon
Creamed Sweetbreads in Patty Shells
Brookfield Sausages
Tiny Golden Pancakes
Scrambled Eggs
Hash Brown Potatoes
Assorted Sweet Rolls
Coffee Cakes   Preserves
Coffee   Tea   Milk

Dinner
On the Cold Buffet
Assorted Fruit Bowl   Cold Ham Platter
Bowl of Carrot Sticks, Radishes, Celery, and Green Onions
Lazy Susan Holding Spiced Peaches, Sweet
Gherkin Pickles, Olives, and Pickled Onions
Platter of Assorted Sandwiches
Platter of Cheese Slices—Cheddar and Swiss
Hard Cooked Eggs, Stuffed
Tossed Combination Salad Bowl
Bowl of Cottage Cheese
Cherry Gelatin with Cantaloupe Balls
Bowl of Onion and Parsley Dip
Assorted Crackers
Cole Slaw Soufflé

On the Hot Buffet
Hot Soup
Braised Sirloin Tips, Mushrooms
Buttered Noodles
Buttered Broccoli Spears

Buffet Desserts
Strawberry Shortcake, Whipped Cream
German Chocolate Cake   Ice Cream

Cold Appetizer
Red Pimientos, Anchovies, Olives, and Fennel Sticks

Hot Soup
Cream of Watercress Soup with Toasted Croutons

Hot Appetizer
Striped Bass sautéed with Almonds and Grapes
Red Bliss Potatoes

Main Course
Broiled Filet Mignon
Sauce Bordelaise

Vegetables
Chestnuts and Brussels Sprouts

Salad and Cheese
Brie Cheese with Winter Greens
Crisp French Bread

Dessert
Pears poached in Red Wine
Macaroons

Coffee
Colombian Coffee

12-6. Well-coordinated banquet menu. From Schmidt. *The Banquet Business.*

design consultants in creating menus that sell effectively.

Even though they are not designers themselves, people who manage kitchens can still help appraise a menu's design (including artwork), typeface (style of printing), and marketing and merchandising qualities. Above all, they have a significant role in ensuring continuing creativity and originality. Constant appraisal and reappraisal of their own and others' menus helps ensure that menu makers do not fall into a rut.

This book cannot go into great detail about layout, but one factor has paramount importance: eye movement. Figure 12-7 indicates a person's normal sequence of eye movements when first confronted with an open menu that has three folds. Since the center is where most people look first, the popular, high-profit items that the manager most wants to sell should be featured there. Otherwise, menus should follow a logical course sequence, from hors d'oeuvres (or appetizers), to soups, to pastas, to salads, to meat and fish entrées, to vegetables. In some operations separate menu cards for desserts and for wines may be justifiable.

Menu Jargon

One advantage of using French on menus is that it is considered an almost universal language for food, at least among chefs. In the United States, French is still widely used in higher-priced establishments. But the average American knows little French, and most menus do not use it extensively. When French is abandoned as a menu language, considerable care needs to be taken to ensure that the menu

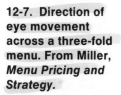

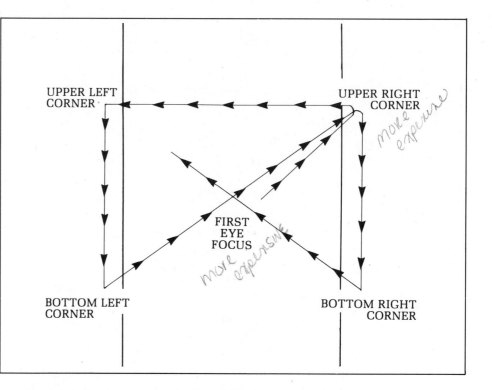

UPPER LEFT
CORNER

UPPER RIGHT
CORNER

more expensive

FIRST
EYE
FOCUS

more expensive

BOTTOM LEFT
CORNER

BOTTOM RIGHT
CORNER

12-7. Direction of eye movement across a three-fold menu. From Miller, *Menu Pricing and Strategy*.

language chosen is explicit and informative. To be avoided are overly flowery, vague, and misleading terms. Instead, use specific and accurate, but colorful terms. For example, instead of just using "Fish" for a menu heading, try "Seafood Suggestions" or "From the Coast." Other headings may include "From our Silver Grill," "Fresh Spring Vegetables," or "Mouth-Watering Desserts." Modes of cooking need to be included when appropriate; for example, the menu should identify charcoal-grilled or broiled dishes. Try using suitable place names—such as Georgia peaches—when applicable.

Basic Food Vocabulary

Although the average American menu uses little French, the French food vocabulary is still useful for chefs because the French names of dishes not only describe the central item, but indicate the method of cooking and the accompanying sauces and garnishes. The competent chef should aim to be familiar with the French name for principal commodities and cooking processes and should also be reasonably prepared to interpret and use reference works that provide further details.

In addition to French, other languages have added terms to the chef's food vocabulary—for example, Italian (minestrone), Russian (borscht), and Magyar (goulash). Many originally foreign culinary words have been used so often that they have been assimilated into English—for example, entrée and sauté.

Describing Cookery Processes. Some menu terms reveal the way a given item has been cooked. For example, *roti* means roasted, sautéed means fried in shallow fat with frequent turning, and *au beurre* means cooked with butter.

National Descriptions. Some foreign terms refer specifically to a (real or imagined) national style of cooking and service rather than just to the type of item. For example, *"à l'anglaise"* inevitably means extremely simple or plain cooking, such as plain boiled beef. *Italienne* suggests pasta accompaniments and Italian-style cooking. In other cases, the meaning of the national description varies according to the food with which the designation is linked. Thus *petits pois* (peas) *à la française* denotes peas stewed with lettuce and onion, while *riz au lait* (rice pudding) *à la française* denotes rice pudding mixed with beaten eggs.

Indicating Shape and Cut of Garnish. Some French terms describe the cut of vegetable garnishes. For example, *paysanne* indicates a rough slicing of vegetables, *macédoine* denotes fruit or vegetables cut into little cubes, *julienne* means in fine strips, and *brunoise* means diced. Finally, *Monte Carlo* describes a round or coin-shaped garnish.

Association Words. Association words indicate the mixture of vegetables that accompanies a main dish. For example, with entrées of lamb cutlets (or other small cuts of meat), *aux primeurs* indicates the presence of first spring vegetables, while *jardinière* means that an assortment of trimmed vegetables, irrespective of season, will provide the garnish.

Geographical Clues. Some association terms are derived from the association of a certain commodity with a particular town or geographical area. For example, *potage Argenteuil* means soup with a type of asparagus originally developed in the Argenteuil area. Similarly, *Florentine* indicates an accompaniment of spinach, and *Chantilly* the addition of whipped cream.

The Chef and New Menu Names

The chef is directly involved in the naming of two categories of dishes. First, there is the dish named after the chef who invents or perfects it. Second, there is the dish named *by* the chef who develops it. Due perhaps to the modesty of chefs, many dishes of the second type never bear their inventors' names. Dishes named after chefs include *filet de sole Dugléré, faisan Carême,* and cold *paupiettes de sole Escoffier.* Such dishes honor chefs by becoming permanently associated with their names. The second category includes dishes named by chefs for historic occasions, patrons, famous people, places, and so on.

Historic Occasions. The recipe for *poulet sauté Marengo* arose from an improvisation forced by a shortage of ingredients on the eve of the battle of Marengo. The dish now serves to commemorate that occasion. Another battle, at Crécy, was linked with carrots, which were reportedly abundant near the scene of the fighting. Dishes with that name refer to the inclusion of carrots.

Patrons and Gourmets. Unlike today's restaurant chef, the great chefs of the past were likely to be privately employed by a famous person such as a king or statesman. Having created or distinctively adapted a dish, the chef often chose a name that would not only distinguish it on the menus of his own establishment, but (he hoped) would ultimately find a lasting place in the culinary repertoire. There could be no better way to help it along than to link it with the famous name of an employer or benefactor. This had the additional benefit, no doubt, of pleasing the patron. *Sole Colbert,* for example, derives its name from Jean Baptiste Colbert, the "father" of France's financial system, who was famed in the seventeenth century also as a patron of science, literature, and the arts —including gastronomy. Talleyrand and Richelieu are prominent among other famous statesmen-gastronomes whose names have graced a number of dishes.

Artists, Writers, and Composers. Many dishes have been named after famous persons of the arts, sometimes because they were active in the kitchen as aspiring chefs themselves. For example, *tournedos Rossini* were named after the great Italian composer. Victor Hugo, Rabelais (Rabelais consommé), and Verdi (Verdi consommé), are among many literary and musical people to give their names to food. Dishes have also been named after famous theatrical, operatic, and concert performers. For example, dishes have been named after Sarah Bernhardt (stuffed eggs, Sarah Bernhardt style) and Nelly Melba (peach melba), who not only won fame in the arts, but also actively concerned themselves with food.

Other Sources of Names. The foregoing indicate but do not exhaust the influences on the naming of dishes. Another example would be naming a dish after the establishment where it was perfected—for example, *pommes* Delmonico and Waldorf salad. Though sometimes fanciful, menu names have seldom been chosen completely without reason or logic.

Recipe for a Good Menu

Yield:
An attractive menu that helps sell the establishment's products so that it can meet its profit objectives

Ingredients:
Getting a clear idea of the establishment's catering policy
Discovering popular items that cater to the desires of potential customers in the establishment's market
Choosing dishes that can be suitably prepared in light of the establishment's equipment, facilities, and staff skills
Compiling a well-balanced selection of foods
Deciding on prices that are both affordable to customers and profitable to the establishment
Writing the menu in colorful but accurate and meaningful language
Designing an attractive layout with visual impact and sales appeal

Method:
There is no one way to achieve all these steps. Skill in menu composition requires market research, study of other successful menus, continual practice, and seeking expert advice when needed.

Conclusion

The art of composing menus may best be perfected by studying others' menus and by continual practice. It requires more than just cooking skill or any other single talent. Creative menu writing requires a chef of discernment and culture—a person who is well-read and has broad interests and social contacts. Such a person will be dedicated to precision in language and will strive always to be practical. No matter how well-balanced and well-prepared the dish may be, there is no point in offering it if it will not sell. The professional chef, therefore, must reconcile personal creative satisfaction with the establishment's need to have a menu that sells and helps achieve profit objectives.

13. Food Purchasing

Chefs at smaller establishments are often responsible for both purchasing and cooking. And even though most chefs at larger places are not responsible for purchasing, it is useful for them, too, to have an understanding of where foods come from and how they reach the kitchen.

Purchasing decisions definitely affect chefs. For instance, increased food costs make managers and professional food buyers progressively more concerned with purchasing specifications and portion control. When they decide to buy precut, uniform-size cuts of meat, for example, the chef's job is definitely affected. The chef becomes responsible for ensuring that the goods received match the purchase specifications and for using the purchased items on future menus. Obviously, the chef must have sound knowledge of the raw materials and commodities that are to be used.

Since there are opportunities in purchasing for kickbacks and various types of fraud, the essential qualification for a buyer is complete personal integrity. The buyer should also be committed to getting the best bargain, in terms of quality and price, that is compatible with the establishment's catering policy. Buying should not be a matter of automatic reordering on the basis of past experience; instead, it should follow thoughtful planning based on stocks held, intelligent forecasting, prevailing prices, specifications, and comparison shopping.

Food Distribution and Buying Knowledge

The people responsible for food purchasing must understand the nature of food-supply channels. See figure 13-1. A few caterers receive food from all of the supply sources shown. For example, larger operations may buy in fresh produce markets and from retail outlets, and additionally may receive regular deliveries from wholesalers and manufacturers. Units of a restaurant chain receive food processed at central kitchens. In general, canned goods and dried foods are primarily distributed by wholesalers, while frozen and fully prepared foods are distributed by manufacturers.

The technical, economic, and trading knowledge that a buyer should have is expressed diagrammatically in figure 13-2. Training, research, and past experience should all be harnessed to identify the best food buys. Both inferior goods and unnecessarily superior ones that cost more should be avoided. The buyer must also be concerned with preventing waste and loss.

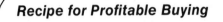

Recipe for Profitable Buying

Yield:
An efficient purchasing system that minimizes expenses, thereby increasing profits

Ingredients:
Select food of a quality that provides an acceptable yield after preparation
Find the specified quality for the lowest reasonable price
Plan for the proper portion size: if too large, much is wasted; if too small, customers are dissatisfied; if irregular, pricing becomes unfair
Buy no more than needed (based on sales forecasts and the amount already on hand); otherwise, the extra supplies will tie up capital
Make sure that all food can be stored properly so that it does not go to waste
Make sure that goods received are of the same quality and quantity as ordered and paid for

Method:
Buyers should be trained and experienced. Above all, they must be honest and dedicated to the establishment's goals.

13-1. Food supply channels. From Fuller, *Professional Kitchen Management.*

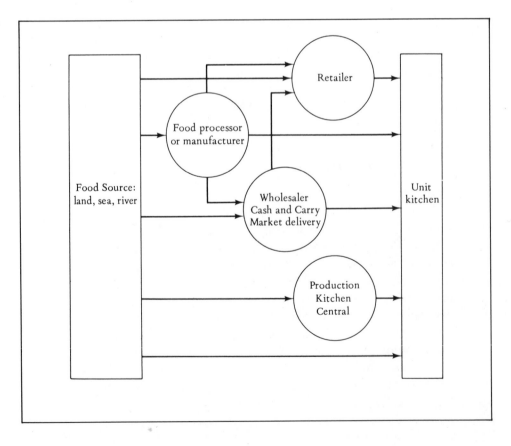

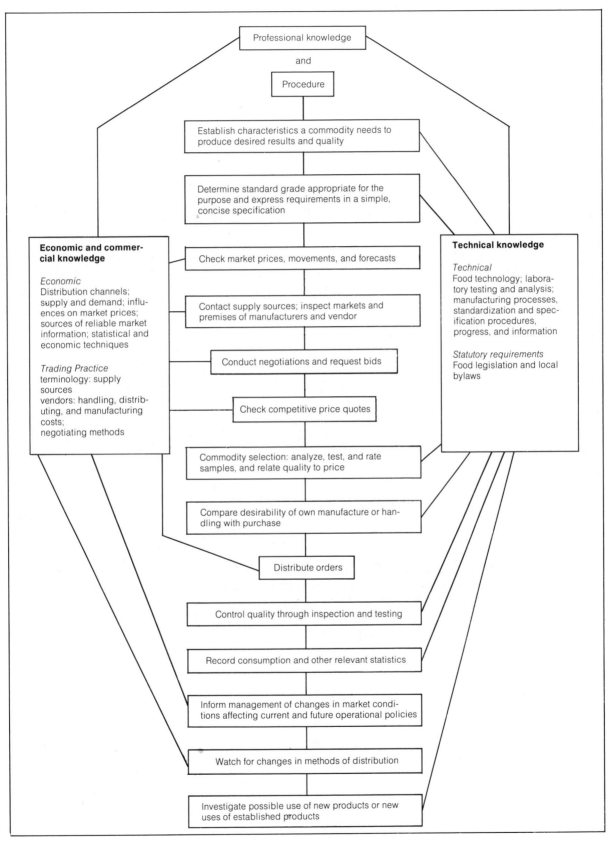

13-2. Chart of food-buying knowledge. From Fuller, *Professional Kitchen Management.*

Specification Buying

A specification has been defined as a "statement of particulars in specific terms." A good specification is fundamental to costing and pricing for profit. A food specification provides:

Buying standards for the operation

A common denominator for market bidding by sellers

Consistency between purchasing and receiving

Each type of food has its own unique aspects which must be considered when purchasing. Therefore, a different specification must be developed for each particular commodity. It should include such details as the item type, quality (or grade), quantity, characteristics (fresh, chilled, frozen, canned, and so on), delivery time, and delivery frequency. The source or country of origin may also be given. Such specifications may need to be changed as a commodity becomes scarcer and more expensive, or more common and cheaper. See figure 13-3.

Asparagus, canned, all green stalks or spears

10 cases

U.S. Fancy or Grade A

24/2's

Quote price per case.

Style shall be stalks not more than 3¾ inches in length; minimum drained weight shall be not less than 12 ounces; size of spears shall be extra large (mammoth). The product shall score 90 points or more. Pack shall be from current stocks. Inspector's certification of grade shall accompany invoice; all cases shall be marked with the certificate number.

13-3. A well-written specification for asparagus spears. Notice that a certificate detailing the federal inspector's score for grade is required and that the product should not grade less than a total of 90 points. The bottom score for Grade A asparagus is 85 points. From Knight and Kotschevar, *Quantity Food Production, Planning and Management*.

Using a Specification

A specification's prime purpose is to inform potential suppliers of a caterer's requirements so that they can properly quote prices. But even for small buys where formal specifications are not really practical, the specification concept can still be used to guide purchasing of the most suitable weights, qualities, and yields. A buyer can then seek the most favorable price per unit. The specifications must also be given to the goods receiver, backdoor clerk, or storage person because effective specification buying demands effective specification *receiving*.

The true worth of a specification depends on its effectiveness—that is, on the actual yield of the product and on consumer satisfaction with

COOKING LOSS

ITEM _____

PORTION SIZE _____ COOKED _____ HOURS _____ MINUTES AT _____ DEGREES

PORTION COST FACTOR _____ _____ HOURS _____ MINUTES AT _____ DEGREES

BREAKDOWN	NO.	WEIGHT		RATIO TO TOTAL WEIGHT	VALUE PER POUND	TOTAL VALUE	READY TO EAT VALUE PER		READY TO EAT PORTION		COST FACTOR PER	
		LBS.	OZ.				LB.	OZ.	SIZE	VALUE	LB.	PORTION
ORIGINAL WEIGHT												
LOSS IN TRIMMING												
TRIMMED WEIGHT												
LOSS IN COOKING												
COOKED WEIGHT												
BONES AND TRIM												
LOSS IN SLICING												
SALABLE MEAT												
REMARKS												

COST FACTOR PER LB. OR PORTION = $\dfrac{\text{READY TO EAT VALUE PER LB. OR PORTION}}{\text{PURCHASE PRICE PER LB.}}$

To find ready to eat value of cuts at a new market price, multiply new price per lb. by the cost factor.

13-4. A form for yield testing. From Peddersen, *Food-service and Hotel Purchasing.*

it. Kitchen tests need to be used to check yield. See figure 13-4. Consumer satisfaction must be assessed by sales history, plate waste, complaints, and so forth.

Scope of Purchases

Buying inevitably tends to concentrate maximum attention on high-cost foods. In most menus these are the animal protein foods, especially meat, poultry, and fish. There are, of course, other expensive luxury items, but these are more rarely used. Animal proteins remain the principal price determinants on menus. Although specifications apply to a wide range of catering commodities, they are therefore particularly needed for meat, fish, and poultry.

Meat

The food buyer should know the structure of the animals from which meat cuts are to be taken so that he or she is better able to ensure that the cuts actually received properly meet specifications. The buyer must therefore be able to recognize the various cuts, to judge their primeness, and to know how they will be cooked.

Beef. The chef has traditionally looked for marbling (the appearance of particles of fat in the lean section of the meat) in beef. These small particles indicate a well-fed animal, and they provide a sort of internal basting during cooking which external basting alone cannot match. Good-quality beef should have bright, firm, and fine-grained lean meat. Its fat should be white or creamy rather than yellow, although this rule is affected by the breed and is certainly not inflexible. Light-colored meat with the appearance of oozing is indicative of toughness, while darker shades with a drier (though still damp) texture is usually indicative of meat having been properly hung. In American food operations, beef for steaks and roasting is labeled with the date of slaughter and is used in sequence to ensure maturity before cooking. It should be held in quarters or in large wholesale cuts in the purveyor's conditioning rooms at 3.33°C (38°F) to 5.55°C (42°F) for at least ten days before it is cut up.

Much meat is now purchased by caterers already cut into joints for roasting, braising, and boiling, or into still smaller cuts for grilling and frying. The expert can recognize the cut of meat by the shape of its bone. Figure 13-5 shows the bone structure of beef, and figure 13-6 shows the basic cuts that can be derived from beef.

Lamb (or Mutton). The appearance of good lamb is pink rather than red, with fine graining in the lean. The fat not only should be creamy colored, but should have a clear, crisp appearance. Pulled apart, knuckle joints of lamb shoulders and legs have a bluish tinge when the animal is young. Mutton will have, by virtue of its coming from an older animal, darker red meat with whiter and waxier fat. The basic cuts of lamb and mutton can be seen in figure 13-7.

Veal. Veal is the meat of young calves. Because of the American emphasis on full-grown beef, veal has not been as popular (or common) as beef. When purchased, the lean part of veal should be clear and pale pink, with the fat firm and pinkish white. Any evidence of softness or

13-5. Primal (wholesale) cuts and bone structure of beef. Courtesy National Live Stock and Meat Board.

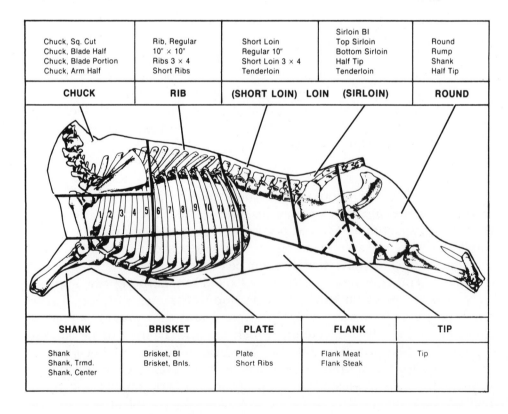

Chuck, Sq. Cut Chuck, Blade Half Chuck, Blade Portion Chuck, Arm Half	Rib, Regular 10″ × 10″ Ribs 3 × 4 Short Ribs	Short Loin Regular 10″ Short Loin 3 × 4 Tenderloin	Sirloin Bl Top Sirloin Bottom Sirloin Half Tip Tenderloin	Round Rump Shank Half Tip
CHUCK	**RIB**	**(SHORT LOIN) LOIN (SIRLOIN)**		**ROUND**

SHANK	**BRISKET**	**PLATE**	**FLANK**	**TIP**
Shank Shank, Trmd. Shank, Center	Brisket, Bl Brisket, Bnls.	Plate Short Ribs	Flank Meat Flank Steak	Tip

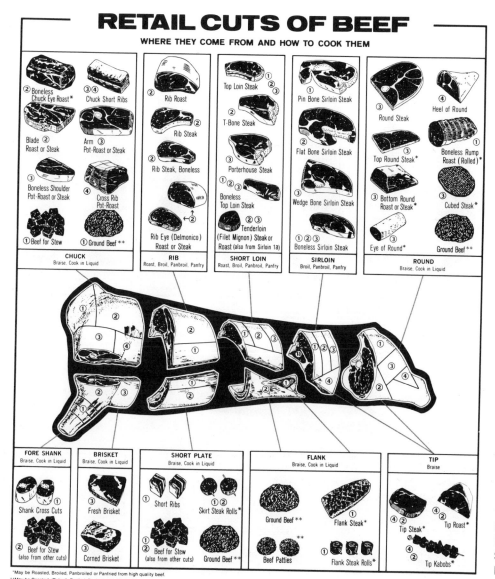

13-6. Retail cuts of beef. Courtesy National Live Stock and Meat Board.

moistness in the fat means staleness; such veal is to be avoided. Positive signs of quality include having kidneys that are well-covered with fat and having bright blue veins in the shoulder. The joints and cuts of veal can be seen in figure 13-8.

Pork. Lean pork meat should be pink, pale rather than bright, and of firm and fine-grained texture, making it resilient to the touch. The skin should be thin and the underlying fat white, firm, and fine-grained. Meat from a young animal should appear slightly moist, but any excessive oozing is an unfavorable sign. In older animals, the flesh is coarser, darker, and of drier appearance. See figure 13-9.

Bacon is prepared from the pork belly. General signs of quality are a smooth, thin, flexible rind, good pink color of the lean meat, and firm,

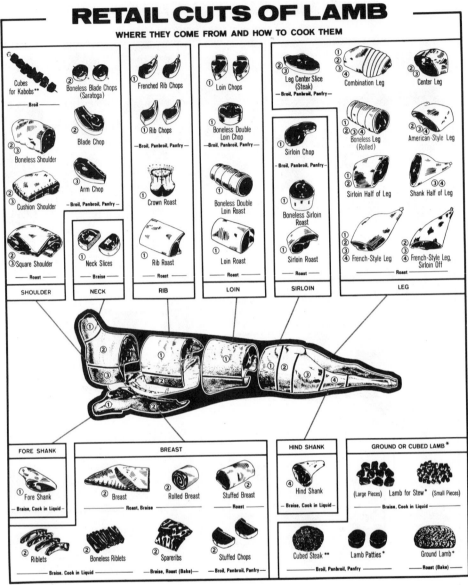

13-7. Retail cuts of lamb and mutton. Courtesy National Live Stock and Meat Board.

clean-looking fat that is tinged with pink from the brining process but does not show any yellow marks. Bacon may be purchased smoked or unsmoked.

Poultry and Game

The prevalence of chilled and frozen poultry, bred to standard size and already cleaned, has reduced the need for examining and selecting birds. Nevertheless, the chef should be able to evaluate the age and quality of all sorts of meat.

Chicken. The skin of a chicken should be smooth and supple, and its breastbone should be soft and flexible. Manipulating the front part of the breastbone between the fingers to test its pliability is perhaps the

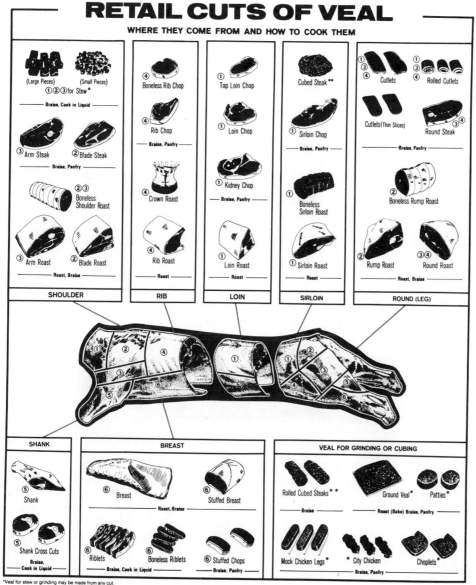

13-8. Retail cuts of veal. Courtesy National Live Stock and Meat Board.

most reliable method of testing the youth and tenderness of a chicken. A hard, unyielding breastbone is a certain indication of an old and tough bird. If purchased uncleaned, other signs of youth are small spurs and combs, small and shiny scales over the legs, and flexible, smooth legs. Some general points to look for in uncleaned chickens, irrespective of age, are plumpness, good appearance of the eyes (particularly avoid those with sunken eyes), unblemished skin of regular color (avoid those of patchy and discolored appearance), and a clean, wholesome smell. See figure 13-10 for the main types of chickens. See figure 13-11 for official poultry identification seals.

Duck. Ducks taste best at about ten weeks old, when they may still be properly described as ducklings. Most are produced on Long Island,

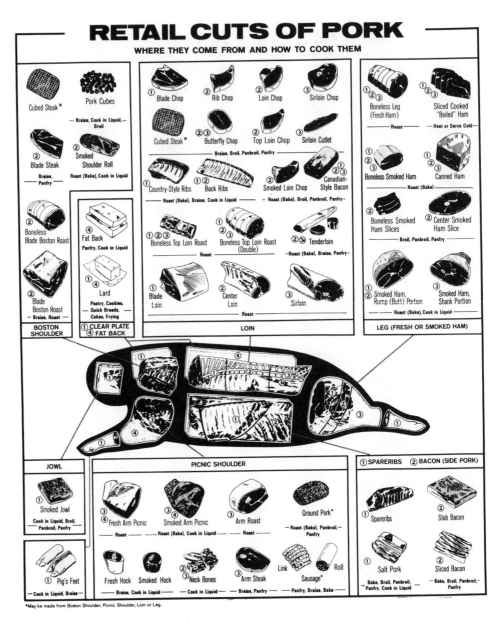

13-9. Retail cuts of pork. Courtesy National Live Stock and Meat Board.

New York, in two major crops per year. In frozen form, of course, they are available all year. The meat should all be dark.

Goose. Geese are in season all year long, and they are usually marketed young (in the first eleven weeks of age), just as ducks are. After that age, their weight gain is mostly fat and their meat becomes tougher.

Turkey. Turkeys are produced and used all year long, but are especially popular at Thanksgiving and Christmas. Turkey hens weigh between 12 and 16 pounds (between 5.45 and 7.27 kilograms) and are regarded as more delicately flavored than toms. Some chefs, however, consider toms superior in tenderness. They weigh between 12 and 30 pounds (between 5.45 and 13.63 kilograms) each. Turkeys should have

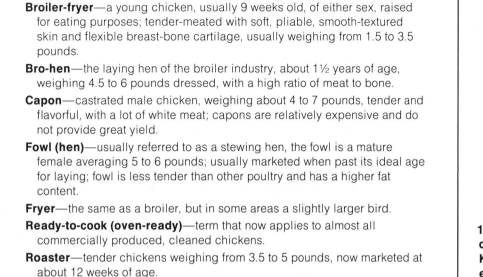

Broiler-fryer—a young chicken, usually 9 weeks old, of either sex, raised for eating purposes; tender-meated with soft, pliable, smooth-textured skin and flexible breast-bone cartilage, usually weighing from 1.5 to 3.5 pounds.

Bro-hen—the laying hen of the broiler industry, about 1½ years of age, weighing 4.5 to 6 pounds dressed, with a high ratio of meat to bone.

Capon—castrated male chicken, weighing about 4 to 7 pounds, tender and flavorful, with a lot of white meat; capons are relatively expensive and do not provide great yield.

Fowl (hen)—usually referred to as a stewing hen, the fowl is a mature female averaging 5 to 6 pounds; usually marketed when past its ideal age for laying; fowl is less tender than other poultry and has a higher fat content.

Fryer—the same as a broiler, but in some areas a slightly larger bird.

Ready-to-cook (oven-ready)—term that now applies to almost all commercially produced, cleaned chickens.

Roaster—tender chickens weighing from 3.5 to 5 pounds, now marketed at about 12 weeks of age.

Stags—usually termed roosters, stags are tough and stringy and weigh 3 to 6 pounds.

13-10. Types of chickens. From Knight and Kotschevar, *Quantity Food Production, Planning and Management.*

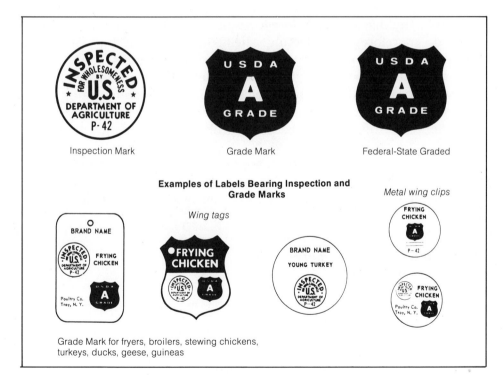

13-11. Forms of official identification for ready-to-cook poultry. From Peddersen, *Foodservice and Hotel Purchasing.*

the same signs of quality as chickens—good odor, plumpness, and cleanness of appearance.

Guineas. Guineas are domestic fowl of the same family as pheasants. They tend to be tough and dry unless eaten when young. They are much darker than chickens, but they may be similarly tested for youth by the softness of their flesh and the pliability of their breastbones.

Birds should weigh 2.75 pounds (1.25 kilograms) or more if they are to be satisfactory for roasting.

Pigeons. Squabs are immature pigeons between 3 and 4 weeks old. They weigh about 0.5 pounds each (0.23 kilograms) and have light-colored, tender meat. Older pigeons are too tough to be very desirable at the table.

Venison. The meat, though dark in color, should have a clean appearance. The accompanying fat should be abundant, bright, and clear. Venison is normally hung for up to three weeks in a cool, well-ventilated larder or cellar. This leaves the meat tender but "gamey"-flavored. A shorter hanging time produces a milder flavor but tougher meat.

Rabbit. Young rabbits, suitable for frying, have tender, fine-grained flesh of a bright pinkish color. Older rabbits, more suitable for roasting, have tougher, coarse-grained flesh which is somewhat darker.

Fish

In buying fish, the most important criterion is freshness. Shellfish present special problems. For one thing, some types of shellfish may cause trouble to diners who have allergies. Shellfish are also susceptible to infection. For example, if sewage is discharged near oyster beds, the oysters may harbor typhoid or hepatitis viruses. If infected oysters are eaten raw, the diseases can spread to humans. Particular vigilance is required, therefore, in selecting shellfish; it should be done only through reliable suppliers. To ensure freshness of oysters, clams, mussels, and so forth, look for tightly closed shells. If the shells are slightly open when first seen, they should close immediately on handling or be rejected as dead. During opening, the shell should noticeably close upon the knife: the stronger its resistance to the knife, the fresher the shellfish.

In addition to shellfish, there are many popular species of fish and crustaceans. See figure 13-12. The same type of fish can often be purchased in many forms. The most common of these are illustrated in figure 13-13.

Recipe for Selecting Fresh Fish

Yield:
The purchase of fresh fish for dishes that are safe and more appealing to the customer

Ingredients:
Eyes should be bright, clear and convex (protruding rather than sunken)
The skin should have its full natural colors unfaded
The gills should be of good reddish color and firm to the touch
All the flesh should be firm, springing back when touched
The flesh should not separate from the bones
It should smell fresh and mild, with no unpleasantness at all

Method:
Purchase only fish of unquestionable freshness. Since it quickly deteriorates, use it promptly or refrigerate at 1–3°C (34°–38°F), storing it away from other foods.

13-12. Popular species of fish and shellfish. From Peddersen, *Foodservice and Hotel Purchasing.*

Species	Other Names	Where Caught	Market Forms
Butterfish		Northeastern U.S.	Whole, dressed; smoked
Catfish	Fidler, Blue Channel	Pond raised commercially, Great Lakes, other U.S. lakes, rivers, ponds, creeks, Brazil	Whole, dressed; fresh, frozen
Lake trout	Togue	Cold-water lakes of North America	Whole, drawn, fillets; steaks; fresh, frozen
Mackerel	Atlantic Blue	New England, Norway	Whole; fresh, frozen
Spanish	American	South Atlantic, Gulf	Whole, drawn, fillets; steaks; fresh, frozen
King	Cero, Kingfish	South Atlantic, Gulf, Pacific Coast	Drawn; steaks, fillets; fresh, frozen
Mullet	Striped, White	South Atlantic and Gulf of Mexico	Whole; fillets; fresh, frozen, smoked, salted Mullet dip
Rainbow trout		Northwestern U.S. (commercial fish farms), Denmark, Japan	Dressed, boned, boned and breaded; fresh, frozen
Sablefish	Black Cod	Pacific Coast	Whole, steaks, fillets, kippered, smoked
Salmon			
Sockeye	Red	Pacific Coast, Alaska	Dressed, steaks, fillets; fresh, salted, pickled, smoked (sardines)
Chinook	Spring, King	Pacific Coast, Alaska	
Silver	Silversides, Coho	North Pacific	
Pink	Humpback	Pacific Coast	
Chub	Fall	Pacific Coast	
Atlantic		North Atlantic	
Sea Herring	Atlantic or Pacific Herring	New England, Middle Atlantic, North Pacific, Iceland, Denmark, Norway, Germany, England, Scotland, Holland, Sweden (virtually worldwide)	Whole, chunks; fresh, salted, pickled, smoked (sardines)
Shad	Buck, Roe, or White Shad	Coastal rivers from Maine to Florida, Washington to California	Whole, drawn, fillets, boned; fresh, frozen, smoked, canned. Shad roe: fresh, frozen, canned
Smelt	Whitebait, Surf Smelt, Grunlon, Eulachon or Columbia River Smelt, Silverside, Jacksmelt, Bay Smelt	North Atlantic, Pacific Coast, Columbia River, and bays from Mexico to Canada, Great Lakes	Whole, dressed, breaded, precooked; fresh, frozen

continued . . .

13-12.

Species	Other Names	Where Caught	Market Forms
Tuna	Albacore, Yellowfin, Skipjack, Blue Fin, Little	Atlantic and Pacific Coasts, Worldwide	Canned, drawn, smoked
Whitefish		Great Lakes, Canada	Whole, drawn, dressed, fillets; frozen, fresh, smoked
Yellow Perch	Lake Perch, Ringed Perch, Pacific Perch	Great Lakes, Canada, Pacific Coast	Whole, drawn, dressed fillets; butterfly fillets; fresh and frozen
Clams			
Butter		Pacific Coast, Alaska	
Hard	Hard Shell, Cherrystones, Quahog	New England, Middle and South Atlantic	
Little Neck		Pacific Coast, Alaska	Live in shell; shucked, fresh and frozen, frozen breaded, raw and cooked; canned
Razor		Pacific Coast, Alaska	
Soft	Soft Shell	New England, Middle Atlantic, Pacific	
Surf	Skimmer	Middle Atlantic, Pacific	
*Geoduck	King Clam, Gweduc, Gwee Duk, Gooey-Duck	Washington's Puget Sound, South of Anacortes and In Hood Canal	
*Ocean Quahog	Mahogany and Black Quahog, Mahogany Clam	New England Coast	
Crabs			
Blue		Middle and South Atlantic, Gulf	
Dungeness		Pacific Coast, Alaska	Live In shell; fresh or frozen; cooked meat, sections, claws; frozen breaded, raw or cooked (cakes, patties, devilled, stuffed, etc.); canned
King		Alaska	
Stone		Florida	
Snow	Tanner, Queen	Pacific Coast, Alaska	
*Jonah		New England Coast from Main to Cape Hatteras, North Carolina	
*Red	Deep Sea Red Crab	New England and Middle Atlantic Coast	
Lobsters			
Northern	Maine Americana	New England, Canada	
Rock		South Africa, Australia	Live in shell; fresh or frozen; cooked meat, cooked whole, tails raw; canned
Spiny		Europe, Australia, North America, South America, Japan, Africa	
California Spiny		California Coast, Mexico	
Mussels	Bay Mussels	New England and Middle Atlantic	Live in shell, frozen in sauces, canned

continued . . .

13-12.

Species	Other Names	Where Caught	Market Forms
Oysters			
Eastern		New England, Middle and South Atlantic, Gulf	Live in shell; shucked, fresh, frozen; frozen breaded raw or fried, canned, smoked
Pacific	Japanese	Pacific Coast, Japan, Korea	
Olympia	Western	Pacific Coast	
Scallops			
Bay		Middle and South Atlantic, New England, Gulf	Fresh or frozen: shucked; frozen breaded, raw or cooked; specialties
Calico		South Atlantic	
Sea	Alaska Scallops	New England, Alaska, Canada	
Shrimp	Prawn	Worldwide. In U.S.: South Atlantic, Gulf, Alaska, Maine	Fresh or frozen; raw, headless; peeled (also deveined), raw or cooked. Frozen breaded, raw or fried, cooked whole.
*Rock		Mexico, Florida	Canned; packaged; split-in-the-shell
Squid	Inkfish, Bone Squid, Sea Arrow, Calamari, Calamary, Flying Squid, Taw Taw	Atlantic, Gulf, and Southern California	Frozen; canned

*Available on a regional basis

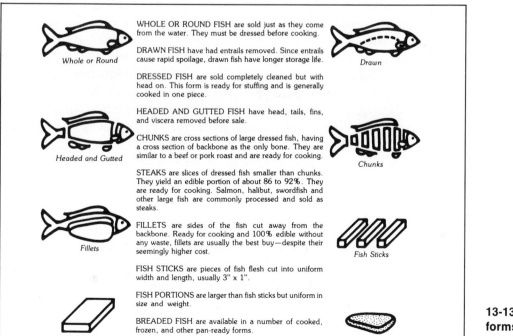

WHOLE OR ROUND FISH are sold just as they come from the water. They must be dressed before cooking.

Whole or Round

DRAWN FISH have had entrails removed. Since entrails cause rapid spoilage, drawn fish have longer storage life.

Drawn

DRESSED FISH are sold completely cleaned but with head on. This form is ready for stuffing and is generally cooked in one piece.

HEADED AND GUTTED FISH have head, tails, fins, and viscera removed before sale.

Headed and Gutted

CHUNKS are cross sections of large dressed fish, having a cross section of backbone as the only bone. They are similar to a beef or pork roast and are ready for cooking.

Chunks

STEAKS are slices of dressed fish smaller than chunks. They yield an edible portion of about 86 to 92%. They are ready for cooking. Salmon, halibut, swordfish and other large fish are commonly processed and sold as steaks.

Fillets

FILLETS are sides of the fish cut away from the backbone. Ready for cooking and 100% edible without any waste, fillets are usually the best buy—despite their seemingly higher cost.

FISH STICKS are pieces of fish flesh cut into uniform width and length, usually 3" x 1".

Fish Sticks

FISH PORTIONS are larger than fish sticks but uniform in size and weight.

Fish Portions

BREADED FISH are available in a number of cooked, frozen, and other pan-ready forms.

Breaded Fish

13-13. Market forms of fish. Courtesy National Fisheries Institute.

199

Vegetables and Fruit

When possible, the chef or a designated subordinate should personally examine fruit and vegetables prior to purchase. If this is not possible (for example, if purchases are handled by mail or phone), examination can and should take place upon receipt of the goods. Even if the goods have already been paid for, defective items should be thrown out or returned rather than used. It is false economy to use bad or doubtful produce at the risk of losing customers.

Recipe for Purchasing Fresh Fruit and Vegetables

Yield:
Fresh and delicious produce for high-quality meals

Ingredients:
Reject overly ripe or withered items
Reject those with bruises, mold, or cut skins
Reject those with signs of insect infestation
Reject greenstuffs with yellow or other discolored leaves
Select clean produce without excessive accompanying soil
Select sound and ripe items
Select those with a rich natural smell
Select items that are properly shaped and unblemished

Method:
It takes time, but the chef and all others who handle fruit and vegetables should briefly inspect the items going into production. Sometimes, a single container holds many good items but also a few bad ones that should be rejected.

As mentioned in Chapter 12, the chef should take advantage of the seasonal availability of particular fruits and vegetables. Figure 13-14 indicates the seasons when a number of popular items are relatively abundant. When placing an order, the chef should make sure to specify appropriate sizes as well as amounts. See, for example, figure 13-15. To ensure freshness, the chef should normally seek deliveries of fruit at least three times a week. Fruit is best stored chilled (at 3.33°C or 38°F), except for bananas, which should be kept at room temperature.

Fruit displayed in the dining room on buffet tables, on serving counters, or in baskets must be checked before each service period, or at least daily. Overripe fruit is unsightly and must be discarded.

Convenience Foods

Convenience foods are processed foods that have been carried to an advanced stage of preparation by the manufacturer and therefore may be used as a laborsaving alternative to less highly processed items. See figure 13-16. Since they cost more, the decision on whether or not to buy them must take into account the advantages of eliminating preparation time, labor, and related fuel costs. Many items from the main food groups are available today in ready-to-use form. See figure 13-17 for examples of the types of food available and the forms in which they are sold.

MONTHLY AVAILABILITY OF FRUITS EXPRESSED AS A PERCENTAGE OF TOTAL ANNUAL SUPPLY

COMMODITY	% Jan	% Feb	% Mar	% Apr	% May	% June	% July	% Aug	% Sept	% Oct	% Nov	% Dec
Apples	11	10	10	8	6	3	2	3	10	15	11	11
Apricots					5	62	31	2				
Avocados	11	11	11	11	9	7	6	6	5	6	8	9
Bananas	7	8	9	9	10	10	8	8	7	8	8	8
Blackberries					13	56	19	12				
Blueberries					2	32	39	23	4			
Cantaloupes	*	1	1	3	8	24	24	22	12	4	1	
Casabas						1	5	16	29	29	18	2
Cherries	*				14	39	42	4				1
Coconuts	8	6	8	5	3	3	4	4	11	14	18	16
Cranberries	1	1							6	21	49	22
Crenshaws				*	3	8	17	27	27	15	2	*
Figs, Fresh					1	15	8	29	24	19	4	*
Grapefruit	12	12	13	12	10	6	3	2	2	8	10	10
Grapes	3	3	3	3	2	6	10	18	19	15	11	7
Honeydews	2	5	7	6	3	7	14	22	21	12	1	*
Lemons	7	6	7	8	10	11	11	10	8	7	7	8
Limes	6	4	4	4	6	15	16	13	10	7	6	9

COMMODITY	% Jan	% Feb	% Mar	% Apr	% May	% June	% July	% Aug	% Sept	% Oct	% Nov	% Dec
Mangoes				2	19	39	29	10	1			
Nectarines	2	5				16	35	34	8			
Oranges, all	12	11	11	10	9	7	5	5	5	6	8	11
Oranges, West	9	9	10	10	9	7	7	7	7	8	6	11
Oranges, Fla.	15	15	14	11	10	6	2	1	*	3	10	13
Peaches	*	*	*		2	26	31	27	13	1		
Pears	6	6	7	6	4	1	6	15	16	15	10	8
Persians			*	5	15	29	31	19	1	*		
Persimmons	1							2	41	39	17	
Pineapples	8	9	12	14	15	17	7	4	2	3	4	5
Plums-Prunes	1	1	1		2	18	25	25	24	3		
Pomegranates								20	63	15	2	
Raspberries					1	21	55	5	6	7	4	1
Strawberries	1	2	5	15	31	26	10	5	3	1	*	*
Tangelos	10								7	46	37	
Tangerines	24	8	3	1						20	44	
Watermelons		*	1	2	11	27	33	21	5	*		

*Less than 0.5 of 1% of annual total
The table is based on unloads of fresh fruits in 41 cities as reported by the U S Department of Agriculture, and on import figures

MONTHLY AVAILABILITY OF VEGETABLES EXPRESSED AS A PERCENTAGE OF TOTAL ANNUAL SUPPLY

COMMODITY	Jan %	Feb %	Mar %	Apr %	May %	June %	July %	Aug %	Sept %	Oct %	Nov %	Dec %
Artichokes	6	7	12	23	15	5	4	3	4	6	9	8
Asparagus	*	2	20	33	28	15	1	*	*	1	*	*
Beans, Snap	5	5	6	8	9	13	12	11	10	8	7	6
Beets	4	4	5	5	7	13	15	13	12	11	7	4
Broccoli	10	10	12	11	9	5	4	3	6	10	11	9
Brussels Sprouts	14	9	5	2	1	1	1	2	11	19	20	16
Cabbage	9	8	10	9	9	10	8	7	8	8	8	8
Carrots	10	8	10	9	8	8	8	7	8	8	8	8
Cauliflower	9	7	7	7	5	5	4	5	11	19	14	8
Celery	9	8	9	9	8	7	7	7	8	9	10	9
Chinese Cabbage	9	8	7	7	6	8	9	8	9	10	11	10
Corn, Sweet	1	1	2	6	15	16	20	18	11	4	3	2
Cucumbers	4	4	5	9	12	14	14	10	8	8	8	6
Eggplant	8	6	7	8	7	8	9	12	12	8	8	8
Escarole-Endive	7	7	9	8	7	9	9	9	9	9	10	8
Endive, Belgian	5	15	15	14	11	4			4	10	9	15
Greens (misc.)	10	10	11	11	8	7	6	6	6	8	8	10
Lettuce	8	7	8	9	9	9	9	9	9	8	8	8
Mushrooms	10	9	10	10	8	7	5	5	6	8	10	11
Okra	*	*	1	4	11	19	23	21	12	7	3	1
Onions, dry, all	8	7	8	9	9	10	9	8	9	8	8	8
Onions, dry, Texas	*	*	6	32	30	14	11	6	1	*	*	*

COMMODITY	Jan %	Feb %	Mar %	Apr %	May %	June %	July %	Aug %	Sept %	Oct %	Nov %	Dec %
Onions, dry, New York	10	9	10	6	2	1	2	12	14	13	11	11
Onions, dry, California	2	2	1	1	9	21	23	14	9	8	7	3
Onions, Green	6	6	8	10	10	11	11	10	8	7	7	7
Parsley and Herbs	6	6	8	8	7	8	8	8	8	10	13	11
Parsnips	13	11	11	9	6	5	3	3	8	14	11	9
Peas, Green	7	8	9	15	13	15	13	9	5	3	2	2
Peppers, Sweet	7	6	7	7	8	10	10	10	10	9	9	7
Potatoes, All	9	7	9	9	9	9	8	8	8	8	8	8
Potatoes, California	4	4	4	3	10	26	24	11	5	3	3	4
Potatoes, Maine	11	11	16	19	16	9	2	*	*	1	5	9
Potatoes, Idaho	14	12	14	14	9	2	*	2	3	8	12	12
Radishes	6	6	8	9	11	12	11	9	8	7	7	7
Rhubarb	6	12	15	22	27	13	3	1	*	*	*	1
Spinach	9	8	10	10	10	8	6	5	7	9	9	8
Squash	7	5	6	7	8	9	10	9	10	11	11	8
Sweetpotatoes	9	8	9	7	4	2	3	6	10	12	17	13
Tomatoes, All	6	6	8	8	11	11	12	10	8	8	6	6
Tomatoes, Florida	12	10	14	16	23	8	*				4	13
Tomatoes, California	2	1	*	*	2	8	19	17	16	19	12	4
Tomatoes, Mexico	13	20	24	22	13	3	*	*	*	*	1	4
Turnips-Rutabagas	12	11	10	6	4	4	4	4	9	12	13	11

*Less than 0.5 of 1% of annual total
The table is based on unloads of vegetables in 41 cities as reported by the U. S. Department of Agriculture.

13-14. Availability of fresh fruits and vegetables in the United States. Courtesy National Restaurant Association.

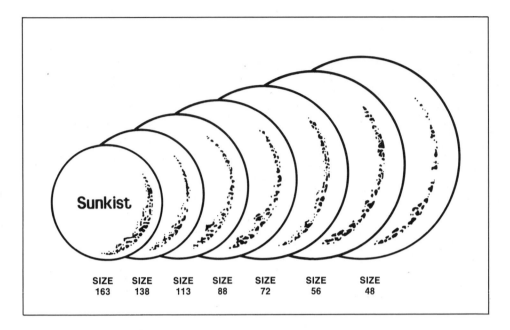

13-15. Available sizes of oranges. Reprinted with permission Sunkist Growers Inc.; SUNKIST is a trademark of Sunkist Growers; from Peddersen, *Foodservice and Hotel Purchasing.*

Sunkist

| SIZE 163 | SIZE 138 | SIZE 113 | SIZE 88 | SIZE 72 | SIZE 56 | SIZE 48 |

Applying Convenience Foods. In deciding which convenience foods to use, the following factors should be considered:

1. *Labor.* The cost and the availability of kitchen labor must be assessed.
2. *Time.* The speed of preparation must be considered in relation to service standards.
3. *Quality and Variety.* Sometimes convenience foods are of higher quality or provide items not otherwise available to enrich the menu.
4. *Space.* Processed foods require less storage and handling space.
5. *Convenience.* The kitchen's operation may be made smoother, and greater flexibility in work schedules may be possible.
6. *Hygiene.* Ready-to-use foods have most, if not all, of their waste matter removed. Elimination of such refuse before food reaches the kitchen reduces food handling and avoids or eases waste disposal problems.
7. *Cost.* Frequently, cost is the deciding factor. Savings realized through the use of convenience foods occur not only in labor, but in food quality, yield, portion size, and waste. This also enables the chef better to control and predict operating costs.

Problems with convenience food systems vary according to the nature of the operation. Chefs, therefore, must take the time to define and analyze the merits of convenience foods for their own particular operations.

Buying Canned Food. Since canned goods can be stored a long time (up to about one year), some chefs are tempted to buy them in large quantities to save on the purchase price. It is unwise, however, to tie up capital and storage space unnecessarily in the form of food stocks. The chef should purchase items that are normally consumed quickly—such as canned fruits, juices, vegetables, and meats—in amounts no larger

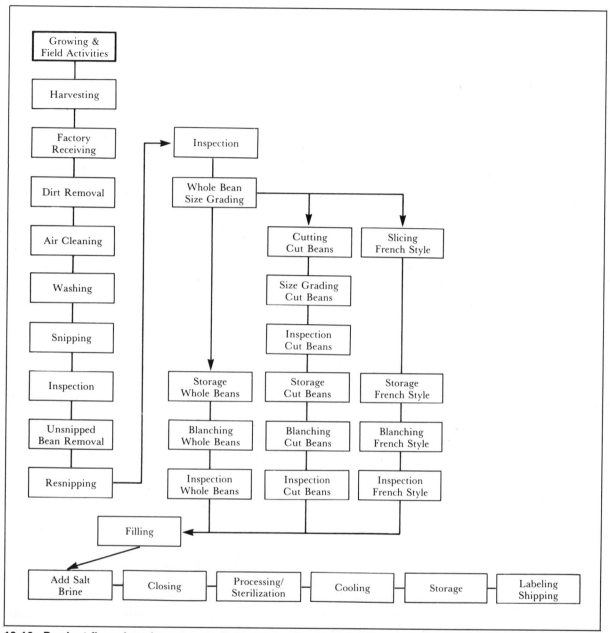

13-16. Product flow chart for green and wax beans. Reprinted with permission, Stewart-Tucker, Inc., Menlo Park, CA; from Peddersen, *Foodservice and Hotel Purchasing.*

than about one month's supply. Cans should be stored at less than 21°C (70°F), but not too close to the freezing point. Cans that are rusted, leaking, swollen, bulging, or badly dented should be discarded.

The differences in quality, cost, and quantity among cans of similar size can be so great as to prevent any real comparison during the first round of purchasing. The buyer should make sample purchases, drain off the liquid, and weigh and portion the remaining contents to estimate real costs per pound and per serving. Figure 13-17 illustrates the great variability in yield by the type of canned food.

Vegetable	Drained Weight (Solids) Percentage	Serving Yield* No. 10 Can (105 oz.) 3 oz. per portion	Comment
Asparagus	62	21†	cuts or spears
Beans, green or wax	60	21	cuts
Beans, kidney	85	29	
Beans, lima	75	26	medium-size
Beets	67	23	slices
Carrots	67	23	
Corn, cream-style	100	35	
Corn, whole-kernel	67	23	
Mushrooms	62	21	
Peas	64	22	
Spinach	69	24	
Succotash	94	32	cream-style corn
Sweet potatoes, mashed	100	35	
Sweet potatoes, whole	66	23	in syrup
Tomatoes	100	35	
Vegetables, mixed	68	23	

*Serving yields will depend on amount of vegetable liquid included. Additional losses may be expected from overcooking and extended holding of vegetable before service.
†Twenty-one servings is calculated by multiplying the desired weight percent (62) by the ingredient's total weight (105) and dividing that number by the portion size (3); 0.62 × 105 = 65.1, 65.1 ÷ 3 = 21.7.

13-17. Drained weight (by percentage) and serving yield for various canned vegetables. From Knight and Kotschevar, *Quantity Food Production, Planning and Management*.

Food Seasonality

It must be repeated for emphasis that in purchasing, as well as in menu planning, the chef must be aware of food seasonality. Fresh meat is available all year long, of course, as is any item that can be frozen. In addition, imports from warm regions can provide fresh fruits and vegetables even during the coldest winter. But to get items at their freshest (and often their cheapest), it is necessary to purchase them in season from nearby suppliers.

Figure 13-14 lists the peak seasons for common fruits and vegetables. The availability of fresh game is dictated by the various states' restrictions on hunting seasons. The availability of fresh fish in plentiful supply depends upon local conditions and commonly cannot be predicted far in advance. Therefore, the wise purchaser keeps informed about developments in local markets.

Conclusion

While the food buyer must remain alert and even critical, it is a mistake not to seek good relations with suppliers. Once dealers of sound reputation have been selected, it is safe to expect reliable goods and fair service. Skilled meat suppliers, properly trained grocers, experienced vintners, and so on have more specialized knowledge in their areas than do most chefs. Developing an atmosphere of mutual confidence can certainly help in securing the expert supplier's skill and assistance in making the most suitable purchase.

This chapter has indicated a number of important factors in food buying. In addition to these, reliable records of perishable and other foods on hand help minimize overbuying. There must also be honest and reliable receiving of goods by a person knowledgeable about specifications and capable of recognizing quality. Conscientious weighing, counting, and quality checking are essential. Otherwise, suppliers and/ or delivery people may be tempted to underdeliver or cheat on quality. Such problems would wipe out any advantage gained by lower purchase cost. Good buying, therefore, must be supported by good receiving.

14. Records and Control

Professional chefs must not only know how to cook good food and manage people well, they must be able to work with numbers. Chefs need not be accountants, of course, and indeed they do not supervise the accounting or financial control section of their establishments. Nonetheless, they do have to remain aware of costs, prices, inventories, and the profit picture, at least as it relates to the kitchen. The records that reveal such details should be based on food and payroll information supplied daily. Only in this way can food and labor costs be related to the exact volume of food and beverage sales produced—a necessary relationship to identify in order to develop more accurate forecasting and pricing arrangements.

Aims of Control

Many kinds of food and beverages are difficult to control because they tempt staff members into theft. But most staff want to do a good job and would appreciate the importance of management controls if they were properly informed about them. Effective management, expressing itself through sound controls, engenders confidence, improves morale, and increases the readiness of workers to accept responsibility. It also discourages weaker-willed staff from committing misdeeds.

The purposes of kitchen and storeroom records and control are:

To ensure that incoming goods agree in quantity and quality with what was ordered

To record receipt of such goods to ensure their safe custody

To control movement of goods from the storeroom to the various sections needing them, or from one section to another

To enable food costs to be compared with corresponding food sales

To prevent or limit losses through deterioration, carelessness, and pilfering

To reduce the tying-up of excessive funds in inventory

The amount and type of kitchen records varies according to the size and scope of the establishment. Smaller establishments need fewer records, and the chef may handle much of it personally. In larger establishments, there is less personal supervision and therefore a greater need for records; the number is sure to be so great that the chef will need aid from kitchen clerks. In addition to records, there must be adequate practical security measures. The most elaborate system of bin cards, for example, is useless if a storeroom is left unlocked and unattended.

Recording Receipts

Exact procedures may vary, but figure 14-1 indicates the basic steps to follow during purchasing and receiving. Figure 14-2 shows a typical purchase order. Such orders should be written on printed, serially numbered, triplicate order forms. The top copy is for the vendor. The second goes to the storeroom clerk in order to verify receipt later. The third is usually sent to the business or accounting office for comparison with the suppliers' invoice (when that arrives) to ensure that

14-1. Flow chart showing use of requisitions, purchase orders, and invoices. From Crawford and McDowell, *Math Workbook for Foodservice/Lodging,* 2nd edition.

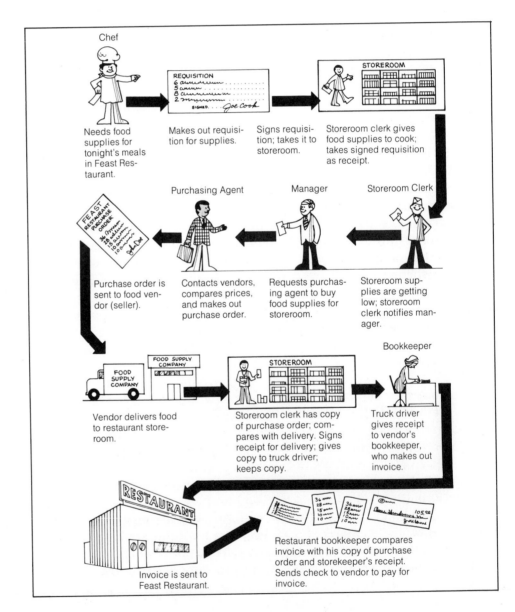

Chef

Needs food supplies for tonight's meals in Feast Restaurant.

Makes out requisition for supplies.

Signs requisition; takes it to storeroom.

Storeroom clerk gives food supplies to cook; takes signed requisition as receipt.

Purchasing Agent

Manager

Storeroom Clerk

Purchase order is sent to food vendor (seller).

Contacts vendors, compares prices, and makes out purchase order.

Requests purchasing agent to buy food supplies for storeroom.

Storeroom supplies are getting low; storeroom clerk notifies manager.

Bookkeeper

Vendor delivers food to restaurant storeroom.

Storeroom clerk has copy of purchase order; compares with delivery. Signs receipt for delivery; gives copy to truck driver; keeps copy.

Truck driver gives receipt to vendor's bookkeeper, who makes out invoice.

Invoice is sent to Feast Restaurant.

Restaurant bookkeeper compares invoice with his copy of purchase order and storekeeper's receipt. Sends check to vendor to pay for invoice.

payment is made only for goods actually ordered and received. Sometimes goods are ordered by telephone, in which case an order form should be sent later as a means of confirmation.

Supervisors of the receiving process should ensure the following points are observed:

1. The receiver is competent and authorized (it should be one person's exclusive responsibility to receive goods).
2. The receiver is familiar with specifications (and has these readily available).
3. The receiving area is large enough and is equipped with scales.
4. Goods are inspected, weighed, and counted to guard against:
    a. commodities not matching specifications (for example, excessive fat and/or bone on meat, excessive dirt in sacked vegetables, yellowing or staling of green vegetables and salads, or fish weighed with too much accompanying ice;
    b. short weight or count (possible pilferage); and
    c. damage or deterioration (for example, broken packs, blown cans, or pest contamination)
5. Goods promptly brought into the storeroom (those left lying around encourage pilferage).

Receipt Documentation

On receipt, goods must be checked for quantity, quality, and price against the second copy (storeroom copy) of the order form and the supplier's invoice (in "blind receiving," the receiver fills out a blank invoice, requiring on-delivery counting and weighing of everything). Most suppliers send duplicate invoices—one to be signed by the recipient and returned to the supplier as proof of delivery, the other to be retained by the recipient. All breakages or shortages should be noted on the carrier's invoice before signing. After certifying the invoice, the storekeeper passes it to the accounting office for retention with the third copy of the order.

Loss or Damage of Delivery

If checking reveals that goods are missing or damaged, then the supplier and carrier must be notified immediately. This is usually done by requesting a credit memorandum. See figure 14-3. To help prevent more serious problems such as deliveries at the wrong time when no one is on duty for checking, the desired time and place of delivery should be inserted on all orders. This then becomes a condition of the contract with which the supplier must conform. The supplier would then suffer any loss caused by goods being left in the wrong place or at the wrong time.

		PURCHASE ORDER				No. 1124

HAPPY COW DAIRY COMPANY
(NAME OF PURVEYOR)
123 Milk Can Lane
(ADDRESS OF PURVEYOR)
New Haven, Connecticut 06511
(PURVEYOR'S CITY AND STATE)

TO PURVEYOR: OUR PURCHASE ORDER NUMBER (ABOVE) MUST BE SHOWN ON ALL YOUR INVOICES AND PACKAGES.

DELIVERY DATE (S):
May 1-31, 1977

DELIVERY INSTRUCTIONS: Deliver fresh Mon. thru Fri. no later than 6 A.M. to storeroom receiving area.

TERMS: 1% 10-Net 30 days

AUTHORIZED SIGNATURE

FOR OFFICE USE ONLY:
CHARGE TO (ACCOUNT): | TOTAL TO DATE: | BALANCE:

SERIAL MODEL, OR CIR SPEC. NUMBER	ITEM	QUANTITY ORDERED	QUANTITY RECEIVED	UNIT PRICE	EXTENSION
300.1	Milk Fresh Homo. 1 gal. Norris	2100 Gal	2250 Gal	$1.04	$2340.00

Date Received for Payment: 6/4/77 RC
Prices, Extensions and Total Verified by: 6/10/77 2643 W. a. H.
Date Paid:
Check Number:
Bursar's Initials:

				SUB TOTAL:	$2340.00
				LESS DISCOUNT:	$23.40
				PURCHASE ORDER TOTAL:	$2316.60

SHIPMENT RECEIVED AND VERIFIED BY:
5/31/77
CULINARY INSTITUTE REPRESENTATIVE   (DATE)

SHIPMENT RECEIVED AND VERIFIED BY:

PURCHASE REQUEST ORIGINATOR   (DATE)

14-2. Example of a purchase order. From Knight and Kotschevar, *Quantity Food Production, Planning and Management.*

Explanation of purchase order columns: The first three lines are used for the name, address, city, state, and zip code of the purveyor.

Delivery date(s): Filled in as required for regular or open delivery purchase order.

Delivery instructions: The specific building, section, or address where delivery is desired.

For office use only: For operations maintaining separate cost accounts.

Terms: Record applicable discount, or other terms as specified by the vendor.

Authorizing signature: Signature of the person authorized to approve purchase orders.

Serial, model, or specification number: On purchase orders for equipment insert the serial, model, or catalog number. On purchase orders for food, use the specification number.

continued . . .

Item: An accurate, complete description of the item desired. If a specification number is used, the description may be shortened since the specification itself gives complete details.

Quantity ordered: Type in the quantity needed and the correct unit of sale, such as 50 lbs., 25 doz., 4 gal., etc.

Quantity received: Write or type the exact quantity received. When using open delivery purchase orders, all delivery slips for the period must be added and the *total quantity received* recorded.

Unit price: Record the dollar and/or cents figure per unit.

Extension: Multiply the number of units received times the unit price and enter the total amount.

Sub total: Add the figures in the *extension* column and enter the total amount.

Less discount: Enter the amount of discount (if any) in red ink.

Purchase order total: Subtract discount from *sub total* column. Enter new total.

Shipment received and verified by: The signature, in ink, of the person actually receiving the merchandise.

Shipment received and verified by (purchase request originator): Some establishments, when purchasing equipment and certain other items, require a purchase order request as authorization to prepare a purchase order. If a purchase order request is required, this section would be signed by the originator of the request. This would relieve the actual receiver from responsibility for the merchandise. This section would not be used on food purchase orders.

OPERATION'S NAME AND ADDRESS

TO: _____   No. _____

ADDRESS: _____

CITY, STATE: _____   DATE: _____

GENTLEMEN: Please send Credit Memorandum for the following:

INVOICE NO.	ITEM	QUAN.	UNIT OF SALE	UNIT PRICE	EXTENSION
				Total	

REASON:

BY: _____

TITLE: _____

14-3. Example of a credit memorandum. From Knight and Kotschevar, *Quantity Food Production, Planning and Management.*

Invoices

When invoices (figure 14-4) are received they should be transmitted directly to the business office, where they can be matched to the office copy of the order form. Prices, as well as the calculations on the invoices, can then be checked. Occasionally an invoice may arrive before the goods. Care must then be taken not to confuse this type with the invoices indicating that goods have already been delivered.

Normally, invoices are summarized on a daily basis by the accounting office and also entered into the accounts of the respective suppliers. Payment is usually made on a monthly basis.

FEAST RESTAURANTS
San Francisco, California

Storeroom Requisition

Charge To __Kitchen__   Date __6-15-80__

Amount	Unit	Item	Unit Price	Extension
3	cn.	Tuna, chunks, 66 oz.	$4.46	$13.38
2	cn.	Coffee, regular, 2 lb.	4.18	8.36
1	gal.	Mustard, prepared	1.46	1.46

Total __$23.20__

Signed __D. J. Golladay__
Approved __R. Grimes__

14-4. Example of an invoice. From Crawford and McDowell, *Math Workbook for Foodservice/Lodging,* 2nd edition.

BIN CARD

Commodity:

Date	Receipt or issue voucher no.	Received	Issued	Balance

Minimum/Maximum stocks . . . .

14-5. Example of a bin card. From Fuller, *Professional Kitchen Management.*

Taking Inventory

Goods taken into the various storage areas may be controlled either through independent bin cards (figure 14-5) or stock record cards for each item. Bin cards are attached to the appropriate bin, shelf, or drawer; their use necessitates a neat arrangement of commodities in the storeroom. Bin cards must be updated any time goods are issued or received. The minimum/maximum stock level entry helps prevent shortages and overstocking. The minimum level is based on the rate of goods usage and the period of time between sending an order and receiving it. The maximum level allows a hedge against tying up too much money, space, and time in handling excess goods.

Documentation must be accompanied by supervision because, even after careful receipt procedures, goods may still be lost through:

Theft from the storeroom

Deterioration of the goods due to poor storeroom conditions

Depredations by rodents and insect pests

Faulty control procedures (issues without requisitions, and so forth)

Whenever the storage attendant is not present, security must be maintained by keeping storerooms locked. If unauthorized access to them is allowed, it is unreasonable to expect any one person to accept responsibility for losses as storekeeper.

Recipe for Effective Stock-Keeping

Yield:
An efficient storeroom operation in which goods are carefully controlled

Ingredients:
Designate the people to have responsibility over the storeroom
Keep all units of the same item together
Keep related items near each other
Keep unrelated items farther apart
Record all receipts, issues, and running balances clearly and accurately
Differentiate the various types of units—for example, between dozen and gross
Periodically confirm the running balances by taking inventory
Report discrepancies (if any), and determine the cause
Keep the storeroom locked at all times when a person responsible for it is not present
Maintain stocks of all items between the minimum and maximum balances

Method:
Train and supervise all staff with regard to security of goods and of the storeroom. At random intervals, make surprise spot checks of the records and of actual procedures to keep staff members on their toes.

In addition to using locks, the storekeeper should take inventory periodically. If the number of a given item on hand does not match the supposed balance on hand in the records, the discrepancy should be reported. If discrepancies are large or recurrent, the manager should take steps to determine whether pilfering, deterioration, math errors, or incomplete records are at fault. The manager should also make unannounced, random spot checks to see if bin cards and inventories are accurate.

Often, deposits are required on containers such as casks, cases, and bottles. Money can be lost if these chargeable containers are not properly controlled. A return and empties book should be kept at the appropriate storeroom for this purpose.

Issuing Goods to the Kitchen

Within the total control system, issued goods have to be valued or costed. In doing this, no unauthorized issues should be made from the storeroom. Rather, a simple internal requisition system should be used. With this system, goods can be released only on receipt of a signed requisition slip. See figure 14-6. Only one senior member of the staff in each *partie* or section should be authorized to sign these requisitions for goods from the storeroom. Once issued, the goods must be promptly entered as issued on bin cards, with the requisition slips being filed in the storage area as vouchers supporting the issues. This system is simplified by allowing routine requisitions only at certain prearranged times.

14-6. Example of an internal requisition form. From Fuller, *Professional Kitchen Management*.

Specimen Internal Requisition Form (Duplicate Pad)

Serial No.: 43881

[Name of Establishment]
INTERNAL REQUISITION

From Section:. . . .   (e.g., Saucier)   Date: . . . .

Please Supply:

Item	Quantity required

Signed...
Section...

CONSUMPTION OF PROVISIONS

$- - - - - -$ ended $- - - - - -$

	Opening stock	Add (net) purchases	Total	Less closing stock	Consumption	% Total consumption	Budget	+ Variance	− Variance
Meat									
Poultry									
Fish									
Ham/Bacon									
Vegetables									
Fruit									
Groceries									
Tea									
Coffee									
Ice cream									
Cheese									

Food Sales

Consumption _____

Gross profit _____

Gross profit percentage $- - - - - - -$

14-7. Form for calculating cost of goods sold. From Fuller, *Professional Kitchen Management.*

Generally, both bin cards and requisition slips are concerned with quantities only. A form like the one in figure 14-7 is required to calculate the value of receipts and issues. With this form the value of goods issued and the gross profit percentage can be calculated on either a daily or a weekly basis.

```
┌─────────────────────────────────────────────────────────────────────┐
│                                                                       │
│                      Food/Beverage Transfer Memo                      │
│                                                                       │
│                                          Date  9/8/7-                  │
│                                                                       │
│     From  Bar                                                         │
│                                                                       │
│     To  Main Kitchen                                                 │
│                                                                       │
│     Quantity              Description           Unit Price    Amount  │
│                                                                       │
│     1            Qt ------ Sherry                  1.89        1.89    │
│     1            Bottle (Fifth) Red Wine for Cooking  1.39     1.39    │
│                                                                       │
│                                                                       │
│                                                                       │
│                                                                       │
│                                                 Total        $3.28    │
│                                                                       │
│     Sent by  Joe — Bartender                                         │
│                                                                       │
│     Received by  Paul — Chef                                         │
│                                                                       │
└─────────────────────────────────────────────────────────────────────┘
```

14-8. Example of a food and beverage transfer memorandum. From Dittmer and Griffin, *Principles of Food, Beverage, and Labor Cost Controls for Hotels and Restaurants,* 3rd edition.

The system should also regulate the return of goods from kitchens to storerooms. This involves the use of a "stores returned" form to record both quantities and values. Similarly, a transfer memo (figure 14-8) should be used to record transfers of items from one section to another.

Sales History

A menu sales history records for easy comparison the number of each menu item sold during a given time period. This is especially important for higher cost entrée items. The simplest method is to tick sales off on the daily menu itself. However, more formal records are desirable for long-term test periods, which are more reliable. In such a case, a record form following the format and sequence of the menu should be devised. The number of each item sold is extracted from sales checks by a cashier or controller and entered on the form. As accuracy is essential, such entries should be spot checked independently from time to time. See figure 14-9.

A good menu sales history helps the chef forecast future sales of the same menu items. This, in turn, helps guide future purchasing and calculation of menu costs. And, of course, unpopular and unprofitable items can be dropped altogether.

Day Monday		Date 10/1/7-		Meal Dinner
Item		Number of Portions		Total
A	ꟷꟷ	ꟷꟷꟷ ꟷꟷꟷ ꟷꟷꟷ ꟷꟷꟷ 111		23
B		ꟷꟷꟷ ꟷꟷꟷ ꟷꟷꟷ ꟷꟷꟷ ꟷꟷꟷ ꟷꟷꟷ ꟷꟷꟷ ꟷꟷꟷ ꟷꟷꟷ ꟷꟷꟷ ꟷꟷꟷ ꟷꟷꟷ		60
C		ꟷꟷꟷ ꟷꟷꟷ ꟷꟷꟷ ꟷꟷꟷ ꟷꟷꟷ ꟷꟷꟷ 1111		34
D		ꟷꟷꟷ ꟷꟷꟷ ꟷꟷꟷ ꟷꟷꟷ ꟷꟷꟷ ꟷꟷꟷ ꟷꟷꟷ ꟷꟷꟷ ꟷꟷꟷ		45
Total				162

14-9. Example of a sales tally form. From Dittmer and Griffin, *Principles of Food, Beverage, and Labor Cost Controls for Hotels and Restaurants*, 3rd edition.

Recipe Detail & Cost Card

Item: Seafood Newburg   Menu: Dinner

S.P. **$5.00**
Cost **$1.99**
F.C. % **39.8%**

Yield: 10 portions   Portion Size: 4 oz of Seafood, + sauce   Date: 6/22/7-

Ingredients	Quantity	Unit	Cost	Ext.	Procedure
lobster meat	1 lb.	lb.	11.25	11.25	Saute all seafood well in melted
shrimps	1/2 lb.	lb.	3.75	1.88	butter. Add sherry & simmer
scallops	1/2 lb.	lb.	4.75	2.38	until wine is absorbed. Add
filet of sole	1/2 lb.	lb.	3.50	1.75	paprika and cream sauce, then
heavy cream	1 cup	qt.	1.80	.45	combine and simmer. Beat egg
cream sauce	3 cups	—		.75	yolks and cream, add slowly to
butter	1 cup	lb.	.80	.40	pan, and combine well. Check for
salt & pepper				.05	seasoning, pour into serving
paprika	1 T			.10	dishes, and add sherry.
sherry wine	8 oz.	qt.	1.60	.40	
egg yolks	6 ea.			.42	
sherry wine	1 oz.			.05	
				$19.88	

14-10. Example of a recipe card for portion control. From Dittmer and Griffin, *Principles of Food, Beverage, and Labor Cost Controls for Hotels and Restaurants*, 3rd edition.

Standardized Recipes and Menu Costing

Standardized recipes provide the basis for control because they record precisely the ingredients and methods used for preparing each menu item and thereby help to ensure consistent quality. They also allow more accurate cost calculations. Each item of the recipe is costed and all the costs are summed. Dividing by the number of portions yields the cost per portion. See figure 14-10. The cost of accompaniments such as garnishes, vegetables, and salads that are served with the item and not priced separately on the menu must also be computed and recorded on a separate card.

Budgeted or estimated costs can be achieved only with strict waste control and carefully maintained production efficiency. Even so, budgeted costs should allow a tolerance of perhaps 5–10% for unavoidable waste and human error. Any larger deviation than that, or any sudden increase in loss, should be investigated.

Portion Control

Portion control does not necessarily mean reducing size or penny-pinching, both of which can swiftly lead to dissatisfied customers. The same principle operates in every business. Nobody expects to get 19 or 21 cigarettes in a packet of 20, nor an extra half-pint in a gallon of gasoline. Similarly, in food and beverage operations, portion control means serving the same size helping to each customer for the same price. It is unfair to serve a 12-ounce steak for the same price as a 9-ounce one, and knowing the serving size and the cost of its ingredients enables management to set a fair price on the food served to produce a reasonable profit.

Without portion control, a sales record may show 30 portions of a dish prepared, only 18 sold, and yet none left over. What happened to the other 12 portions? Were oversize portions served? Or were any eaten by staff (or visiting friends) without record of them? Without portion control, it is difficult to say, and difficult to prevent such costly losses.

14-11. Average range of portion sizes for a complete meal. From Fuller, *Professional Kitchen Management.*

	Average minimum		Average maximum	
Appetizer	50 g	(2 oz)	75 g	(3 oz)
Salad	50 g	(2 oz)	75 g	(3 oz)
Soup	175 g	(6 oz)	200 g	(7 oz)
Vegetable	50 g	(2 oz)	75 g	(3 oz)
Potato	115 g	(4 oz)	115 g	(4 oz)
Meat	75 g	(3 oz)	150 g	(5 oz)
Bread & Butter	50 g	(2 oz)	75 g	(3 oz)
Dessert	115 g	(4 oz)	150 g	(5 oz)
Beverage	200 g	(7 oz)	200 g	(7 oz)
Total	880 g	(32 oz)	1,115 g	(40 oz)

Portion Size

Portion size is decided after the chef has considered the type of customer to be served, the price the customer expects to pay, and the amount of profit required. An average stomach is said to accommodate about 0.9 to 1.12 kilograms (2 to 2.5 pounds) of food comfortably, both liquid and solid. This may provide some guidance to portioning, especially in institutional catering where it can be more economical to give seconds to a few rather than to fill garbage cans with plate waste from a majority of customers. On the basis of stomach capacity, courses and items might break down as shown in figure 14-11. Of course, these are average figures only. Appetites vary tremendously, just as body sizes and activity levels do. Even if fewer courses are served, there is not necessarily a need to increase the portion size of the remaining items.

Portion Guidance

Once managers have decided on portion sizes, they must communicate these to kitchen staff and also provide them with the physical means of controlling size. These include:

Workable standard recipes

Visual guides to plate and dish layouts

Weighing scales for expensive items such as meat and fish

Serving implements of suitable size (ladles, serving spoons, scoops, and so on)

Serving dishes of suitable size, so that the set portion does not look too large or small in comparison to the dish

Meat cuts (steak, chops, chicken, and so on) accurately weighed by grams or ounces, or purchased to preportioned specifications

Training in carving or in using slicing machines

Clear distinction between *table d'hôte* and *à la carte* portions (where applicable)

See figure 14-12 for some illustrative portion control equipment.

Visual Aids and Training

To exercise portion control, it is not enough to have portioning equipment and a sales documentation system. The staff must have training in how to make the system work. Particularly valuable are charts illustrating item preparation along with instructions, lists of ingredients, cooking times, and garnishes for standardized recipes. Films or slides may also be used.

The best basis for an effective system of portion control is simplicity, staff cooperation, and relevant training. Also, management must supervise portion production as well as portion service to prevent collusion between waiters and members of the kitchen staff. But in spite of this necessary emphasis on preventing pilfering, portion control is basically not a negative concept or procedure. Rather, it ensures that the price of a dish is neither less nor more than it should be.

Item	Application	Approximate
Baking dishes	Baked dishes	Sizes up to 40 cm (16 in)
Butchers' knives	Raw meats	20, 25, 30, 35 cm (8, 10, 12, 14 in)
Butter pat machines	Butter pats	6 g (¼ oz) upward
Casserole dishes	Stews and casseroles	225 g (8 oz)
Cheese cutters	Slicing cheese	up to 30 slices per 450 g (1 lb)
Cooks' knives	Slicing: meats, etc.	20, 25, 30, 35 cm (8, 10, 12, 14 in)
Custard cups	Custards, trifles	150, 175, 200 g (5, 6, 7 oz)
Disposables		
foil cases	Entrée and pie dishes	various
paper cups	Tea and coffee	200, 225 ml (7, 8 oz)
paper soufflé cases	Jams, sauces	14 to 142 ml (½ to 5 oz)
Extendable trellis cutter	Multicutting sweets	
Hand and power slicers	Meats, bread and butter	various
Individual creamers	Cream	28, 71 ml, (1, 2½ oz)
Individual pie dishes	Meat and fruit pies	11, 13 cm (4½, 5 in)
Iron spoons	Stews, etc.	25, 30, 35 cm (10, 12, 14 in)
Juice glasses	Appetizers	71, 142 ml (2½, 5 oz)
Ladles	Sauces, soups	28 to 284 ml (1 to 10 oz)
Milk dispensers	For tea and coffee	21 and 284 ml (¾ and 10 oz)
Pastry markers	Pie-cut marking	6, 7, 8 cuts per pie
Perforated spoons	Vegetables (e.g., beans, peas)	33 cm (13 in)
Pie tins	Baking pies	7.5 to 23 cm (3 to 9 in)
Pudding basins	Puddings, meat and sweet	100 g to 1.35 kg (4 oz. to 3 lb)
Pudding roll tins	Puddings	30, 35 cm (12, 14 in)
Ramekins	Ramekins and soufflés	54, 113 g (2¾, 4½ oz)
Scoops	Ice cream, solid purées	12, 16, 20, 24, 30, 40, 60 scoop measures per 1⅛ liter (1 quart)
Small weight scales	Portion weighing	12 g to 1.80 kg (½ oz to 4 lb)
Soup bowls	Soup	18, 20, 21, 23 cm (7, 8, 8½, 9 in)
Soup, fish, meat, and entrée plates	Soup, fish, meat and entrées	18, 20, 21, 23 cm (7, 8, 8½, 9 in)
Steak molds	Minced beef, hamburgers, etc.	100/125 g (4 oz) upward
Sundae dishes	Composite ice cream dishes	50, 100, 175, 225 g (2, 4, 6, 8 oz)
Sweets, cheese, and bread-and-butter plates	Sweets, cheese, and bread and butter	15, 16, 18 cm (6, 6½, 7 in)
Tea and coffee cups	Tea and coffee	142, 198, 227, 255 ml (5, 7, 8, 9 oz)
Tea measuring machine	Tea for pot service	450 g, 0.90 kg (1, 2 lb)
Woven wire vegetable servers	Peas, sprouts, etc.	50, 75, 100 g (2, 3, 4 oz)

14-12. Types of portion control equipment. From Fuller, *Professional Kitchen Management.*

	Loss	Edible
Beefsteak		
entrecôle (on the bone)	40%	60%
fillet (on the bone)	10%	90%
rump (on the bone)	30%	70%
Crab	70%	30%
Duck (eviscerated)	30%	70%
Chicken (eviscerated)	25%	75%
Fruit	3–50%*	
Ham (on the bone)	15%	85%
Lobster	65%	35%
Round fish	25%	75%
Salmon	25%	75%
Sole	50%	50%
Veal	25%	
Vegetables	6–60%*	

*Loss varies according to quality. Cheap fruit and vegetables can have a high real cost when their trimming waste is evaluated. Similarly, peeling and trimming need careful supervision.

14-13. **Examples of loss in food preparation. From Fuller, *Professional Kitchen Managment*.**

Yield Testing

Yield tests have long been relied on to help identify appropriate portion sizes. The greater the amount of original material that is lost in preparation, the most expensive each ounce of final yield becomes. The cost per ounce of final yield is therefore more important for pricing than the cost per initial ounce. The selling price per unit of measure is significant, especially for expensive items. A customer might like a 100-gram (4-ounce) portion of smoked salmon, for example, but be unwilling to pay for more than a 25-gram (1-ounce) serving. If most other customers are in the same financial position, a menu offering only a 100-gram serving will guarantee few sales.

Figure 14-13 provides examples of percentage losses in commodities of various kinds. These are average figures only. The exact loss naturally depends on the individual product's quality. Again, it is the cost per ounce of yield that counts. This principle applies not only to high-priced items, but also to foods of more modest unit cost (for example, vegetables and fruits) that are purchased in large volume.

Beverage Yields

Tea and coffee are available in various packs, sizes, and weights. The exact yield depends on the blend and strength. Consequently, the figure below gives only approximate guidance:

Tea. For infused tea, 60 grams (2.4 ounces produce 5 liters (1.32 gallons). Assuming use of 2-deciliter (7-ounce) capacity cups, and allowing 0.25 deciliters for sugar and unfilled space, 5 liters will yield about 28 cups. Using 2.5-deciliter (9-ounce) capacity cups, and again allowing 0.25 deciliters for unfilled space, 5 liters of tea will yield about 22 cups.

Coffee. For black coffee, 120 grams (4.7 ounces) produce 1.5 liters (0.40 gallons). Assuming use of 2-deciliter (7-ounce) cups, and allowing 0.25 deciliters for cream and sugar, 1.5 liters will yield 10 cups, while 2.5-deciliter (9-ounce) cups will yield about 7 cups.

Waste Control

Vigilance against excessive loss in preparation must never be relaxed. In costing recipes it is essential to account for bone, fat, and skin in meat, and for corresponding inedible parts and trimmings in other commodities.

Recipe for Minimizing Food Waste

Yield:
An efficient operation that reduces food costs while keeping quality high

Ingredients:
Carefully select popular items for the menu so that they will be sold
Use sales forecasting to prevent overproduction
Purchase supplies that give the best price per ounce of final yield (convenience foods that are waste-free are often most economical)
When planning portion sizes, food costs, and prices, take into consideration any shrinkage or evaporation during cooking
Ensure that prepared dishes are appetizing and of satisfactory quality, so that customers will eat them
Establish standard portion sizes that minimize plate waste; more than an average of about 0.08 kilograms (0.18 pounds) of plate waste per person might indicate a problem
Do not use expensive leftover food in cheap dishes (for example, do not grind up steak for hamburger)

Method:
When the manager, the chef, and the staff realize that throwing out plate waste is like throwing money into a garbage can, they will be more motivated to do something about it. Stress this point during training and put up posters to remind everyone of it.

Calling Orders from Kitchen to Restaurant

In some restaurants, especially those conducted on traditional *partie* lines, a kitchen clerk known as the *aboyeur* (barker) is stationed at the pick-up counter throughout the meal service period. On receipt of waiters' checks, the *aboyeur* announces in a loud voice (in order to be heard above the kitchen clatter) the requirements of the order. The announcement normally consists of:

Naming the chef or the *partie* being addressed

Stating the number of portions required

Stating the name of the item (for example, lamb cutlet)

Naming the style of cooking (for example, grilled)

Listing the garnishes, dressing, or sauce (if any)

The chef or assistant must then acknowledge the order.

When an order has been completed, the barker places the check through a slit into a locked box. For control purposes, all of these checks can be compared with sales revenue at the end of the shift.

Gross Profit Percentage

Gross profit is the difference between total food cost and total income. This difference may be expressed as a percentage, and percentage targets may be applied to each item or meal. Such percentage targets or guidelines help encourage kitchen compliance with record keeping, cost calculating, cost constraints, and other control procedures.

In the percentage method of control, food is charged to the kitchen at cost price, and the chef is required to produce a given percentage of profit on each item produced. Any deviations noted from this percentage are investigated and the cause(s) ascertained. A form like that in Figure 14-7 aids control and shows variances when items are expressed as percentages of total consumption. (The alternative, the selling-price method of control, charges the kitchen with commodities at selling price and compares those figures to actual receipts of cash).

Percentages and Performance

To calculate net profit, labor costs and all overhead expenses such as rent and energy must be subtracted from gross profit. If these costs are not controlled, the savings in food costs may be wiped out by losses elsewhere. The ratio of food costs to other costs varies from one operation to another, of course. In a typical operation 35% of the selling price is food costs, which yields a 65% gross profit. Labor costs may run another 30%, with overhead at 25%. This leaves a net profit of 10% (100% − 35% − 30% − 25% = 10%).

In some operations, however, labor costs may equal or exceed food costs. Low-food-cost items such as soup, stew, and pasta dishes may seem more profitable, but when labor costs in preparing and serving them are considered, they may cost as much as high-priced items such as roasts and steak. Figure 14-14 shows how food and labor costs affected profit margins at a subsidized cafeteria run for company employees. With average selling prices, food costs, and labor costs taken into account, the total possible margin of profit for the menu in Table A of figure 14-14 is $2.75. For its six menu items, the food cost is 41% and labor costs average 30%. Looking at specific items, however, reveals that high labor costs make soup and apple pie into profit losers. If they are

14-14. The effects of food and labor costs on profit. From Fuller, *Professional Kitchen Management.*

Table A: Food cost, labor cost, and selling price

	Food cost	Selling price	Food cost % of sales	Gross profit after food cost	Labor cost	Labor cost % of sales	Profit after food and labor cost
Soup	0.03	0.30	10	0.27	0.47	157.0	−0.20
Stew	0.30	0.90	33	0.60	0.47	52.2	0.13
Half chicken	0.50	1.50	33	1.00	0.47	31.3	0.53
Roast beef	1.00	2.50	40	1.50	0.47	18.8	1.03
Steak	2.00	4.00	50	2.00	0.47	11.8	1.53
Apple pie	0.05	0.25	20	0.20	0.47	188.0	−0.27
Total	3.88	9.45	41	5.57	2.82	30	2.75

Table B: Comparative result after substitution

	Food cost	Selling price	Food cost % of sales	Gross profit after food cost	Labor cost	Labor cost % of sales	Profit after food and labor cost
Soup	0.03	0.30	10	0.27	0.47	157.0	−0.20
Stew	0.30	0.90	33	0.60	0.47	52.2	0.13
Half chicken	0.50	1.50	33	1.00	0.47	31.3	0.53
Roast beef	1.00	2.50	40	1.50	0.47	18.8	1.03
Spaghetti	0.25	1.25	20	1.00	0.47	37.6	0.53
Apple pie	0.05	0.25	20	0.20	0.47	188.0	−0.27
Total	2.13	6.70	31.80	4.57	2.82	42.1	1.75

Table C: Comparative position after re-presentation and repricing

	Food cost	Selling price	Food cost % of sales	Gross profit after food cost	Labor cost	Labor cost % of sales	Profit after food and labor cost
Soup	0.03	0.30	10	0.27	0.47	157.0	−0.20
Half chicken	0.50	1.50	33	1.00	0.47	31.3	0.53
Roast beef	1.00	2.50	40	1.50	0.47	18.8	1.03
Steak (2)	4.00	7.50	53	3.50	0.94	12.5	2.56
Apple pie	0.05	0.25	20	0.20	0.47	188.0	−0.27
Total	5.58	12.05	40	6.57	2.82	23.4	3.65

ordered as supplements to the profitable main courses of steak or roast beef, the final combination does leave a profit. But on plain orders for stew or pie, or soup and pie, the house takes a net loss.

Lowering food costs by substituting cheaper items does not necessarily help. For example, if low-food-cost spaghetti replaces steak, the total food cost drops, but so do the total income and the profit margin. See Table B of figure 14-14.

On the other hand, if high profit items are reduced in price so that more are purchased, the profit margin for each one is reduced, but the greater number of sales ensures a greater total profit. See Table C of figure 14-14.

Pricing Money Losers

Operations with high rents and labor costs may price money-losing items on *à la carte* menus so that they bear their fair share of overhead. Appetizers or drinks, for example, may be set at high prices, while entrees are priced at relatively lower levels. For one thing, this encourages a customer to order a complete meal instead of just pie and coffee. But even if that result does not occur, this type of pricing ensures that each customer pays a share of overhead.

Applying Percentages

Managers and chefs should not be too rigid about applying percentages, at least as long as they are turning a profit overall. For example, restaurants in inexpensive areas with low overhead costs tend to have relatively high food costs—around 50%. Conversely, luxury restaurants in better areas with higher operating costs tend to have lower food costs—around 35%. (It should be obvious that the actual total cost for luxury food is greater, but since other costs are even higher, the percentage attributable to food goes down). Also, despite varying percentages, both may make a profit as long as they cater to their customers' preferences.

In addition to quality, the number of menu items may also affect the food cost percentage. Generally, the more menu items there are, the higher the food cost is, unless convenience foods are relied on. Percentages are also affected by selling prices, which must reflect customers' expectations and competitors' prices as well as food costs themselves. As long as the overall average of food costs is in line, therefore, the chef should not worry about a few items that are not making much money.

Nevertheless, the food cost percentage remains a valuable guide to spotting defects and losses in food and beverage operations. For example, if the food-cost percentage is too high, check for unwise purchasing, faulty receiving, commodity waste, pilfering, poor hygiene, spoilage through overlong or careless storage, overproduction and spoilage in production, poor menu planning, and inadequate control. On the other hand, if the food cost seems too low, check for poor food quality, loss of customers, and inflated labor costs.

Inclusive Prices For Food and Accommodation

At some establishments, there is a single charge for both lodging and meals. The problem then becomes how to divide up the total in a sensible way. Either a dollar amount can be set aside for food, or a set percentage of the total received for food can be taken.

The more precise method is to value meals at an appropriate selling price and deduct this from the total figure. This ensures that an adequate amount of money for food is obtained; the remainder can then go to lodging. Alternatively, the chef can take a percentage of the total and multiply it by a desirable food-cost percentage to see how much can be spent for food. Then the chef can decide on an appropriate menu level. The trouble with this approach is that the level may turn out to be lower than what would have been planned had the other method been used.

Conclusion

A chef does not perform all of the above calculations personally but nevertheless must remain responsible for conscientious and accurate record keeping within the kitchen, at the service counter, and in the storerooms. Such controls are necessary to disclose deficiencies in purchasing or storage, and losses caused by other forms of waste or pilferage. Control helps achieve a satisfactory profit.

To many people, however, all record and control systems can at times seem irksome. Therefore, the system should be as unobtrusive as possible. Simplicity is the key to a good control system. The methods chosen should not involve too much staff time nor make errors likely. Too elaborate a system (as many retailers in other businesses have found) can cost more in operation than it saves in materials. But a simple, straightforward system can help keep employees happy as well as save money.

Recipe for Effective Control

Yield:
A well-controlled system that runs smoothly toward established profit goals

Ingredients:
Select employees for integrity
Assign responsibility for property and/or procedures to specific individuals
Make available the record forms and kitchen tools (as for portion control) that are needed
Train employees in how to use the system
Make unannounced spot checks to see how well staff members are following the system
Reward staff members who develop ideas on how to cut losses and improve the system

Method:
The most important principle is to keep the system simple enough for everyone on the staff to be able to understand and use it. Otherwise, it might sound great in theory, but just waste time and confuse workers.

Illustration Acknowledgments

Many of the illustrations in this book originally appeared elsewhere and were adapted for this book. All are credited in their captions. Complete bibliographical information for the sources cited follows.

Crawford, Hollie W., and McDowell, Milton C. *Math Workbook for Food-service/Lodging.* 2nd ed. New York: Van Nostrand Reinhold Company, 1981.

Culinary Institute of America. *The Professional Chef's Knife.* New York: Van Nostrand Reinhold Company, 1978.

Dittmer, Paul R., and Griffin, Gerald G. *Principles of Food, Beverage, and Labor Cost Controls for Hotels and Restaurants.* 3rd ed. New York: Van Nostrand Reinhold Company, 1984.

Dunn, Martha Davis. *Fundamentals of Nutrition.* New York: Van Nostrand Reinhold Company, 1983.

Eshbach, Charles E. *Foodservice Management.* 3rd ed. New York: Van Nostrand Reinhold Company, 1979.

Fuller, John. *Professional Kitchen Management.* London: Batsford Academic and Educational Ltd., 1981.

Keiser, James R. *Principles and Practice of Management in the Hospitality Industry.* New York: Van Nostrand Reinhold Company, 1979.

Knight, John B., and Kotschevar, Lendal H. *Quantity Food Production, Planning and Management.* New York: Van Nostrand Reinhold Company, 1979.

Lundberg, Donald A. *The Hotel and Restaurant Business.* 4th ed. New York: Van Nostrand Reinhold Company, 1984.

Miller, Jack E. *Menu Pricing and Strategy.* New York: Van Nostrand Reinhold Company, 1980.

Peddersen, Raymond B. *Foodservice and Hotel Purchasing.* New York: Van Nostrand Reinhold Company, 1981.

Richardson, Treva M., and Nicodemus, Wade R. *Sanitation for Foodservice Workers.* 3rd ed. New York: Van Nostrand Reinhold Company, 1981.

Schmidt, Arno B. *The Banquet Business.* New York: Van Nostrand Reinhold Company, 1981.

Waldner, George K., and Mitterhauser, Klaus. *The Professional Chef's Book of Buffets.* New York: Van Nostrand Reinhold Company, 1971.

Wilkinson, Jule. *The Complete Book of Cooking Equipment.* 2nd ed. New York: Van Nostrand Reinhold Company, 1981.

Index

Notes

Notes

Notes

Notes

Notes